The Sacraments of Daily Life

The Sacraments of Daily Life

by
Bernard J. Kelly, C.S.Sp.

Sheed & Ward
New York · 1943

IMPRIMI POTEST:

    D. MURPHY, C.S.S.P.,D.D.
        PRAEP. PROV. HIB.

NIHIL OBSTAT:

    ARTHUR J. SCANLAN, S.T.D.
        CENSOR LIBRORUM.

IMPRIMATUR:

    ✠ FRANCIS J. SPELLMAN, D.D.
        ARCHBISHOP, NEW YORK.

New York, May 31, 1943.

PRINTED IN THE UNITED STATES OF AMERICA
BY BURR PRINTING HOUSE, NEW YORK

TO

JESUS AND MARY

King and Queen of the Sacraments

INTRODUCTION

WHILE THERE IS NO GREAT DEARTH of spiritual literature at the present day the need of a book on the sacraments remains. That this should be so is all the more surprising when one recalls that the sacraments are the channels instituted by Our Lord Himself to convey grace to our souls. The normal path of progress in spirituality—that is to say, of growth in grace— is the sacraments. All our ascetical and spiritual practices, if they are to be of value to our souls, should lead to the sacraments, except in so far as they will happen to follow them as the fruits of their reception and expressions of the life they give. To grow in grace we should understand the sacraments. We should endeavour to cast our prayer in a sacramental mould. We should live and act as the grace of the sacraments inspires us. To do this is to accept grace as Our Lord wishes it to be accepted and to live it on the terms under which He gave it. He, Who knows better than we do the inner mystery of His grace, wished that it should be sacramental.

The plan of this book is simple. The first four chapters deal with the sacraments in general in so far as they are means of union with God in Three Divine Persons. The fifth chapter, dealing with the relation of Christ to His sacraments, is central for the understanding of the whole. Everything that follows depends upon it, and the preceding chapters find their full meaning in it. It might be well to read it first before the rest of the book, on condition however of reading it again in the place given it, where it forms a necessary bridge between the first and second parts. The latter half of the book considers the sacraments in detail and some closely allied questions. The sacraments of Orders, Matrimony, and Extreme Unction, are left over till the very end of the book, as being somewhat more restricted in their application to life than the other sacraments. In all the chapters a certain amount of brevity has been aimed at. The more obvious points were omitted to make room for what was of greater importance from the spiritual standpoint. The reader is asked to forgive such omissions, even if they do result in absence of scientific exhaustiveness.

HOLY GHOST MISSIONARY COLLEGE
Kimmage
Feast of the Annunciation, 1941.

CONTENTS

The Sacraments of Daily Life

1

THE QUEST OF GOD

"My soul hath thirsted after the strong living God."
(PS. 41, 3)

THE CHILD IS FATHER to the man—an axiom that is at the root of all intelligent education. For as the child develops so will the man be. The man is the moral and intellectual heir of the child. There have been but few men who have succeeded in cutting adrift from bonds that tied them since childhood to willed and accepted vice. The mind formed from childhood in a mould of sin lacks the elasticity, the independence of initiative, required to enable it to mould itself anew. All this and more is meant when we speak of the child as being father to the man.

But there is another sense in which the axiom may be understood—and in which it is no less axiomatic—though it be not the one commonly accepted. The child is father to the man in that the man, grow though he may in real or imagined worth, is nothing more than a big child. His field of action is wider than that of the child; more may depend upon his intelligent or non-intelligent attitude in the face of society; his fellows have a right to expect him to contribute to the common well-being to an extent to which a child would be unable to do so. But if we abstract from the wider field, from the material magnitude of the task that falls to the share of the man, and concentrate our attention on what really counts —the emotional reaction to events and the affective colouring

I

of the willed reaction to them—we find that the forces that count in the life of the average man are to an alarmingly great extent precisely those that stand out so clearly in the child and that appear so petty in the eyes of the grown-up spectator of the child's first steps upon life's stage. The man who grows irritated when his children quarrel about the right of one to monopolize a toy sees nothing petty in his own impatience if some member of the family unwittingly uses his favourite chair or egg-spoon; the man who laughs superiorly at the rapidity with which children grow tired of playthings expects to be taken seriously when he tells his friends that he has sound reasons for giving up ventures that have merely lost the attractiveness of novelty; nor does he see any incongruity in complaining that children are too fond of play and too little inclined to work and in spending his own evenings in interminable games of golf or bridge, though there is so much that could be done for the poor and the ignorant. What an appalling total of complacent fatuity would be spared the world could men be brought to look on themselves as least of all likely to be living at the level of rational life at those moments that they believe they are making their manhood and superiority felt. There are few sadder sights than the man who does not see when his actions are those of a child.

There is one moment in the child's existence when it reveals the great secret of human nature. That moment comes when the baby hands make their first feeble effort to draw to themselves an object which, in some as yet confused fashion, they have perceived to be good. For it is of the very essence of man that he turn outside himself to seek the perfection of his being, and the outstretched arms of the child are mute testimony to needs that seek satisfaction while life lasts. Man enters the world a tiny bundle—and how frail a bundle—of flesh and blood. The flesh will grow, the blood stream become abundant, bones will harden, if nourishment be received from the outside world. The child if left alone will perish. The child has a soul, an intellect, a will. But no thought arises in the intellect, no desire inflames the will, unless the world manifest itself to the child through the media of the senses. If even one of the senses fails to operate, a whole realm of thought will remain forever outside the child's ken. If it has never heard, the beauty of music will remain unknown; if it has never seen, the glory of the sun-stained sea will be a mystery. Growth of body and of soul, growth of limbs, of intellect, and of will, are dependent on what the outside world can be brought to contribute; and without its contribution there can be not even a stunted growth.

In this the child lays bare the secret of the man. For the man also finds his perfection through contact with the best that the world can give. The human being is as it were a sponge. It is a power of absorbing, of assimilating. The faculties of man, his intellect and his will, are his own. But the object upon which these faculties are to exercise themselves, finding in that exercise their perfection and development, is not in man, is not his. His soul is made for truth and beauty and goodness. But to find them it must turn to beyond its own narrow bounds. The hands that the baby stretched out eagerly to what it perceived in so ill-defined and provocative a form remain stretched out even when the baby has grown into the man. The term of desire may be clearer, may be better understood, but it is always something that will be attained by reaching out and straining. The basic laws of human nature outlive the changing phases that the years call forth.

If it be the law of the nature of man to seek perfection, contentment, and happiness, in vital contact with reality, one question immediately becomes imperative. What is there in the universe that is most worthy of man's striving? In what object will he find a power to quicken and to inflame, whose touch will send pulses of life and being coursing through his very soul? The question may seem to be a new one. But all that is new in it is the formula. It is the age-old question of the end of life; the question that the philosopher asks when the problem of Ethics has taken definite shape in his mind; the problem that each and every man must face when he comes to the cross-roads of life, when it first dawns upon him with staggering insistence that life must have a purpose and that he may fail to achieve it. Whether we speak of the end of man or of the purpose of life, or even if we come to no more precise formula than that of the seriousness of life, in every case we mean ultimately to imply that life must have a goal and that on the attainment and suitability of that goal will depend the success or the failure of life.

Were we to attempt to tell the goal of life from what we see to be the objects actually pursued by mankind we should be bewildered by their diversity. There is hardly any object of no matter how little intrinsic worth that has not been made the term of the striving of some immortal soul. Among the welter of diverse ends there are however some that stand out both for their frequent recurrence and for their suggestiveness. Though they are not man's true end, the very fact that they are so often mistaken for it by man seems to indicate that they must bear it some resemblance and that they may serve to point out where man's true end lies.

The first of the objects in which we see men put their final end is riches. To encounter examples it is not necessary to search out the confirmed miser. There are ever so many average persons whose one aim in life, from the moment that they began to fend for themselves, is to arrive ultimately at the possession of a certain modest, but sufficient, competence. Very often the money is sought not as end but as means to something else. We shall consider this shortly. But it can be and often is a real end. A man, or the mother of a family, may begin by wishing to provide for the future. To do this requires money. At first the money is sought as a means to ensure future happiness and comfort. But after a time it begins to take a place which is no longer subordinate. The eternal preoccupation with money, the daily experience of all that money can do and of the little that can be done without it, results gradually in the conviction—though it may remain ever at the level of what is grasped only implicitly—that money is of value for its own sake and that sacrifices should be made whose only justification is that they result in greater riches. Has it not often happened that a hard-working and industrious man has come to impose privations on himself and his family on the plea that money must be saved to provide for the children long after the need for strict economy had ceased to exist?

There is no need to speak in detail of the really avaricious. The folly of their lives is evident, though there may be many who while admitting the folly would find it hard to say in what exactly it consists. But in the last analysis it is something that is not far to seek. It is merely an intensification of the folly of the ordinary man who overestimates the value of money. It consists in mistaking for an end something that by its very nature and by its whole nature is a means.

To make money the end of life is to presuppose that money is an end of some kind, that is to say, that it has an intrinsic worth which is its own independently of what it may be used to acquire. Now the whole value of money consists in its worth in exchange. It is something which may be exchanged for something else. The "something else" is what we really desire. The money is of value only in so far as it is a means to obtaining what we need. It is then legitimate to acquire money to the extent to which it may be of use; it is legitimate so to regulate one's present life as to provide for having the money needed for later eventualities. But the end is never the money, but rather what the money renders accessible to us. Money may be sought in view of food, education, lodging, as end. Of itself it is never more than a means.

From this it follows that the precise evil of miserliness and avarice in all their forms consists in the fact that they doom their victim to final frustration. He has been led to concentrate his life on something that is incapable of satisfying the meanest genuine desire. At the end of life he will realize that he has been a failure—that he has followed the road that leads to nowhere. Even before life reaches its close the sense of the futility of his aims will come home to him from time to time. There will always be the knowledge too that his aim in life is one that may be missed through circumstances over which the victim has absolutely no control. Riches amassed in the course of a lifetime may be lost in a day. Is not this thought alone sufficient to show that the pursuit of wealth can bring no deep and constant peace? And beyond this thought there is the other more terrible still—even if riches be gained and hoarded, that cannot satisfy the soul's thirst, for they were made to be the instruments of life, not its purpose.

Though riches be not the end of life the fact that so many men are absorbed in their pursuit indicates that there must be something in riches that makes them akin to man's true end and thereby gives them the outward show of desirability. What this something is becomes clear if we admit that man's final end must be something worth having, something which, in itself, is of value. Riches may be mistaken for a real end because it is not so difficult to come to imagine that they have a real worth of their own independently of what may be acquired by their means. Were this possibility not present they could never be constituted an end. The fact that they have been made an end brings clearly to view what must be a property of the true end, and so provides a means for identifying it. Whatever it be, it must be something of intrinsic value, something of intrinsic worth.

There are, and have been, men who sought riches as a means to power. Do not they suggest a new question—is the end of man power? The test of the final end which we obtained in the preceding paragraph does not seem to exclude power as final end. For power has value; power is of worth.

A man has power when he is able to impose his will upon his fellows. If power be absolute there is no limit to the extent to which others must subject themselves to him who is in power. If it be incomplete or relative, then there is no limit set to it within a certain sphere. Thus a man may have power to do all that money can do, though the things that can be done by force of personality and nothing else remain impossible to him. Another may have power to do whatever influence, or birth, or intelligence, can do. The power of another may be just that given to a quick tongue backed up by a vindictive mind. But whatever be the power in question the thirst of power can so absorb the interest of a man that he will make it the effective goal of his life. Actions will be weighed against the loss or gain of power they will involve.

Even if this process be not fully conscious it will be real enough to be perceived at times when the opportunity for exercising power presents itself. For then, the man infatuated by the desire of power will feel a joy so gripping, will be carried away to so great an extent by the consciousness of his momentary triumph, that he could not fail to notice the utterly inordinate nature of his reaction to the experience of power were he not so intoxicated by it as to have almost lost awareness of its true insignificance—and possibly of his own also.

For power cannot be the end of man, no more than riches. Power too is a means, not an end. Power is a means of acting, just as riches is a means of obtaining. But whereas to act is nobler than to have, the temptation to put one's end in power is subtler—and we may add more reasonable—than that to put one's end in riches.

Power is a means or principle of acting. The whole value of power is that having power our field of activity is widened. To seek power just for the sake of being respected is stupid. The fact that other people respect us will not make us any better in ourselves. To seek power as a means of opening new fields to our activity is not stupid. That is the end of power. But to seek the power itself as the end and to forget the essential importance of the field of activity that it opens to us is a perversion of right order, and it is that that constitutes the evil of regarding power as a final end. The mere possession of power is not a point at which a man can halt in the journey of life. He has the power that he may use it, and its whole value lies in its use. The man who has power in influence may use it to benefit society by getting worthy men into responsible positions. The man who has intellectual power and eloquence may use it to flay vice or to defend morality.

These are examples of the good use of power. If it be used to create employment for shiftless relatives or to heap ridicule upon what is praiseworthy it is being diverted from its purpose. What should be a means to good becomes the instrument of evil.

If it be so clear that power is just a means to something else, not an end in itself, how is it that so many give their whole lives to the conquest of power? There is of course the reason that anything that feeds pride appeals to a man, and he is happy to have that appearance of being somebody which power gives even if in reality he be of but little worth. But there is another reason which goes nearer to the root of things and it is that power can create the illusion of personal perfection. We are all apt to credit the great and the powerful with qualities which they do not possess. Their idlest word becomes weighty with mature thought. Their peculiarities of behaviour, as often as not due to carelessness, are considered the hall-mark of worth. Power creates the illusion of personal perfection in the eyes of those who are subject to power. It creates the same illusion in the eyes of its bearer. It is not a far call from hearing oneself spoken of with reverence to thinking that there may be after all a reason for reverence. Power begins by blinding the lesser breed; it finishes by blinding the giver of the law. The ultimate reason therefore for the quest of power is the instinctive conviction that man's happiness, his final end, is something that perfects himself, fills him with a sense of well-being, constitutes him a centre whence others may draw support and guidance—gives him in other words the reality which is the fount of true power.

Our analysis of power has shown that it cannot be the goal of life. But it has been far from fruitless. It has revealed, as did our analysis of riches, where man's true end and happiness must lie—in the possession of something that confers fulness of life and being, that makes of man a source where others may draw and have their fill.

It may seem strange at this point to ask one more question—can the end of life be friendship? Yet this question follows logically on what we have just said. For friendship is based on personal worth which blossoms forth into love of one's friend and the relationship with him of mutual esteem and support. Friendship too, unlike riches, is something of real value, something of worth. It can be an end. In fact it is deceitful to use friendship as a means to personal gain or to the advantage of a third party. Friendship which ceases to be an end in some real sense ceases to be friendship.

There are many who make of some form of friendship the end of life. Friendship may take different forms. But though they differ in name, and even to a certain extent in idea, they are all but kinds of friendship. The child's relationship to its father or mother is one of friendship. There is in it however that note of reverence which distinguishes it from the friendship vowed to a brother or sister or to one not connected by blood. The fact that there are modes of friendship does not vitiate the essential unity which underlies all its manifestations.

If we understand friendship in this wide sense, examples of people who have made friendship the end of life will rise spontaneously to the mind. We have all known at some time or other the mother whose only aim in life was the well-being of her son; and how she toiled and suffered that he might be spared what she had had to endure; and how she regulated her desires and her aversions by the sole consideration of how they were likely to react upon her son. There have been children too—though this unfortunately is some-

what rarer—who have lived for their parents, have rejected
the chance of a home life of their own because they felt that
their parents needed them, and have experienced their whole
lives through the effects of the sacrifices that their filial devotion imposed on them during their early years. Sisters have
been known to become the slaves of brothers, looking for no
greater recompense than the knowledge that they were loved
in return. Friends have died that the life of a friend be saved,
and the pain of death was considered light in view of the
imperative rights of friendship. The fact then that friendship may be made an end is abundantly clear.

What is it that makes friendship so attractive? An easy
question to ask and hard to answer. Like all elemental things
friendship is known better by living it than by reading about
it. Friendship, we are told, is a state of mutual love based on
similarity (of life and interests), and issuing in a perpetual
interchange of riches, above all else those of the spiritual
order. A cold definition—and yet it describes a thrilling
reality. To have a friend is to face life in the strength of
two, not one; it is to establish a little world of one's own
where there is nothing that is not to the heart's desire. The
friend is one on whom reliance may be placed; one whose
word gives added life and strength; one whose love brings
consolation and courage. A friend is a guarantee of victory in
life's warfare; his undisturbed companionship is the greatest
reward of the hours of hard-won peace. Is there anything
that a man could desire more soul-satisfying than to live in
the company of friends? Should not his whole aim be to
acquire friends, and friends of choice, that their friendship
may light up the lonely ways of time and their worth bring
satisfaction to the heart that power and riches left athirst?

Friendship is something good and noble. Still more than

riches and power it must be an ingredient of true happiness. But alone it does not tell us where true happiness lies. For the value of a friendship is the value of the friend and of his love. And so we are forced to quest once more the goal of life and seek the being in whose friendship it consists. The friend we seek must be worthy of our love; his friendship must be ennobling, must perfect us. Who is this friend?

Who is this friend? This is the question that knocked for so long at the heart of a St. Augustine and found its answer in words of piercing beauty: "Late have I loved Thee, O Beauty ever old and ever young, late have I learned to know Thee. And behold Thou wert in me and I sought Thee outside the portals of my being. Thou wert with me; but I, alas, was not with Thee. I with my untutored taste turned to the beauty Thou hadst made, and the work of Thy hands drew me away from Thee who gave that work its being. But Thou hast spoken and pierced my deaf ears. Thy splendour has shone forth and enlightened my darkness. I have tasted Thy sweetness and my soul desires no other food than Thee." [1] It is God that the soul seeks. God is the riches that satisfy; God gives power and fulness of being; God is the friend with Whom we may live every day and every moment of every day. It is God that we need. It is to God that the infant stretches out its arms in inarticulate yearning. It is in God that the man will find strength and peace.

"O God, my God, to Thee I watch at break of day" (Ps. 62, 1). The soul thirsts for God and there are so many things which we in ignorance and perversity offer it instead of God. We offer it money when it cries out for the Author of all riches. We offer it the ghost of earthly power when it seeks

[1] This is a free paraphrase of the well-known passage of the "Confessions."

to be full of the substance of the power of God Omnipotent. We offer it the satisfaction of being loved by men when it could be loved by God Himself. And the soul rejects our offers; for God, Who made it greater than all that we can give, made it big and wide enough to hold Himself within its embrace. "In a desert land and where there is no way and no water . . ." (Ps. 62, 3)—so wanders the soul that has not God. Full though the world be of the created, it is desert to the soul that experiences desires that the created cannot satisfy. Though there be roads, and wide ones, which lead to earthly goals, the world is a trackless waste to the soul that needs God and is as yet unconscious of the term of its need.

"O God, my God to Thee I watch at break of day," "Late have I loved Thee, O Beauty ever old"—and let us add to these the words of the Apostle of the Gentiles "And I live, now not I; but Christ liveth in me" (Gal. 2, 20)—are not these three expressions of that thirst for God that rages, consciously or unconsciously in every human soul? And yet how seldom is that thirst quenched as it was in the case of David the King, or of St. Paul, or Saint Augustine. Three great saints in the Church of God who had been great sinners! Perhaps it is that the intensity of their cry to God is due to their having at one time been far from Him—to having known what it was to pursue a goal with all the single-mindedness of a passionate nature and then to find that their pursuit had been vain and that it was God that they should have sought. A generous soul snatched from the pursuit of evil and shown that it is God that it must thenceforth desire is capable of an extraordinary singleness of purpose in its quest of God. It has sought happiness outside God and has found the horror of the abyss. False pleasures have no positive attraction for it any more. Habit may drag it now and then from its new-found path, but the will remains firm; for the will has been taught by sad experience that outside God there is no real good. And so, such a soul does not fall into the self-deceiving duplicity of the average man who wants God and everything else that he can have as well; in fact who professes to want God before everything else, but who misses no opportunity of gaining a little more of the things of the world at the risk of having a little less of God for all eternity. "A little less of God"—the expression comes so readily to the mind and there is no dread felt at the thought of not being able to enjoy what alone is worth enjoying to the fullest degree.

One may ask what this has to do with the sacraments. It will of course be admitted that the sacraments being given us to get us into heaven, and heaven being essentially the possession of God, that there is some kind of a remote connection between the two subjects. But the truth of the matter is that the connection is far from being remote, for the sacraments are the signs of our approach to God at the very moment of their reception and the sincerity of our desire of the sacraments is the measure of the sincerity of our desire of God. It is then far from irrelevant to recall in a general way the fact that we need God, and the less pleasant fact that we refuse again and again to face up to the need and to devote our whole energies to the search of Him Whom our soul desires.

The story of the rich young man of the Gospel is familiar to us all. "Good master" he said to Our Lord, "what good shall I do that I may have life everlasting?" (Matt. 19, 16). He had heard of the everlasting life where God would be the possession of the soul. He had even advanced a certain

distance along the road leading to God; for when Our Lord
spoke of the commandments that he must keep he replied,
"All these have I kept from my youth" (ib. 20). He desired
to advance still further. ". . . what is yet wanting to me?"
(ib.). Then came the, to him, startling reply. He must seek
God and God alone, seek God sincerely, walk the road that
leads to God without turning to the left or to the right,
knowing that only God is worth the pains of the search: "If
thou wilt be perfect, go sell what thou hast, and give to the
poor, and thou shalt have treasure in heaven: and come,
follow me" (ib. 21). In the reaction of the young man to this
clear-cut indication each and every soul may see mirrored its
own vacillation and insincerity. "And when the young man
had heard this word, he went away sad: for he had great
possessions" (ib. 22). He wanted God, but not so much as to
want nothing else as well. The possession of God would bring
happiness, but the sorrow of parting with his possessions
would cut deeper than the balm of that happiness could penetrate.

We need God just as that young man needed Him. We
also are insincere—some more so, some less, but all to some
extent. It was a sudden instinctive sorrow that taught the
young man that, without perhaps being aware of it, he was
not content with God alone. We feel within ourselves the
same sorrow and it is the same message that it whispers into
our ears. He felt sad at the thought of losing his riches. Are
not we sad time after time? And is it not the loss of something that is not God that causes our sorrow? Let there be
here no tendency to exaggerate. It is but natural—and con-
sistent with a supernatural life built upon a natural one—
that the loss of something of value should cause pain. This
is by no means inconsistent with a sincere quest of God. But

the pain which shapes and moulds itself into a feeling that life has really lost half its sense and all its sweetness, into the stark conviction that the real value of things can never be the same now as it was before—this is proof that even if we do desire God we do not desire Him as the fulfilment of all our hopes. His throne is shared by something else, and when we lose that something else, though He remains upon His throne, there is beside Him an empty place the thought of which works in us a great void.

"Rejoice in the Lord always; again, I say, rejoice" (Phil. 4, 4). To seek God is already to find Him. As St. Catherine of Siena reminds us, the way to God is Christ, and Christ is Himself God. To come to God through Christ is to come to God in the company of Him Whom we seek. What cause then have we for sorrow? We may lose wealth, we may lose power and influence, we may lose friends. But if we are sincere in our thirst for God we possess God in spite of every other loss, and having God, our willed reaction to life can only be confidence and joy. There is a common belief that a sad saint is a sorry saint, and it is one that hides a wealth of truth. A saint has nothing to be really sad about—sad, that is to say, with a sadness that cannot be redeemed by a higher, absorbing, joy and peace. The soul of Our Lord was sorrowful even unto death (Matt. 26, 38). Yet there was room in His Heart for the peace of the prayer ". . . not as I will, but as thou wilt" (ib. 39). St. Francis could find perfect joy in the midst of the harshest trials.

Joy—spiritual joy compatible with physical pain—in the midst of suffering is then a simple test of the reality of our thirst for God. Pain, when we have still God, is proof that God is not all that we want—proof that we think joy may be found outside Him. And still, the attempt to find joy outside of God is doomed to failure. For the heart of man is bigger than man can understand. Man looks around the world and after a certain period of experiment believes he has found just what will satisfy him. Man, we noted at the very beginning of this chapter, is little more than a child, and an experience of childhood can be used to illustrate the inanity of his hope. It has happened more than once that a little boy— beginning to be not quite so little—has been mortally insulted by a well meaning aunt, who, coming to see him after a few years' absence and forgetting that little boys grow up, presents him with a toy train just at the time of life when he would love to have a really good tennis racquet. The aunt means well, but she simply does not realize that the horizon of a little boy can widen to the extent of making what once gave pleasure now appear insulting. The man who tries to satisfy himself with what the world can give treats himself as does the aunt her young nephew. In fact he treats himself still worse, for she errs through ignorance, whereas he, though knowing that nothing short of God can yield ultimate satisfaction, metes out to his own soul but the paltry playthings of an earthbound mind. Man is too big to be content with the best this earth can give. Man comes from the hand of God and God made man so great that nothing short of his Maker can equal his capacity to yearn. The fact of having a soul widens man's horizons beyond the limits of earth— beyond the limits even of created spirits—makes of them a mighty sweep opening on the Infinite Itself.

Our hearts have been made for God and they can find no rest until they rest in Him. The life of the man who is all that a man can be is never static. It is a life of striving, of progress, of peaceful yielding to a mighty urge. To feel at home on earth is to have missed one's true home, for we have no home but the Bosom of our Father. The theological term for one still on earth, "Viator" or "Wayfarer" is one which we can never too well understand. We are wayfarers. We have no right to rest, no right to halt, no right to say the air we breathe is pure enough for us, the landscape we see all that we desire. For far away we glimpse a better land, whence breezes blow that send the blood coursing madly in our veins. Deep within us we know that there is something better than aught we have experienced. Deep within us we hear a voice whose appeal cannot be resisted, for it is the voice of the Maker to the thing He has achieved, the voice of the Father to His child.

2

UNION WITH GOD

*". . . in this we know that he abideth in us, by the Spirit
which he hath given us."*

(1 JO. 3, 24)

MAN HAS NEED OF GOD. The pages of Holy Scripture tell us
how some among the sons of men have succeeded in their
search for Him. Out of the multitude of these happy ones—
happy in that they have attained the Source of all happiness—
let us select for a moment's consideration three well-known
figures.

There is in the first place Nicodemus—he who came to the
Lord by night. He had not much courage. He had just
enough to lead him to venture on the least compromising of
all possible courses. He hardly had much love. For love
makes heroes of the sorriest stuff. But there was one impulse
that led him on in spite of cowardice, in spite of his niggard
love. He felt, or rather saw, that this Man Who had arisen in
Israel was a problem, that this Man simply did not fit into
any of the categories of men he knew so well and could dismiss from his thoughts as being of no great import to life.
There had been borne in upon his mind the conviction of his
own intellectual insufficiency and his visit to the Lord was a
cry of an intellect that sought light and satisfaction. "Rabbi,
we know that thou art come a teacher from God . . ."
(Jo. 3, 2).

Then there is Mary Magdalen. She sat, it is true, at the
feet of the Master and listened to Him Who had the words

of eternal life. But it is another moment in her life that stands out in our minds when we think of her. We see her kneeling at the feet of the Good Shepherd, bathing those feet with her tears and wiping them with her hair. And we hear the voice of Him she serves: "Many sins are forgiven her, because she hath loved much" (Lk. 7, 47). Forgiven are her sins—sins of frailty, perhaps, sins of a passionate and loving nature that sought to still desire in every way that earth could teach. She had at length found Him her soul desired. He had come to her more as the All than as the Teacher—as One loved rather than as One known.

If we pass beyond the pages of the Gospels we find the third among those who found their Lord of whom we wish to speak. It is St. Paul. Consider him at the moment of his conversion. He is thrown from his horse and falls blind and helpless on the ground. God has revealed Himself to him as the Omnipotent. St. Paul—there can be no doubt of the fact—learned the truth and goodness of the Saviour. But somehow we see in him what we do not see in either Nicodemus or Mary Magdalen a special revelation of the Power of God, of that Divine Omnipotence Which alone is equal to the task of drawing out of man all that man has in him to be and to give. St. Paul tells us of his Jewish upbringing, of his education, of his zeal for the Law. He appeared to be lacking in nothing that went to make the perfect man. All that training and innate power could give was his. Full of his own excellence, relying on the justice that was his through the observance of the Law, he plunged into the arena of life sure of being right and of doing right. God met him on the road to Damascus and Paul learned that wisdom and name and external righteousness are but dust in the estimation of God. "I count all things to be but loss for the excellent knowledge of Christ Jesus my Lord; for Whom I have suffered the loss of all things and count them but as dung that I may gain Christ: and may be found in Him, not having my justice which is of the Law, but that which is of the faith of Christ Jesus, which is of God . . ." (Phil. 3, 8–9). From that moment Paul was nothing in the life of Paul. There would live, work, and triumph in him Christ and Christ Crucified. The weakness of Paul would give place to the strength of Him Who was "Christ the power of God and the Wisdom of God" (1 Cor. 1, 24).

These three figures are the key to the understanding of how man may find God and be united with Him. They are the key to the mystery of grace. For man is intellect and man is will. More than that—for that may be said with equal, or greater truth of the angels—man is hope; man is the optimist, the striver, the fighter, the wayfarer.

Man is intellect. Placed in the universe, that immense question mark, that ceaseless cry of "What am I, Whence do I come, Whither do I lead you?", the mind of man needs light. Around hover the shadowy forms of half-suspected truths. He strains in the darkness trying to give them shape, piecing together the fragmentary details lit up by stray and fitful flashes.

Man is will—a need of the good. Within himself he finds no satisfaction. Outside himself are things that beckon, that smile, that greet, that disappoint. He turns from the one to the other, ever restless, ever searching; and the will rejects find after find for it meets imperfection everywhere.

Man is hope. How else could he continue the struggle? At one moment buoyed up by the delusion that he is wise enough to make his way through life alone, at another by the assurance that things may not after all prove to be so very difficult, he flounders as best he can, constantly changing the grounds of his belief that all will be well according as stay after stay is struck from beneath him.

By faith our intellects possess the Truth of God and the God of truth—not fully, of course, but as becomes the intellects of wayfarers. Faith is a power of believing on the authority of God Himself. It is, in other words, a share in God's power of knowing. What He holds true we hold true. What God sees to be false we reject. We cannot see the intrinsic reason for acceptance or rejection—that will be our privilege in Heaven—but we are infallible in accepting and infallible in rejecting if we accept and reject through faith. We are raised at once above the darkness and error of earth. There are now certain matters about which we cannot be wrong. We have now standards by which to judge all things. God allows us to look at the world as it were through his eyes. We see what in it is of real value; we see what is dross. We know that the grace of a single soul is more than all the material universe—that there is something in the tiny baptized child that is worth more than gold or precious stones. We are sure of that. We could never have guessed it had we not the gift of faith. We know that God is present on our altars. It is God Who has revealed this to us. We know what God does when His minister pronounces over us the words of absolution. We know that there are Three Persons in God and that One of Them became Man. He looked a man like so many others; and yet we who have the faith and we alone can look at Him and grasp the truth of Him and know, as God knew, that He was God. Faith is then a share in the knowledge of God. It is union with the All-knowing, contact established with God by way of intellect.

By charity—love—we adhere to God the All-Perfect, the

Being Who alone is worth possessing. The will is in man a power of, so to speak, staking one's all on some object or other. The will is the seat of love. The act par excellence of the will is love. To be united to an object by way of the will is to love it—in other words, to submit oneself entirely to its spell. A man is at the mercy of what he loves. If he loves money he subordinates his life to the cult of money. Anything in him that is incompatible with money and the possession of money must be eliminated or stifled. Does he wish to educate his children—the first and determining consideration is the cost. Does he feel ill and broken-down in health—he cannot take a holiday that would involve any great expense. There are poor to be clothed, schools to be built—these things are all very good but there is no sense in making any contribution that would encourage people to apply again. Such a man as this does not live. He has no life of his own. Money has dragged him down to its own level, made him its slave—or rather he has used his will to fix all his desires and aspirations on money, and uses the same will to keep himself its plaything.

By charity we have the power of fixing our wills on God and of compelling every power and faculty that is ours to turn itself Godwards. We are enabled to give our lives the one direction that it is worth while to have. The man who has charity lives as it were with his face ever turned upwards to God. Rays of God-sent light are beating down on that upturned face. There is warmth too—the warmth of Divine Love. One loves and is loved in return. The man is all for God; and God, we may say with reverence, is all for the man that loves Him. Here is union, here is Godwardness, here is a life flowing with steady sweep and unswerving course, growing in breadth and fulness as it nears its boundless goal.

Man, finally, is hope; man is striving. And man strives in virtue of the possession of some driving force within him. Life is beset by difficulties of innumerable kinds. Some difficulties are such that they can be overcome by mere physical strength and endurance. The man who has strength and endurance places in them his hope of victory in life. Others call for gifts of intellect, and these gifts can in their turn be the stay of hope. Perseverence, determination, ambition—a man may hope to win through with the help of any or all of these. And yet who can fail to see the frailty of a hope supported by such props? Ambition is a powerful driving force, but there are difficulties it cannot surmount. The most ambitious of men cannot force himself into a position that the rich are determined will not be his. Determination is of value only if the determined one have other gifts to use with determination. Perseverence is very much the same. Intellectual power will bring man far; but how rare it is to find it wedded to strength of will and patience. Even the ideal man—the man endowed with every gift that nature can give—will encounter opposition that he will be powerless to crush; he will encounter temptations that he will be powerless to resist—for our struggle is not just with flesh and blood but with princes of darkness; he will encounter problems that admit of only an approximate solution or that refuse to fit at all into his scheme of things. Who can face sickness, helplessness, life-long physical pain, in the strength of mere stoicism? Who can think on death—not just push it into the background, which is to admit defeat—and face the prospect with confidence? Man, backed up by nothing more than his native wit and strength, feels himself too small, too insignificant to have been launched into the universe. He is one, and a frail one, against the unknown and the unknowable. His defeat is not even likely to be honourable, for the child in him will cry when life's screw is pressed too tight.

The virtue of Hope endows us with the strength of God; the resources of Omnipotence are ours in all that concerns living our own individual life as it can and should be lived. "My God, I hope in Thee for grace and for glory." The grace of God is with us in this world. And that grace is God Himself working in us, making Himself with temptation issue lest we fall on the way (Cf. 1 Cor. 10, 13). We fight no longer with our own weak weapons but with the might of God. Our striving is confident, sure of reaching its term, equal to the task of meeting any opposition whatever. God's Omnipotence will give grace in this world and glory in the next. We could never attain to the joy of eternal happiness through our unaided human effort. That is a crown to be won by an effort that is divine. We hope for this happiness—this glory—because we know that God lives and fights for us within our souls and "that the sufferings of this time are not worthy to be compared with the glory to come, that shall be revealed in us" (Rom. 8, 18). God is united to us, then, by Hope. Hope is contact with and sharing in Omnipotence.

By the three Theological virtues of Faith, Hope and Charity, we enter into union with God—with His Truth, His Goodness, and His Power. But there is, over and above this union, another and deeper union, one which transforms the very substance of our souls, making us—what is far more than to be capable of acting like and with God—sons of the Eternal, sharers in His Nature. This is the union established between God and man by sanctifying grace.

"In the beginning was the Word, and the Word was with God, and the Word was God . . . in Him was life, and the life was the light of men . . . as many as received Him, He gave them power to be made the sons of God . . . who are born not of blood, nor of the will of the flesh, nor of the will of man, but of God" (Jo. 1, 1–13). In these words St. John reveals the manner of man's elevation to a sharing in God's Nature.

In the beginning was the Word Who was God. In Him was the Life of God and the Nature of God in all Their fulness. In Him was the Life that man longed to share in and the Nature that man would fain graft on to his own. The Eternal Word determined to give man what he sought and united to His Own Divine Nature, in the unity of His Divine Personality, a human nature like in all things to ours, sin only excepted.

By this act of taking flesh unto Himself—the Incarnation —the Divinity of the Word was communicated in a most wonderful manner to the Sacred Humanity. There was, in the first place, the anointing of that Humanity by the Personality of the Word. The Sacred Humanity was the Humanity of the Word. There was no fibre in It that did not belong to the Word. It had no personality of Its own other than the personality of the Word. It existed by the selfsame principle—the Divine Existence—that was the principle of the existence of the Word. Just as the human body is pervaded by the human soul in such wise that there is no particle of bone or flesh, no drop of blood, in which the soul is not, without its presence causing bone and flesh and blood to be unreal bone or unreal flesh or unreal blood, so also the Sacred Humanity was pervaded through and through by the Person of the Word, anointed and gladdened by the unction of a Divine Personality, while remaining as truly human as is the nature of any man or woman that treads the earth today. This was the first communication of the Godhead to the Humanity of Our Saviour.

The second communication was necessitated by the first. It was only fitting that the human nature of Our Lord, belonging as It did to a Divine Person, should receive every endowment of which It was capable and that might serve to make It a worthy consort of the Divine Nature with which It was united in the unity of the Person of the Word. The Word was God from all eternity. He had therefore, also from all eternity, the Divine Nature. He was a Person Who was God. By taking to Himself a human nature He became man. This made of Him a Person Who, as well as being God, was also man. There consorted therefore together in this Divine Person two natures, a Divine Nature and a human one. The human was called to co-habit with the Divine, to be along with the Divine the nature of a Divine Person, and this so truly that were we to ask of Jesus of Nazareth toiling in Joseph's workshop "Who are You?" the answer could only be "I am The Word, The Second of the Three Who are Holy, Omnipotent, Eternal."

To fit the Sacred Humanity for this unspeakable dignity It was endowed with the plenitude of Sanctifying grace. Without ceasing to be a human nature It was perfected, made like to the Divine Nature, to the fullest possible extent. The assumption of the Sacred Humanity by the Word had not added any organic part—if we may so speak—on to the Sacred Humanity. This assumption was an actuating, a perfecting, which consisted rather in drawing a human nature to the Word and flooding it with the light of the Word than in adding some new, hitherto non-existing, and created perfection to It. The Personality of the Word was not united to the Sacred Humanity so as to form with It a new whole. But grace—even the grace of Christ—is something new, something other than the Word and the Divinity and Personality of the Word. It is a created likeness of the Divinity which added to a human nature makes it like the Divine Nature. Grace becomes an intrinsic constitutive part of the being it sanctifies. It perfects, beautifies, elevates, makes like God, makes worthy to consort with God.

The Word was Son of God by nature. He was Son of the Eternal Father, born of Him from all eternity, ever being uttered by The Father as His Image and the Splendour of His Substance. The Divine Nature of the Word was then the Nature of One Who was Son of The Father by right of birth. With It was associated by the Incarnation a Human Nature, and it was because of this union that the Human Nature needed to be perfected. Hence it follows that the created perfection of the Human Nature—that is to say, the grace with which it was endowed—must have been in some way a grace of sonship, a grace enabling the Human Nature of Our Lord to consort as in some measure like with like, with the Divine Nature of the Eternal Son. To be at ease as member in a society of antiquaries one must be an antiquary. To fill with credit a chair in a university one must be of the stuff of which professors are made. In some such way we may say that the Sacred Humanity, invited by a Divine Decree, to be with the Divine Nature the Nature of a Divine Person Who was also Son of the Father, must have been lifted up, perfected, adorned, and made—in so far as it was possible for a human nature—like to That other Nature Whose company it was to share in the close intimacy of a personal bond.

"As many as received Him, He gave them power to be made the sons of God." The created grace of Our Saviour was given to Him as being Our Head. The Incarnation took place that man might be drawn to God. Every grace poured out on the Incarnate Word was intended ultimately to reunite man and God. "And of His fulness we have all received." He gives to us of the fulness of Sanctifying grace that is in Himself, Our Head. Our grace is derived from His. Our grace is then in its turn a grace of sonship. It makes us sons of God—not natural sons born of God by generation, but adopted sons made like to God by the infusion of sanctifying grace into our souls, by a process of regeneration: "who are born of God." Our adoption is then a reshaping of our whole being. It does not consist merely in giving us new powers, nor in giving us new objects on which to exercise our old powers—though it does incidentally do all this. It consists primarily in adding to our intrinsic worth, in engrafting on to us something of the Divine. It makes us, in other words, to be like God.

Grace and the Theological virtues of Faith, Hope and Charity, are the principles of our union with God in this world. By them we are united to the Truth, Power and Goodness of God and are made like Him as children are of their father. From these four principles there springs that marvel of our regeneration known as Inhabitation. God lives in our souls. He is there as a guest. "If any one love me . . . my Father will love him, and we will come to him, and will make our abode with him" (Jo. 14, 23). "You are the temple of the living God" (2 Cor. 6, 16). This union is the union of friend with friend. God is our Friend and Father. His Power, with which we are united, is the Power of a Friend; His Truth is the Truth of a Friend; His Goodness is the Goodness of a Friend. God is enshrined within us as in a living temple the very stones of which are called to worship and to love. We are no longer alone. We are with God and God with us.

Such is in merest outline the idea of our godlikeness. It is the more than adequate answer to our thirst for perfection and development. Yet, though this thirst be common to all men—and though reflective men can see that it is ultimately a thirst for God—it is a matter of no slight difficulty to grasp in what precisely our godlikeness consists. There are people who would admit readily all that has been said of it in the last few pages. They do not err therefore in what it does include. But they err, not infrequently, in supposing that it includes as well certain other things which are really incompatible with it, and in giving pride of place to the elements they have themselves introduced. We may take as example of this the case of Our First Parents.

It is a significant fact that Our First Parents did not sin through rejecting the idea of a deification of their natures. They felt the need of the Divine. They knew that it was a need to be answered by contact with the Godhead. And they accepted this necessity of turning outside themselves to God when they agreed to the serpent's suggestion: ". . . in what day soever you shall eat thereof, your eyes shall be opened: and you shall be as gods, knowing good and evil" (Gen. 3, 5). In what then did their sin consist? It consisted, not in wanting to be like God, but in wanting to be like Him independently of Him. Adam wished to know good and evil like God, but without the intervention of God. He wished to be like God, but not to draw his similarity to God from God as its source. There follow in the book of Genesis terrible words describing the effect of this perverted thirst for the Divine: "And the eyes of them both were opened: and . . . they perceived themselves to be naked . . ." (Gen. 3, 7). They had sought fulness of being and they learned instead that to follow their own paths led to nakedness.

It is easy to think that one has clothed oneself with God

and really to be naked. Contact with God is Faith, Hope, Charity, Grace, and Inhabitation—that and nothing more. That and nothing more—though it is far more true to say "that and nothing less." Yet though this latter be more true, the first expression is more faithful to what men commonly believe. They wish to be united with God in all the ways we have just examined, but they wish as well some mode of union they have thought out for themselves and which varies from man to man. Some wish their godlikeness to include the feeling of power, the feeling of being master of one's fate and captain of one's soul, and the joy of gazing unruffled at the storms of life without experiencing anything of their unkind breath. In fact they believe that in this especially does union with God consist. But their feeling of power is illusory. The power that union with God gives is the power of Hope, of childlike trust. It is not a power that will be our very own. It is a power that is the Power of a Friend and that is ours to borrow only, not to hold.

There are some also who hope to find in godliness an intellectual illumination that will teach them the secret of refuting all error. Their mistake does not consist in the desire to know. They ought to desire to share in God's own knowledge—even in the Knowledge which He has of Himself. But they go astray in desiring a knowledge which will be at the same time the secret of successful refutation. They want a knowledge that will confound others—not just a knowledge that would confound them if they paused to examine it, but one that will confound them whether they will it or no. They have succumbed to the attractiveness of what is really a gratia gratis data—the gift of persuasive words ("sermo scientiae" 1 Cor. 12, 8)—to the extent of becoming eventually unable to admit the existence of genuine sanctity in anyone who does not submit himself to the spell of their peculiar views. In other words, they have missed the meaning of supernatural holiness.

And finally there are those who test sanctity by what they term sincerity. The sincere man is the man of God. They are sincere. They wish nothing but that God's interests be promoted. They believe that all holy and sincere men must see that that and nothing else is the motive in all they do. And so they forge their way through life, standing out, they believe, head and shoulders above the rest of mankind as men of God, sincere and God-fearing, whom all equally God-fearing men should allow to pursue their way unmolested. But they are molested. They meet with opposition. And the judgment they will pass on the opposing parties is a foregone conclusion. No really good man could stand in their way. Perhaps the people who oppose them are in good faith; but viewed objectively their actions are guided—or led astray—by passion, by ignorance, or by insensibility to God's real mind! Poor blind devotees of pigheaded sincerity! They have never understood the lesson of Calvary.

Calvary is the great key to the understanding of grace as it enters into the texture of this world. For on the Cross there hung One united as never mere man will be to The Godhead, and That One showed forth as despised and the most abject of men. Our Lord, torn and bleeding, Our Lord the apparent failure, Our Lord Who had failed to draw the multitude, Our Lord Who was silent when invited to refute, Our Lord Who, the most sincere of men, could say of those that opposed Him "Father, forgive them for they know not what they do"—it was this same Lord Who was full of grace and truth. He, in the midst of humiliation, contempt, failure, was the most perfect of men, was steeped in the Divinity. What clearer lesson can be conceived than this of the fact that the kingdom of God is something that is within us, is something this world can neither feel, nor taste, nor weigh? The godlikeness of the wayfarer is compatible with pain, with social failure. It is compatible with the loss, with the absence, or with even the direct antithesis of what is of value when judged by earthly standards. And the reason is simple: it is not a thing of this world. The soul that has grace has God. It has reached the Term of its desire. But God is hidden within it and no one but He knows just how closely He has united Himself with His creature. To say that grace is hidden is not to say that it is not operative. The soul in the state of grace is really and effectively in contact with the Truth and the Power and the Goodness of God. This contact is real—but it is not visible to intellect or sense. It is an object of knowledge to faith alone. Faith knows that the soul in the state of grace is in continual contact with God, is continually full of God. With the knowledge of faith we must rest content till the day of Beatific Vision opens on our wondering minds.

Grace is something of inestimable value hidden within us. This mystery of an unperceived and unperceivable treasure is not however without parallel in the natural order. The normal man admits that the newly born child differs from a young animal. Yet it has no operation which an animal has not or could not have. As far as external appearances go it is nothing more than an animal. What then is it that distinguishes it from all animals? It is that we recognise in the child—or believe that there is in the child—some secret force, not as yet operative in a visible and tangible manner, but which still gives the child that worth that raises it above the whole brute world and which, one day, will manifest itself in acts of intellect and will. Grace is hidden in our souls somewhat as the rational is hidden in the tiny babe. We cannot see or touch grace. But it is within us as a germ of life, already to some extent operative—just as it is the rational soul that is the principle of the little life that the child actually exercises—and waiting but the day when the toils of flesh are cast off to burst forth in all the splendour of its amazing powers. We cannot see the rational in the child; but we know it must be there, for it is of children that men are formed. Neither can we see the grace within our souls; but we know it is there, for something must work within us that weight of glory that sends us darting after death into the bosom of Our God.

Man has need of God; man finds God through grace. The spiritual life is the life of grace and of growth in grace. But there must be a certain mechanism by which grace is acquired, a certain pageantry on days when grace wells up within us. Is the acquisition of grace a matter of simple contact between God and man without the intervention of any rite or instrument? Is growth in grace a matter of joy to the individual soul alone and is the Church to be deprived of the gladness that is the state's when marching men and singing people vaunt their loyalty and pride? The answer to these two questions is the dogma of the Sacraments. The Sacraments are the pageantry and causes of growth in grace. It is under these two aspects that we shall consider the first four Sacraments we have selected for special study: Baptism, Confirmation, Holy Eucharist, and Penance. These four have been chosen as being those which are received normally by all men—two of them being received frequently. They enter into all lives; they cannot but have an important rôle to play. What is this rôle?

3

THE SACRAMENTS: SIGNS OF UNION WITH GOD

To HAVE MENTIONED in the same context sacraments and pageantry, as we did just now, will, not improbably, be a cause of scandal or annoyance to more than one reader. For there is in our countries a steady current of thought which regards pageants and such manifestations of one's mind and dispositions as mere weak sentiment. What is of real value is the mental attitude; its manifestation is—at any rate if it become obtrusive—nothing more than childish display. One should love one's country and if necessary be ready to die for it, but why indulge in the vulgar fuss of singing anthems and saluting flags? By all manner of means let us love God; but to love Him is a matter of the spirit; any kind of display whatever is simply out of place—a mute indication that the author of the display has no deep and inner sense of God and his relations to God.

It is by no means my intention to discuss this attitude here under all its possible subjective aspects. Thus, there are people of a retiring or shy or unsociable character who dislike display because of the sensitive revulsion they experience at the bare idea of contact with it. If their attitude be due to nothing more than affective reasons it is to that extent irrational and inapt to instruct the searcher after truth. The cases that are of real interest to us are those of people who object to display on intellectual grounds, who can give—or believe they can give—reasons why display is unworthy of a man, and a slight rush or ebb of colour in the cheeks should be the limit in what is allowed by way of registering intense emotion. Instead of answering their difficulties directly let us simply consider the arguments for the admission of some kind of symbolism into life.

There is in the first place the argumentum ad hominem: as a matter of fact the opponents of display object not to display itself but only to those forms of it which they do not happen to find congenial. If they meet a friend they shake hands with him. They are not content with the intellectual conviction existing on both sides that they are friends. Their friendship seeks a visible, sense-perceptible, expression and outlet which is the handshake. If they go to condole with a friend on the occasion of his mother's death they say something, they manifest their sympathy by signs of grief. They are not content with having masses offered for the repose of the mother's soul without at the same time letting the bereaved son be aware of the fact by placing mass-cards on the coffin. They have as well, not infrequently, other little failings in the matter of display, such as wearing dress clothes on solemn occasions and smiling at a good joke. In other words they do not object to display or pageantry at all. They object to certain forms of it; and this not because they are forms of pageantry but because they are manifestations of emotions which seem not to deserve publicity. They object possibly to incense because it speaks to them of nothing but sickly sentiment, and to regimental parade as it expresses nothing higher than the soul of a machine. But they are quite willing to admit, and do admit in practice, the utility of those other forms of symbolism which they think free from vulgar or inacceptable implications.

So much will suffice for the argumentum ad **hominem.**
The positive reason for accepting symbolism is so oft repeated
in scholastic philosophy that it is usually accepted by students
without the tribute of a moment's reflection. If then we go
to the extreme of exposing it once more, that is only in order
that those who do not accept it in practice may be led to see
that their position is sub-human, that instead of having risen
above the herd by their attempt at a more spiritual code of
life they have really failed to get the best that can be got out
of their human organism. In other words we contend that
whoever wishes to live his spiritual life free from ritual and
symbolism is on the wrong path, and that progress in spirituality for him will depend, other things being equal, on the
degree of his sincere effort to integrate them into his life.

Man, we have been often told, lives on the frontiers of
two worlds—the world of pure spirits and the world of the
things of sense. He is below the lowest of the angels and
higher than the most noble of the brutes; but he is neither
so far below the one as to have no share in the life that
quickens its being nor so far above the other as to feel nothing
of the limitations of its meagre mode of existence. Man is
neither imprisoned angel that strives to burst its bonds nor
exalted brute infected with a brain. He is man, something
unique in creation, spirit united to matter and finding strength
and life in the disciplined harmony of the two. It is not in
the scheme of things that man should find perfection by
attempting to act as if he were an angel, by treating what
is of sense in him as if it were outside him. It is not in the
scheme of things either that he should find deep and genuine
joy in the expansion of nothing more than what is in him of
sense. Man's quest of perfection, of God, or whatever we
may wish to term the goal of his life, must be based on

courageous realism; and the reality he must accept is that he has come into the world a being of soul and flesh and blood and that to ignore the claims of either soul or flesh or blood is not to perfect but to dismember self.

The life of man is a quest of God; and God must be sought with soul and flesh and blood if the quest is to be a human one. We may speak in an analogous sense of the angelic quest of God that fulfilled itself at the dawn of their creation. That was a quest of Spirit by spirit. An act of knowledge and an act of love and the angels were eternally, immutably fixed in the possession or the loss of the Almighty. No element of sense entered in to sway will or obscure vision. God had given them but intellect and will and what He expected of them was the homage of their piercing intellects and the love of their fervent wills—that and nothing more. We may also speak of a quest of God in the brute creation. "All ye works of the Lord, bless the Lord; praise and exalt Him above all for ever" (Dan. 3, 57). It is a silent voiceless quest, one of which the subject can have no awareness. Every being of the lower creation, every animal, plant, and lifeless thing has its own end, tends to what is proportioned to its nature. There is then within them all, frozen in, walled up, a spark of desire of the good, and ultimately of God, the Source of all goodness. But their desire is of God as found in His creation, not as He is in Himself—a desire of those works of His hand which share in the being of their Maker and of the Maker as shared in by the works of His hand. They have no power to raise a voice in praise; they have no power to change the theme of their appeal; they have no voice, no sought-for theme, theirs is as it were the long low murmur of a distant sea.

The voice of man raised up to God is not a confused sound

coming from afar. God is near to man, nearer than we can think. We are not as are the stones by the wayside, mute witnesses to the Power and Majesty of a Creator. Nor do we, as do the angels, turn to God in acts of intellect and will alone. It is true that we feel as do the angels the imperative urge to give voice to the stream of religion welling up within. But the voice must be one of flesh and blood expressive of thought and love. Else there remains some portion of our being that has not been pressed into the service of the Most High. All that is within us must praise the Lord, body as well as spirit, mind as well as matter. For all that is in us is the Lord's and spirit may not bid the flesh be still when it is the Glory of the Lord that the flesh would hymn.

There is besides the fact of this right of the Lord to the explicit homage of all that is in man the no less certain fact that the human spirit is unable to essay the sustained flight of its powers without the cooperation of sense. We know that without some kind of imaginative activity there can be no act of intellect, and consequently no act of will. This bare minimum must be admitted by all orthodox students of scholastic philosophy. We cannot think of God, nor pray to Him—in the more common forms of prayer at any rate—without accompanying imagery. To attempt to eliminate this imagery is to dry up all prayer at its source. But to admit the necessity of this sensory contribution to spiritual activity is not yet to have exhausted the rôle of sense. The intellect draws its concepts from sense-perceptible things; the will is inflamed to love when it tastes the sweetness of these same things. Should there then ever be question of a willed fixation of the intellect on a definite thought, of orientation of the will originating in the willing subject, things must play their part in providing fixation and orientation. It will be impossible to fix will or intellect by mere manipulation of imagery. There must be a certain external stimulus, a certain thought-out ceremony expressive of the mental state we wish to induce, forcing us as it were by its very life and realism into that attitude of mind that shadowy imagery could never sustain.

To know or love at all demands concomitant imagery; to give a fixed orientation to intellect or will demands as well adaptation of the external stimulus. This latter point it is, we believe, that the pseudo-spiritual neglect. And yet, it is hard to see how they reasonably deny that there be such a point; for most men admit it in daily life. A man far from home but wishing the memory of his mother to remain ever fresh within him keeps her photograph in some place where it will frequently strike his eye. He does not consider it sufficient to rely on memory alone. The image of his mother stored up in his memory is sufficient to enable him to think of her at any particular moment he may wish to do so. But if he wish to think of her habitually, to keep the drift of his thoughts habitually on his mother in spite of the distractions and absorbing interests of his daily work, then he knows that it is not sufficient to entrust the matter to a fickle memory but that he must arrange some thing in such a way as to call her to his mind time after time—and the photograph is nothing more than such a thing. Tying knots on handkerchiefs, forming useful associations of ideas—such practices are examples of the application of the same psychological rule: to give mind or will a stable bent it is necessary first of all to make environment subservient.

St. Thomas meant all this and more when in the first article of the sixty-first question in the third part of the Summa Theologica he advances in his usual calm and unemphatic way the words: "Sacramenta sunt necessaria ad humanam salutem triplici ratione: quarum prima sumenda est ex conditione humanae naturae, cuius proprium est, ut per corporalia et sensibilia in spiritualia et intelligibilia deducatur"—"the sacraments are necessary for the salvation of man for three reasons, of which the first is based on human nature which has as distinctive mark that it arrives at the knowledge of intellectual and spiritual things by way of things of sense." It is not sufficient to have the imagery that must accompany all thought; there must be things to go upon—"corporalia et sensibilia." And this follows from the very "conditio humanae naturae." It is a necessity rooted in the nature of man. It is not a mere case of a possible course of action. It is a necessity imposed by the very logic of things, an inescapable condition of coming at the measure of knowledge and understanding of spiritual things that it is within the power of man to attain.

Man must therefore be assisted in his ascent to God by the symbolism of things. This symbolism has two principal manifestations: the sacrifice and the sacrament. Let us consider first the sacrifice as being more readily understood from the precise angle of its symbolic character.

The soul that has arrived at some true idea of Who God is sees that He is a Being of infinite majesty. God is Master of the soul and of the world. He made all things from nothing. There is absolutely nothing that is that does not come from God. Were we, while considering any being, to abstract from what in it is due to God, there would be nothing left for us to consider. And this dependence on God is not a merely historical fact. He did not bring things into being and then leave them to their own devices; He did not—for He could not—give them a power of permanence which would dispense with His further action. The continuance of a thing in being is just as much dependent on God as was its first becoming. All that is comes from God—being and permanence in being; thought, word, deed; brain that thinks, lips that speak, and arm that does.

The soul filled with this thought turns her eyes to God and knows that she is nothing. She, nothing, gazes at Him Who is, at Him Who pervades her whole being, at Him Who holds her within His mighty grasp, Who knows the nothingness she but has glimpsed. And the soul lowers her gaze and cries: "My God; all that is in me is Yours; I will to depend on You; I accept my dependence on You."

Here is a fundamental state of soul; a state that needs to be burned into the being of the Christian. It is not a state that it suffices to experience in a fleeting way on rare occasions. Nor is it a state that one does not need to deepen; it is fundamental—the measure of our spiritual stature is in some degree the measure of our understanding of sacrifice. For these two reasons then—the fact that the idea of sacrifice should be kept constantly before our minds and the fact that the idea of sacrifice is one we must penetrate as far as in us lies—we are forced by the psychological necessity of which we have just spoken to externalize our spirit of sacrifice, to allow sacrifice to express itself in a concrete and sense-perceptible form.

The idea which we wish to incarnate is that we and all things belong to God and that we on our side are willing to accept this dependence. How can this be expressed concretely? By the traditional idea of sacrifice as a gift made to God—"haec dona, haec munera, haec sancta sacrificia illibata." All that is belongs to God. We, to express our recognition of the fact, withdraw some one of the things of this world from the use of man and offer it to God. It was always God's. God always owned it. But we had considered it hitherto as for our use—as belonging to us in some way as well as to God. To offer it in sacrifice to God is to abdicate our claim to the thing in question as far as is within our power, the better to express the priority of God's claims on it over ours.

It is not hard to see how such a rite as this is richer in suggestiveness than the bare intellectual admission of dependence on God. We offer in sacrifice a material object. The act of offering proceeds from a spiritual conviction. Sacrifice therefore comprises two elements: the thing offered and the attitude of the offerer. But the offerer himself is soul and body. Hence an act expressive of the total offering of himself to God is most appropriate if it contains both a spiritual and a bodily element. Both these elements are found in sacrifice as it has just now been described. There is a spiritual element—the attitude, or act, of the soul. There is as well a bodily element—a sense-perceptible thing, taken from among the things destined by God for the support of our human bodily life and therefore standing in a very real way for the body. Our offering then is one in which the whole man takes part. It is not the offering of soul alone, nor is it the offering of a merely corporeal being. It is the offering of a being that is both soul and body. It is the offering of a thing as symbol of thought and will, the conviction of a mind expressing itself through forms of flesh and blood.

Sacrifice deepens our conviction of dependence on God. It is true that there are moments of greater or less duration in the life of every sincere Christian when his soul feels as it were plunged into the Majesty of God. There is a stark, eye-to-eye realization of what God is and what man is. Does a symbolic act add anything to such moments as these? The question is a deeper one than I should wish to answer; it is venturesome to set limits to the workings of the graces of prayer. But there can be no doubt that even when weighed against such moments as these the rite of sacrifice presents a possibility of illumination of absolute worth. For the rite is something that may be elevated by grace to the dignity of a revelation. In itself it is of infinite suggestiveness. There is in it the idea of something altogether cut away from the use and service of man. The thing offered is a holy thing. We see in it, as it were, God in the actual exercise of His dominion, laying claim to what is His by right of ownership. The thing is now God's. It looks much as it ever looked; but the hand of God has touched it. We too are God's. Appearances do not betray the fact—but we really are God's. Is not this symbolism a field where grace may find free entry? Can it not even happen that an interior illumination such as those of which we have just spoken, will find its ultimate completion in the shock of contact with the symbolism of sacrifice, in such wise that the conviction of dependence on God will serve as spur to the intellect illumined by grace to probe the depths of meaning of this act so expressive of dependence?

Sacrifice is then the first of the two symbolic expressions of a fundamental state of soul. The second is the sacrament. For the sake of unity of treatment let us consider the sacrament as implied in some way in the sacrifice, though this is not the usual avenue of approach to the problem. In so doing we lose nothing of the essence of the sacrament and show all the more clearly its symbolic character.

Sacrifice is an offering to God symbolic of our dependence upon Him. If the offering be one pleasing in His sight God becomes well-disposed in our regard. Seeing that we recognize the fact that all that we have comes from Him He confers still greater gifts upon us, for He knows now that His gifts instead of drawing us away from Him will only make us turn all the more fervently to Him, depending as we shall on Him not only for our being but for His additional gifts as well. The complement of our sacrifice—of our gift to God—is a gift of God to man, an increase in spiritual stature conferred by God on the soul that has turned her face upwards to Him in the act of sacrifice. Sacrifice and growth in grace—the gift of man to God and the gift of God to man— these are the essential phases of the spiritual life. But if sacrifice has its symbolism should there not be a symbolism of spiritual growth as well?

The symbolism of spiritual growth is the sacrament. The sacrament is a sign of a spiritual reality at work within us and making us holy. The spiritual reality of which it is the sign is not so much an efficient cause or agent of our holiness— though, as we shall see, such an agent is indicated as well— but what is known in scholastic terminology as a formal cause, namely grace. The sacrament is a sign of the grace that is within us and which is the principle of our spiritual life. Every different grace, every mode of life, has its own sign, its own sacrament, in such wise that the growth of the soul in grace and the various necessary phases of its growth are indicated and brought home to the soul by symbolism. There is an exterior sign to remind the soul of every vital stride it makes along the road to heaven. It is not left to words alone to remind it of the progress it is making. There are signs as well, and signs that are richer in content than many words.

Just as the sacrifice has an analogue in the peace offering which inferior or conquered people make to their masters or conquerors there are striking analogues to the sacrament to be found in daily life. The initiation ceremony as practised among certain pagan tribes is one. The young man who has just attained the age of manhood is taken apart from the rest of the tribe and after a period of trial and instruction in tribal lore and rites undergoes a ceremony of initiation into the life of the tribe. The ceremony does not make him a man. Whatever was needed to complete his manhood over and above what age could give him was obtained in the period of instruction. The ceremony then has but one aim: to represent symbolically the fact of arriving at manhood in such a way as to impress the importance of the fact on the young man himself and to intimate it officially to his fellows.

There are similar examples to be found in civilized life as well, though they have not usually the intense earnestness of the pagan rite. Societies usually have their own badges; a member of the society wears the badge, partly to remind himself that he is a member of the society and partly that other members may know him as one of theirs. We dress in black in times of mourning. Those who see us in black understand why, and the fact of being in black tends to restrain in us any tendency to conduct that would be out of keeping with the nearness of death. Policemen have a special uniform. Instinctively we have not the same respect for a detective in plain clothes as for an ordinary policeman. As a matter of fact both have the same authority, but only the one has a special dress in sign of his authority, with the result that it is only in him that authority becomes as it were palpable.

In the life of grace there are different functions and different stages of initiation. The sacraments are their signs. The first stage is spiritual birth—birth to the life of grace. Its sign is the sacrament of Baptism. To be present at a Baptism is to have brought home to one with extraordinary vividness the fact that a spiritual transformation is taking place. The water of Baptism flows upon the child's head and the words are pronounced: "I baptize thee in the name of the Father and of the Son and of the Holy Ghost." The work of cleansing, of washing, operated in the soul escapes our eyes of flesh. But the reality of the sign is inescapable. That really has happened. That cannot be forgotten. Even for the child that has had no experience of the event the fact of the event is beyond doubt, and it is one that can easily be reconstructed in later life, especially after having seen other Baptisms. The sacrament is therefore both sign and reminder of spiritual birth. It keeps the fundamental fact that we have been cleansed from sin and endowed with grace before our minds. It tells us too in some way what it is that has happened to us: that our life of grace is a cleansing, a purifying. It is, in other words, as we have already indicated, a support and stimulus to our faith.

Birth to the life of grace is followed logically by growth in grace. And the growth of a living organism depends on suitable nourishment. The spiritual life is a matter of union with God. Growth in spirituality is growth in union with God. It follows that there must be some sacrament to symbolize growth in God, absorption in God, transformation into God. This sacrament is the Blessed Eucharist. Under the image of bodily nourishment the idea of spiritual nourishment is conveyed to the mind. Food builds up the body. Bread is the essential food of our peoples, wine is the normal drink of many. Bread and wine are then the substance of our bodily food. Growth in bodily life depends on consuming them. But bread and wine transformed into the Body and Blood of Christ by the power of the words of consecration are the sign of something higher than bodily growth; they are the sign of spiritual growth, of growth in God, of being nourished by the Substance of God Himself. To approach the Holy Table is to make an act of faith in the reality of the interior transformation that deeper union with God effects in our souls. It is to confess that union with God is growth, is transformation into God, is strength and life and well-being of soul.

The grown man is distinguished from the child by the fact (which is one among many) of his greater obligations in the face of society. The man is expected to be a man, to contribute to the good of the body politic, to leave the world something better than he found it. The child is expected to leave the world something better than it found him. There will come a time in the spiritual order too when a man will feel that he is bound to take his stand in the presence of—and even in the face of—an organized world that may be hostile to what he stands for. He must be willing to be the soldier of his faith. What is more, he must be willing to allow the consciousness of the fact that he is the soldier of his faith to be burned into his soul by submitting to a ceremony of knighting. He will come before the ruler of the spiritual realm to which he belongs and kneeling before him he will be anointed with the oil of the brave and strong, will bow beneath the outstretched hands where broods the Spirit of Fortitude, will suffer gladly a blow as reminder of the conflict that awaits. He rises from his knees a knight of the Most High, ready to do and to dare in the cause of his holy faith. Within he is a man. The sacrament has been the sign of his manhood. It is something that he will remember when the din of battle begins to break upon his ears. Not only is he a knight in virtue of the spiritual power that is within him—and of which he has no immediate consciousness—but he has been dubbed knight in a way that strikes the senses amid the splendour of liturgical ceremony. The day of his knighting stands ever before his mind's eye, a perpetual reminder of the grace that is in him and the work there is for grace to do.

In conclusion, there is the sacrament of Penance. The average Christian is little inclined to consider this sacrament from the point of view of its symbolism—and the same may be said of the Blessed Eucharist as well. It is more natural to think of it as a cause, as something that effects the forgiveness of sins just as the Blessed Eucharist really contains Him Who is the food of our souls. But symbolism is present in Penance as in any other sacrament. The life of grace and union with God, mirrored in its beginnings, growth, and maturity, in the sacraments of Baptism, Holy Eucharist, and Confirmation, is subject to decay and weakness. We may grow cool towards God; we may even sever all connection with Him. We know that even after we have offended God He is willing to restore us to His friendship. He wills not the death of the sinner but that he be converted and live. We know also that to be restored to the divine friendship means nothing more than to possess once again sanctifying grace and charity, the love of God, which is its first consequence. God can, in other words, restore us to His friendship by an operation which does not fall in any way under our powers of observation. We should, of course, know by faith that we were once more His friends; at least we could conjecture on the basis of principles which our faith tells us to be true that this was the case. But as we have so often seen before, there would be the difficulty of forming in our minds a vivid image of what had happened when grace was given to our souls once more. Spiritual realities do not lend themselves to vivid representation unless they be made concrete in some way. The sacrament of Penance is the concrete representation of what takes place in the soul of the converted sinner. The sinner comes to a God Whom he has offended. He comes admitting his fault and begging pardon. He comes to his judge, though to a merciful One. To portray all this Penance is instituted as a tribunal. The sinner going on his knees confesses his sins to the priest and receives forgiveness. God has forgiven the sins by an invisible operation. But there is the visible rite to remain stored up in memory and to deepen his conviction of the hidden change in soul-state. The one is the image of the other. What is enacted in words that can be heard takes place really within the silence of the inner castle of the soul. Faith is quickened by the rite; the sinner feels keenly the nature of the change the divine mercy has wrought in him who had knelt and acted as becomes a culprit, and he returns to the world contrite, a sinner who to the homage of a contrite heart has added submission to a voice of pardon.

The symbolism of the other three sacraments does not concern us at the present moment. They have their symbolism too, else they would not be sacraments. But it is not our purpose to treat of them here. What has been said may appear forced and academic. If it has been no exaggeration to say that people do not ordinarily consider Penance and the Blessed Eucharist from the point of view of their symbolism, it might almost be added that the same could be said to some degree of any of the sacraments. And yet, the symbolism of the sacraments is something we should not neglect. The rite is intended by God to awaken and quicken faith—and through it, hope, love and contrition—to give insight into the nature of the spiritual effect of the sacrament. The Blessed Eucharist is received under the appearance of food. Does our faith thrill with the conviction that Our Lord is really our spiritual food, that it is He that our souls need, that without Him we die? Yet, that is the message of the sacrament. Do we come to confession as culprits, as people who have been guilty of a crime, as criminals in the spiritual order? Yet that is what the sacrament of Penance should tell us. Do we feel the urge to serve God? Are we class-conscious of our divine sonship and of our commission in God's army? If not we have failed to grasp the lesson of the rites of Baptism and Confirmation. To ask one final question: do we come hungry to Holy Communion? Do we come to it as feeling the need of partaking of the Body of Our Lord and of drinking His Blood? If not, is not our active participation in the external rite a sham, for the rite is a sign and the sign should have a meaning?

Far from being a fruitless study the question of the symbolism of the sacraments could well be made the matter of a distinct and fruitful treatise. We shall refer to it in passing in later chapters. It will inevitably happen that the idea of sign will be dwarfed by that of cause. It is not inopportune however to draw attention to it, lest it be so dwarfed as to be quite lost sight of. We approach the sacraments with mind and will. They are signs precisely that the mind be enlightened and the will inflamed.

4

THE SACRAMENTS: CAUSES OF UNION WITH GOD; SACRAMENTAL GRACE

"Oh how great is the multitude of thy sweetness, O Lord."
(PS. 30, 20)

GOD IS THE GOAL OF HUMAN EXISTENCE. Human life is intended to be a quest of God. But in point of fact man's quests are often far from God, and in these quests he sins. And St. Paul has hard words for the man who seeks his happiness in anything outside God: "For know you this and understand, that no fornicator, or unclean, or covetous person (which is a serving of idols), hath inheritance in the kingdom of Christ and of God" (Eph. 5, 5). Covetousness—in fact, any sin at all—is, in the mind of St. Paul, a species of idolatry. It sets up in the place of God and on His throne, an object which has no right in itself to our homage, no right to be the goal of desire. In doing this it degrades man. It makes him like those who worship gods of stone and wood and leads him to share in their shame. "For professing themselves to be wise, they became fools. And they changed the glory of the incorruptible God into the likeness of the image of a corruptible man, and of birds, and of fourfooted beasts, and of creeping things. Wherefore God gave them up to the desires of their heart, unto uncleanness, to dishonour their own bodies among themselves. . . . And as they liked not to have God in their knowledge, God delivered them up to a reprobate sense, to do those things which are not convenient (Rom. 1, 22 sqq).

If man rejects God and seeks to perfect himself through contact with the world God rejects man and leaves him the world and its bitterness. There is in created things no power of discipline, they cannot give to man a sense of his dignity for they have no dignity themselves. They cannot restrain those forces within him which when unleashed will drag him to the level of the beasts; for he feels that he is their master, that he is greater than they and that the only restraint they can put upon him is the restraint that he himself wills the better to satisfy his thirst. Man cut adrift from God is truly spirit chained in a dungeon of flesh that knows that to burst its bonds is to thrust itself into the horror of the abyss.

Sin is the quest of the creature divorced from love of the creator. Man must strive. Man must turn outside himself whether it be to slake his thirst for God at the fountains of the Saviour or to dull it at the stagnant pond of the created. Turn somewhere he must. To turn to things while at the same time turning his back on God is to sin. Sin is then really a simple thing to glimpse, though it be at the same time the great mystery of iniquity. It is easy to see the choice it involves between the Infinite and the finite. Its mystery is the full horror of the slight offered to the Infinite in preferring the finite. That is something we cannot grasp. When we offend a dear friend we are appalled at the enormity of what we have done. To say that a gulf has opened between the two is all too inadequate to express the reality, the void, the heart-break, the sense of wanton and irreparable destruction —irreparable, for what has been done remains a fact even when seen through the joy and tears of reconciliation. Slighted human friendship is something we can hardly understand. But what if the one offended be God? What if the gulf yawn now between me and Him Who holds me in being? What if to offend is to measure nothingness with Infinity, creature with Creator? That is a mystery. That eludes our straining eyes. That is beyond the horizons of the angels themselves. They only know that the brightest of their number sinned and that he was lost.

Sin is a disordered pursuit of the finite good. What is disordered in it is its implied rejection of God. And as God has many claims upon us and upon all that He has made so we may reject Him by refusing to submit to one or other or all of them. God is our Friend. To sin is to reject His right to our love. God is Lord and Master. To sin is to reject His right to service. God is Lord of His creation. To sin is to reject His right to dictate the terms of its use. And though sin be most properly an offence against God's right to our love there is a peculiar instructiveness in considering sin as an offence against God's right to service and respect in the use of the works of His hands.

To turn from God to creatures is to withdraw creatures from what should be their state of subordination to their Creator. We may love and search out all that is good and attractive in God's handiwork if only we love God still more— if only we admit that His handiwork comes from Him and belongs to Him and that He is far more lovable than aught that He has made. But to attribute to creatures a worth and desirability apart from their value in God is to withdraw them as it were from their condition of being His servants and make of them possible rivals to His Divine Majesty. We may go still further in this analysis of sin and say that to withdraw things in this way from God's dominion is to arrogate them to ourselves. For ultimately the meaning of the inordinateness of our desire of them is that we subject them to ourselves and to our need of satisfaction rather than to

God. To God they belong and they should be used only in accordance with His wishes. To sin is to misuse them for the sake of some personal gratification. It is to make what should be the occasion of our turning to God an occasion for gratifying self. It is to submit creation to the indignity of being the slave of the whims of man. It is to snatch God's workmanship from His grasp and submit it to man's capricious sway.

Sin involves then some misuse of creatures. The cure for sin should in consequence comprise a reshaping of our attitude to creatures; while consisting essentially in a reestablishing of relations with Almighty God it should not neglect to rectify our attitude to created things, making us see them in their true light as works of the hand of God. Grace is the cure for sin; grace makes us friends and children of God. But that there might be included in the bestowal of grace a rectification of man's attitude to things, God in His wisdom and mercy has decreed that grace should come to us normally through the channel of material causes; He has, that is to say, given us as the normal means of obtaining and growing in grace those sacraments which we saw in the previous chapter to be signs of our sanctification.

If sin involves a subjection of creation to misuse by man, the sacraments involve in a no less striking manner the subjection of man to God present in a new and wonderful way in inanimate creatures. The sacraments are signs of grace. This fact already involves a certain divine presence—the presence of the object signified in the sign that signifies it. But we know—and we know it on the infallible authority of the church—that the sacraments of the New Law do not merely signify grace. They contain it as well. God is present in the sense-perceptible sign as really effecting in us what the sign signifies. The sacrament of Baptism signifies cleansing from sin. But in addition God uses it to purify us in very truth. The sacrament is cause as well as sign, and this is true not only of Baptism but of all the other sacraments as well.

It is good to think for a moment of what this fact involves for the pride and self-centredness of man and how it thereby is a remedy of sin. Man seeks to perfect himself through the arbitrary enslavement of creation to his whim, and God has so disposed things that his true perfection is to be found only in submission to this same creation in so far as it is the instrument of the Divinity. In a world where we would wish to be masters we are forced to admit that there is something greater than we. God has not chosen to deal with us as Spirit with spirit. He wills to touch and heal us; but His touch is conditioned by our faith and humility. Naaman the Syrian sought to be cured by God of his leprosy, but hearing that the cure consisted in washing in the waters of the Jordan he became indignant asking were there not equally good rivers in his own country. God asks something similar of us. We must believe that His power is concealed in things of sense. There are so many ways that we could wish to treat with God. We could wish to get His grace normally in prayer, in a contact with God where sense would play absolutely no part. But this is not to be. We are sinners. We tend to abuse God's creation. We must then be forced as it were to take the right view of things. We must have brought home to us with inescapable logic the fact that we are not the centre of the universe; that there are God and His creation as well and that the price of the abuse of the works of the hand of God is to be obliged to quench our thirst at the fount of this same creation, now more than ever sanctified by the touch of the Creator.

The sacraments consist of words and things. But not every

word that man can utter nor every act and object has been
raised to the dignity of entering into some sacrament. In fact
the number of things and words that have been so elevated
are but few. There is but water and bread and wine and oil
and a few out of all the possible words that man can utter
that compose the matter and form of the sacraments. It
might then be objected with a certain show of reason that
there seems to be but little point in instituting sacraments to
correct our abuse of such insignificant matters. If the sacraments be necessary in order to rectify our attitude to the
material universe how can it be sufficient to select for this purpose only a few of the kinds of things the universe contains,
and these perhaps not the ones which seem the most likely to
incite us to sin?

What we must grasp if we are to answer this objection
is that the sacraments are intended to change our outlook not
merely on the things and words that constitute them but on
the whole material universe as well. The things and words
used in the sacraments are symbolic of the vast world of
objects, actions, and words that surrounds us. Out of this vast
world certain elements have been selected to bear in a special
way the healing power of the Almighty to mankind. These
elements form the sacraments strictly so called. But they
point to another sacrament. God is in the world. He directs
all that happens. His providence is ever active making all
things work together unto good to them that fear Him. The
heavens tell His glory, the birds and flowers His beauty,
the sea His unending Peace. That is what we mean by speaking of the world as a sacrament. It is meant to lead us to God.
In reality it has no voice of its own to call us to itself; it has
but the echo of a divine whisper that invites us Godwards.
And this is something we can forget—something that must

be brought home to us by the mystery of a striking presence of God in His works. To believe that God's power is operative in the water that flows on the head of the little child is to remind oneself that He is as truly—though in a different manner—in the stones that make the church and in the light that streams by the open door. Man is forced to live in the midst of stones and light and suchlike things. They are his natural surroundings. Is it not in his best interests to learn that God is where he too must be; that he need not leave his congenial milieu to find God; that God is not hidden in the frozen, white-lit regions of the spirit, but that He walks the earth as He did two thousand years ago; that the sacraments contain the lesson and the proof that Christ is near to us, even at our doors, and that what hides Him from our eyes is the very "this-world-ness" of the flesh and blood that clothe His glorious Divinity?

The sacraments are then a clear-cut indication that our holiness is to be a human holiness—ascent to God of flesh and blood mounting by the ladder of the Sacred Humanity. This latter point is one we shall consider later. Before passing on to it there is another question that suggests itself; if the reason for the sacraments be to recall to our minds by a striking example the sacramental nature of the world, why should there be many sacraments; would not one suffice? Or the same objection might be proposed in a different form: if each sacrament gives grace should not one suffice; it could be received over and over again as often as grace would be lost or growth in grace desired; but at any rate it does not appear that there is anything that one sacrament can do that the others could not do equally well? The answer is at once simple and profound. It is true that the sacraments all give grace—and union with God. But each sacrament gives a grace peculiar to itself. There is, in other words, over and above the general idea of grace, the idea of a grace of the sacraments, or sacramental grace, and it is this latter that the sacraments effect in our souls. Let us examine this matter a little more closely.

Grace is the principle of our union with God. Whoever is united with God has been united with Him through grace. No creature can by its unaided efforts raise itself to the level where the clear vision and love of God are its share. Vision and love of God as He is in Himself is the life of God. Others may share in it only to the extent to which He invites them, to the extent to which He makes it possible for them by the gift of a share in His Nature. Thus, whether it be angel or man that we consider, union with God is a matter of grace.

If grace be the principle of union with God, it follows that grace is essentially the same in all that have received it. Some may receive more, others may receive less. But in every case it is question of receiving more or less of the same thing. The life to which man is elevated by grace is of the same kind as that to which the angels were elevated. For each it is a life centred on God, and than that there can be no higher. The angels may see more of God than we shall. They may love Him with a more intense and generous love than we. But that is not a power of doing something different from what we can do. It is a power of doing what we can do but of doing it better than we can do it. Some men have keener vision than others. But keen vision is still vision and weak vision is no less vision. There is no question of the keen-sighted man being as far raised above his less gifted fellow-men as man is above the brute. And—what is still more strik-ing evidence of our essential equality with the angels in the matter of the life of grace—there is no reason why a human being should not even be higher in grace than the highest of the angels. So far is our grace from being inferior to that of the angels that it may even be more intense than theirs; and that this is true of the grace of Our Blessed Lady is beyond all question, while there is no reason to exclude the possibility of some of the saints being higher in grace than at least some of the angels.

While insisting in this fashion on the essential similarity between the grace of man and of the angels, it is necessary to admit a certain accidental difference; and this is of prime importance as an introduction to what we shall have to say shortly in explanation of the idea of sacramental grace. Grace raises us to union with God. But the grace that is in us is a grace that has come through the loving mercy of a Redeemer. We came into the world sinners and enemies of God. We came into the world deprived of a grace we should have had. And grace, when it comes to us, comes as to forgiven enemies, as to creatures who had need of the mercy of God. Our union with God is not a mere elevation of simple creature to the Divine level. We are less than mere creatures. We are farther removed from God than by the mere fact of having been drawn by Him from nothingness. We are less than dust; we are proud dust—"superbe cinis." To raise us to Himself God has first to lift us from the depth of sin. He found us broken and perverted; made to enjoy His life and lying shattered and helpless amid the wreckage of a creation our pride had caused to fall. Our grace does more then than to unite us to God: it heals us; it restores us to life; it gathers tenderly the fractured members of our beings and makes of them a new creature that thrills with a new life. Grace does this; a grace that is essentially the grace of the angels though its work in us seems so strange and new compared with its work in them. But in truth there is no strangeness, no novelty. For it heals us by uniting us to God; restores to life by giving the life that is in God; builds up again our members by making them one and harmonious in God. Grace does all this, for it is grace that bridges the gap between God and what is not God. Whether it heal or merely elevate it is essentially the same kind of grace; for it heals in God and elevates to God.

The grace of the angels is not a grace of healing. The angels who sinned received no second offer of life. An angel is too simple, too earnest, to come to a decision that may be altered. Man is weak and may be taught; man has received from God the mercy of the power to regret and to reform. An angel may regret, but it can never reform. And so it is that the grace of the angels is never a grace of healing. The angels that fell, fell beyond hope of salvation. The grace of the angels is a simple grace of elevation; it lifts up to God beings who had never been turned away from Him. The angels had been below God—far below Him as the creature is below the Creator. But they were never His enemies. They had no sin to forgive. Grace raises them without redeeming them, for they were never exposed by sin to the danger of eternal ruin. And yet their grace is like unto ours; for though it does not save it unites to God. It is only man whose elevation is effected by a work of salvation.

This is a central point for the understanding of sacramental grace: that grace while remaining of the same kind (as it does in men and angels) can differ accidentally through its performing diverse functions, but all in subordination to and in view of the great central one of uniting creatures with God. For if there be a difference in function between grace as operative in the angel and in the soul of man, there appears to be no reason why the graces of the different sacraments should not also have functions in which may be distinguished over and above the common one of uniting the soul to God, other minor ones depending on the circumstances in which union is to be effected. We hold then that the grace given by any one of the sacraments does all that we saw should be attributed to grace: causes union with the Truth of God, the Power of God, and the Goodness of God; causes similarity in nature with Him and makes Him inhabit our souls. But to these, the constitutive elements of union with God, each sacrament adds something that is its own. It is in virtue of this something that we are entitled to speak of sacramental grace.

The graces of the different sacraments will be considered in detail in the sections allotted to them later on. For the moment we intend merely to say enough to indicate what sacramental grace is and why it is so termed.

The first sacrament received in point of time is Baptism. The rite is one of washing. Hence, to apply the principle laid down in the preceding chapter, the interior state implied—and effected by the sacrament, since it is cause as well as sign of grace—is one of being washed in the spiritual order, of being cleansed from a stain of sin and guilt. The washing in question is not that however of an inanimate object. What is washed is a living soul. The washing purifies the principle of life within. Hence it is a washing that is also a rebirth. It is the entry into a mode of life from which we had been before excluded by the taint of unforgiven guilt. Baptism is then a cleansing that is a rebirth; that is what it signifies and that is what it effects. The grace given in Baptism must consequently be the grace of union with God coming to us as forgiven sinners who enter thereby upon a new kind of life. It is a grace of the forgiven sinner. It comes to us as to creatures who had been far from God, who had turned away far from Him. Under this respect it adds nothing to the idea of the grace of redeemed mankind considered as distinct from that of the angels. But in this there is nothing to surprise us. For the grace of the Redeemer comes normally through the sacraments. And hence it comes in what we might term its most elementary expression in that sacrament which first of all establishes contact with the Redeemer. But under the respect of a new birth it is something entirely peculiar to Baptism. It is a grace destined to increase; it is a grace destined to develop into the full vigour of the life of glory in heaven; it is a grace that makes of us even here on earth, new men, a new creation, destined to walk in the newness of the life that is in us. And yet it is a grace that though complete in all that pertains to the essence of grace is still but a germ, is meant to wax and grow strong through ever fuller incorporation into Him Who is the True Vine.

Baptism gives us the germ—the beginnings of the life of grace. And this grace is something living, something that develops in a way that harmonizes with the laws of growth of all living things. Now there is one sacrament that signifies nourishment and growth, the Blessed Eucharist. It nourishes us by giving us a grace that is effected in us through the very presence of the Author of all grace. But here once more the grace given is not just the grace of union. It is the grace of the redeemed—for does it not come to the redeemed—but it is as well a nourishing grace, the grace of growth, the grace that presupposes the germ of life within the soul, and that has as its peculiar end to strengthen and mature it. It is the natural complement of the sacrament of Baptism. The

Baptized soul, we may say, has been baptized precisely in view of the Blessed Eucharist. We have been given life that it may develop and reach its full expansion in us. We are incorporated into Christ that we may grow up in Christ through eating His flesh and drinking His Blood.

It is easy to have a false idea of the grace of the Sacrament of Confirmation. It is known to be the sacrament that makes us to be strong and perfect Christians; and the sign of anointing with imposition of hands is one which indicates arrival at the state of spiritual manhood. Does it not seem to follow from this that it must be the greatest of the sacraments; that it marks the climax of our spiritual growth; that reception of the Blessed Eucharist after Confirmation can have no purpose other than that of repairing the loss of strength consequent upon the toil of daily life, seeing that there is no possibility of bringing the soul beyond the state of spiritual maturity? To give a full answer to this question now would be to anticipate—at the expense of order—much of what we shall have to say about the Sacraments of the Blessed Eucharist and Confirmation. It is sufficient for our present purpose to mention that the maturity conferred by the grace of Confirmation is to be understood in function of social obligation rather than of completed growth. The grace of Confirmation is the grace of the soul united to God and commissioned by Him to bear testimony to the faith that is in him if the need arise; to work actively for the spread of the faith if he receive the call from his Bishop. It is not a grace that excludes all possibility of further development. It is rather one that marks a new stage in responsibility. It makes the soul of the Christian into the soul of the knight. This new title of nobility is a call to battle for the love of Him Who conferred it.

The grace of Baptism is the grace of fallen and redeemed man. The grace of Penance is the grace of man who has fallen by his own personal act, of the man who lifted by Baptism out of the mass of sin-weighted humanity, plunges himself by his own free will still lower than is his place by birth. What distinguishes the grace of Baptism from the grace of the angels is that it is a grace of the fallen and the forgiven. What distinguishes the grace of Penance from that of Baptism is that it is the grace of those who have fallen freely after the forgiveness of Baptism and who return to their Father with humble and contrite hearts. The sin of Adam is in us only a sin of human nature. We as individuals did not have any part in it. Hence the grace of Baptism is one that heals our nature by restoring grace to it and strengthening it to fight against the darkness of our understanding and the weakness of our will. But the sins that Penance was instituted to forgive are the sins that we ourselves have committed. Its function is then not simply to restore the grace lost, to make things precisely as they were before, but to give the grace of a new pardon, to give a grace that is in some way the embodiment of a humble and contrite heart; it is, in other words, to give the grace of friendship, but of that peculiarly tender and delicate friendship which is known to those only who have tasted the bitterness of remorse and the undeserved sweetness of forgiveness.

These four sacraments give then each its own peculiar grace. All unite us to God. Taken together they unite us to Him in all the different material settings of human life. (It is of course understood that this statement is strictly true only if it be understood as embracing all seven sacraments.) In addition to this they entitle us to the Divine assistance in the performance of the works appropriate to the respective graces. The soul endowed with the grace of Baptism has a right to be helped by God to live in a way worthy of a child of God. That is what is meant when we say that sacramental grace includes a right to actual grace. When God confers on a soul any dignity, He in His love enables it to live in a manner in keeping with its state. When He makes us His children He gives us the Spirit of Childhood. Similarly He gives strength to those whom He has chosen to be His soldiers. In fact the sacrament of Confirmation is popularly conceived as consisting in this donation of strength, in this special outpouring of the Holy Ghost, who will be our support in the hour of Battle. The grace of Penance implies that God will help us to avoid sin in the future. What is still more, and this is a point that is usually overlooked, it implies that He will enable us to live our lives henceforth as beings who have rejected His offered friendship and who are firmly resolved to make amends in the future by scrupulous fidelity to the faintest suggestions of His good pleasure. Holy Communion calls too for actual grace, the grace of loving God. To taste that the Lord is sweet is to long for deeper intimacy with the Lord. This is to love Him. Holy Communion makes us long for God, makes us long to be incorporated still more fully into Our Lord. The actual grace it demands is the grace to long, to desire, to love, to forget self that Christ may be all in all. The fruit of Holy Communion should be a life that is a lived act of love.

Thus far we have seen the broad lines of the sacramental system. The detailed consideration of all seven sacraments will be the matter of the following chapters. It is however altogether necessary to introduce these chapters by a section dealing with the relation between the sacraments and Our

Lord and Saviour. This will be the theme of what follows. It will happen inevitably that all that has been said up to this will appear trivial when compared with the intense reality of the action of Our Lord upon our souls, and His marvellously co-ordinated control of the sacramental system. Yet no apology is needed for having delayed so long on the way. For the thirst of God and union with God find in Our Saviour their full meaning. It is, in addition, He Who has given signification and efficacy to the Sacraments. It is then in the idea of His position in the sacramental system that we shall find the unifying principle underlying all that we have said hitherto. But before unifying it was necessary to indicate the several parts.

5

THE SACRAMENTS: FOUNTS OF
THE SAVIOUR

"You shall draw waters with joy out of the Saviour's fountains."
(IS. 12, 3)

WE LIVE IN AN AGE of catch-word and catch-phrases—nothing
very new perhaps in the history of mankind but still something sufficiently striking to be worthy of mention. One
group of these catch-phrases depends on the use of the word
"integral." Education is some kind of "integration"; modern
life aims at the development of the "integral" man; aesthetic
experience "integrates." It is by no means my intention to
imply that the word—not forgetting its derivatives—is void
of meaning. In fact it can have, and frequently does have,
a quite pointed application. But when we come to its application to the spiritual sphere, and when we meet an expression
such as "integral Christianity" we cannot but sense an unpleasant fuzziness. For the term is used, more frequently
than not, to mean just the radical application of any spiritual
idea whatever. If a man is convinced that the future of the
Church lies in the liturgical revival he forces the refinements
of liturgy down the throats of the faithful and calls that
integral Christianity. Should he happen to be a believer in
the sanctifying power of the man of action he has nothing but
contempt for whoever feels drawn to prayer and quiet—once
more in the name of integral Christianity. It would be pointless to refer to this matter were it not that the idea of integral
Christianity is a fruitful one and worthy of more thoughtful

application. For there is such a thing as not being an integral Christian. It is possible to keep some corner of one's soul free from the touch of religion. It is this that the slightly fanatical exponents of spiritual theories have in mind when they find people who consider their contentions as valid only with certain reservations. But there is another sense that the expression may have as well. Integral Christianity may refer not to the submission of the whole man to an ideal but to the submission of the man to the whole ideal—it may even reach the point of being the submission of the whole man to the whole ideal. That there is such a thing as a whole ideal in addition to there being a whole man is what enthusiasts are prone to forget, and it is one of the applications of this truth that we wish to stress in the present chapter.

One cannot speak of integral Christianity unless in reference to a system of truths having Our Lord as centre. Christianity without Our Lord—and how many there are in practice who adhere to such a system—is not Christianity at all! Our Lord did not come on earth just as a teacher of an ethical or moral code. And yet, there are more than one or two that seem to believe that what He stood for is summed up adequately in the Sermon on the Mount. He came as the Way, the Truth, and the Life. He came as the Truth. He came to teach us. But His teaching was not so much "Do this and avoid that" as "I have given you an example, that as I have done to you, so you do also" (Jo. 13, 15). Right action for the Christian is Christlike action. What should attract us is not the beauty of an act nor the challenge it throws out to the complacency of the world, but its degree of approximation to what Christ did or what He would do. He teaches us and is the Truth; but He is the Way and the Life as well. We are not just copies of Christ, we are extensions of Christ.

Christianity is Christ living over again in man. Moral action is His action in us. Right is what He prompts us to do. Activity which does not spring from Christ may be indifferent if considered in itself, but it is not Christianity; it is bedizened humanity.

The Sermon on the Mount apart from Christ is not Christianity. Its poverty is the poverty of Christ, the poverty Christ inspires us with. Its meekness is the meekness of Christ, not the serene endurance of the stoic. Christianity centres on Christ. That is the one thing never to be forgotten. And so it is necessary to point out a little of the insufficiency of what we have said so far about the sacraments. Life is not just a quest of God; it is a quest of God in and through Christ. The sacraments are not just signs of grace; they are signs of the life of Christ that is in us. The sacraments are not just causes of grace; they are the instruments of Christ; they are the means Christ uses to lay hold on us and make us Christlike. What is the quest of God without Christ but refined paganism? What are earthly causes of grace without Christ but magic? Hence it is that we must retrace our steps somewhat; not denying or whittling down what we have said so far, but giving it life and depth by integrating it into the Christian Synthesis Who is Our Head.

If you read once more the seventh chapter of the Apocalypse of St. John, especially the last four verses, you will get some idea of what Christianity really is. There is recounted that wonderful scene of the signing of the just, and the multitude that no man could number standing before the throne and in the sight of the Lamb. And St. John knew not who they were that stood clothed in white robes and with palms in their hands. But one of the ancients spoke to him saying: "These are they who are come out of great tribulation, and have washed their robes and have made them white in the blood of the Lamb. Therefore they are before the throne of God, and they serve Him day and night in His temple: and He that sitteth on the throne shall dwell over them. They shall no more hunger nor thirst, neither shall the sun fall on them, nor any heat. For the Lamb which is in the midst of the throne shall rule them, and shall lead them to the fountains of the waters of life, and God shall wipe away all tears from their eyes" (Apoc. 7, 14-17). There are few more glorious images in the whole range of symbolism than that of the Lamb that rules the faithful and leads them to the fountains of the waters of life. That is Christianity. That is life in Christ. If it be He Who rules the glorious in heaven and if it be He Who leads them to the vision of the Godhead, how much more is it not true that He is Ruler and Leader of us who are wayfarers. All our life is in Him; all our hope of approach to the Father is in Him; and this not merely in an historical sense, not merely in virtue of the death He died two thousand years ago, but in virtue of the activity He exercises on each and every one of us here and now, in every thought, word, and action that has eternal value. For us men, whether wayfarers or in glory, God is in Christ.

Our first parents, Adam and Eve, sought God. They wished to be like unto God. The idea of frustrating their capacity and thirst for the Divinity never once appealed to them. They saw too clearly to think that they could be happy to the full extent to which that was possible to them without borrowing life and vigour from some divine source. But they sought God outside of God; they sought to become God-like independently of Him Who was God. They refused to accept God's plan for them whereby their godlikeness could be realized only through humble and loving contact with Himself. They refused to draw from the source God had indicated to them. In their rejection of the Source of Godlikeness they barred to their posterity the road they themselves had first refused to take. Their children were left with their capacity for God, with their thirst for Him; but the old road to God was barred and man could build no new one. The Redemption consisted in establishing a new way, a new road, for man to God. Christ is the bridge that spans the gulf between creature and Creator. Christ is the new source of Our Divinization. He is the new fount of the Godhead. No longer do we become Godlike through immediate contact with the Father, conversing familiarly with us in a garden of delights. God has made a new offer of the Divinity to us; but this second offer is made in His Incarnate Son. And this explains that phrase, that invitation, that cry in which the Word becomes as it were palpable in the flesh of Jesus: "If any man thirst, let him come to me, and drink" (Jo. 7, 37). Poor human mortals, you need God. You are but children after all. Come to me. God is in me; I, the Word am in God; I, the Word, am God.

Were there no other reason besides, this one alone is more than sufficient to compel man to turn to Jesus. But there is another reason as well, and one that grips all that is noble and human in us. Christ came on earth to win for Himself a kingdom, and we are that kingdom.

It is a mistake to consider sin and grace as things, inanimate forces, and nothing more. They are things, it is true; but there is behind each of them a person: there is behind sin the person of Satan; there is behind grace, God and Christ. Sin does not fight with grace, but Satan armed with sin engages God and Christ armed with grace. Adam fell tempted by Satan; and Satan tempted him because Satan hated God. Satan was at war with God. He could not attack God in person; but he could attack Him in His friends and His possessions. That is why he tempted Adam; and that is why the fall of Adam was but the first stage in a battle that has raged unseen in our midst since that day. Satan's act of aggression resulted necessarily in a fight to the finish for God's territory of souls.

If we bear this in mind we are not surprised when we see that the first scene recounted in the Gospels after the official opening of Our Lord's ministry by the baptism of John is His encounter with Satan in the desert. Satan was Lord of the world up to that moment. It was with perfect truth that he said, speaking of the kingdoms of the world: "To thee will I give all this power, and the glory of them; for to me they are delivered, and to whom I will, I give them" (Lk. 4, 6). But he senses the presence of a rival, and at once enters the fray. Why did Our Lord—Who was God—permit him to do this? Why, unless it was that Our Lord knew that He really was the rival of Satan and that in wrestling with him in the desert He would make clear to His disciples of later years that He had come as the strong man armed and that His quest of souls was to be understood as a crusade waged by one Man—though that Man was God, He was no less man—against the unbridled fury of the Prince of darkness. From the day of the temptation in the desert Satan hated Our Lord as he had never hated Him before. Now he could say that he knew who He was, the Holy One of God; now he could realize that the continued possession of the kingdoms in which he gloried depended on the destruction of that Man, Who might be more than man. Satan tempted; and the lesson taught him by the temptation was that nothing less than the death of Him Whom he had tempted would make his kingdom secure.

Calvary was the final stage in the struggle between Our

Saviour and Satan. Mors et vita duello conflixere mirando: on the hill of Calvary Life and Death struggled. Life would win; but at what a price! Our Lord would become King and Victor; but by submitting to the shame of the cross: "He humbled himself becoming obedient unto death, even to the death of the cross. For which cause God also hath exalted Him, and hath given Him a name which is above all names: That in the name of Jesus every knee should bow, of those that are in heaven, on earth, and under the earth: And that every tongue should confess that the Lord Jesus Christ is in the glory of the Father" (Phil. 2, 8–11). It was by the very death that Satan had intended to guarantee his power that Our Lord overthrew him. Our Lord's death was not a defeat. It was a victory. He laid down His Life of Himself. No man —and no spirit—took His life from out His grasp. He laid it down in homage and love. We, by the sin of Adam, were chained down to the life that is of this world. He by despising that life earned to be the fount of the true Life. We had been enslaved by the devil through our submission to the charm of the passing things he uses to deceive us; He freed us by exposing the devil's wiles in open show, by that sublime contempt of all that is not God, which was His, hanging naked upon the tree of shame. He had always been God; He had always had within Him the fulness of grace and truth. But now He had that fulness as a Victor-King. He had won in battle the whole human race, and the fulness that was within Him was His to give to man. Regnavit a ligno Deus: God reigned from the wood of the Cross. The cross, intended by the king of this world to set the seal of folly on all Our Saviour stood for was the throne from which He willed to reign. The struggle between Life and Death was really over on Calvary. And yet there remained some sense of incompleteness. The Cross was a victory; but was it one man could understand?

We know how the body of the Lord was taken tenderly from the Cross and laid in the tomb. Perhaps there were some even then who knew their Master was now more than ever their King; His Mother at least knew it. But even they were sad. For He seemed to have failed. They had seen rise up in their midst a Man, Jesus of Nazareth, a Prophet, mighty in work and word before God and all the people. And they had hoped that it was He that should have redeemed Israel. But the chief priests and princes delivered Him to be condemned to death and crucified Him (cf. Lk. 2, 419–21). Yet in spite of doubt and grief there echoed in their memories something He had said while He was yet living, something about a third day. Was it possible that the real victory of the Cross might be completed by an official manifestation of power and a triumphal entry into the kingdom?

The resurrection was the sign and clear declaration to mankind of the Power of Christ. He had pointed to this sign time after time in the course of His life. "Destroy this temple" He had said, "and in three days I will raise it up" (Jo. 2, 19). These were not words uttered by Our Lord on an occasion of little importance. They were His answer to a challenge: "What sign dost thou shew unto us, seeing thou dost these things?" (ib. v 18). Our Lord on Calvary would be really Fount of life. But man could hardly realize that. And so it was necessary that man should be given a sign that it was so, a sign that man could not doubt, a sign that would prove to man that Our Lord had laid down His earthly life of Himself and that when He would He could take it up again. This sign was the resurrection from the dead. The dead Christ was really Master of life and death, for life and death obeyed His will.

After forty days came the Ascension into Heaven. Now while there are many souls who arrive at a certain understanding of the mysteries of the Death and Resurrection of Our Saviour, not a few fail to grasp the import of His Ascension into Heaven. It seems to them, on the rare occasions when the Ascension is at all an object of thought, that it means no more than that Christ suffered and died and is now in glory, and that we too, if we suffer in union with Him and die in His love, will one day have the joy of sharing in the happiness that is now His in Heaven. The Ascension is the promise of a reward and a stimulus to desire, and that is all.

The mind of the Church is different. In the antiphon of the Magnificat of Vespers of the feast of the Ascension she sings: "O King of Glory, Lord of Power, Who today hast risen in triumph above the heavens, do not leave us orphans, but send to us the Spirit of Truth, the Promised of the Father." The Ascension is the enthronement that followed the battle for the kingdom of souls. Our Lord ascended into heaven as King, to sit there in glory at the right hand of the Father, sharing even as man in the government and vivification of souls. In praying Him to send us the Holy Ghost the Church asks Him to rule us even at this moment. For the sending of the Holy Ghost is the work of our sanctification, the work of snatching us from the sway of the Prince of darkness and translating us into the kingdom of the Son Whom the Father loves; and to say that Christ sends the Holy Ghost from His throne in heaven is to say that He as God, and even in a certain way as man, is the source of all holiness; that the God-man is the King from Whose throne grace is dispensed. Christ sitting at the right hand of the Father is the centre from which our life flows.

This same idea is the one that serves as theme to St. Paul's beautiful Epistle to the Hebrews, though the application differs in material detail. In this epistle St. Paul explains the place of Christ in our lives on the analogy of the Judaic priesthood. Christ is the great High-priest who has offered sacrifice for us on the hill of Calvary. But His priesthood does not cease with His Death, no more than did the priesthood of the Jewish High-priest cease with the offering of the victim. There must be an entry of the priest into the Holy of Holies. Sacrifice is a gift of man to God. It is intended to placate God, to make Him well-disposed to men. There must follow, as its natural complement, a gift of God to man, some sign and token of the divine good-pleasure, and this too may pass through the hands of the priest if in him there be the full and unstinted plenitude of priestly mediatorship. The entry of the high-priest of the Old Law into the Holy of Holies was symbolic of the passing of the gift of God to man through the hands of the priest. The high-priest returned to his people charged as it were with proofs of God's munificence.

With Christ this was not to be mere symbolism. His sacrifice was followed by an entry into the real Holy of Holies —the court of heaven—on the morning of His Ascension. Seated there at the right hand of the Father, King and Master of the Treasures of the Godhead, He completes His priesthood by bestowing upon His subjects the life He earned for them by the sacrifice of the Cross: "But Christ being come an high priest of the good things to come, by a greater and more perfect tabernacle not made with hand, that is, not of this creation: neither by the blood of goats, or of calves, but by His own blood, entered once into the holies, having obtained eternal redemption. For if the blood of goats and of oxen, and the ashes of an heifer being sprinkled, sanctify such as are defiled, to the cleansing of the flesh: how much more shall the blood of Christ who by the Holy Ghost offered himself unspotted unto God, cleanse our conscience from dead works, to serve the living God! And therefore He is the mediator of the new testament" (Hebr. 9, 11–15).

This idea is so striking that it may be permitted to quote one more text: "Who in the days of his flesh, with a strong cry and tears, offering up prayers and supplications to him that was able to save him from death, was heard for his reverence. And whereas indeed he was the Son of God, he learned obedience by the things which he suffered: and being consummated, he became, to all that obey him, the cause of eternal salvation" (Hebr. 5, 7–9).

Whether, then, we consider Our Lord as King or as Priest, the conclusion that is forced upon us is the same: it is from Christ reigning glorious now in heaven that life and union with God come; for Christ, to reign is to make souls godlike; for Him, to be priest is to be the Mediator through Whom we receive all that comes to us from God. And Christ reigning in Heaven is the same Who died on the cross. St. John tells us that: for He Whom he saw in the midst of the throne and of the four living creatures and in the midst of the ancients was "a Lamb standing as it were slain" (Apoc. 5, 6). The royal insignia of Christ Our King are His most Precious Wounds; They are His title of nobility. It is not merely the same Person Who died on the Cross Who is now our King; it is the same Person in the glorified perpetuation of His hour of victory: "Jesus Christ, yesterday, and today; and the same for ever" (Hebr. 13, 8). Our Lord remains ever the

Lamb That was slain. He reigns as the Lamb That was slain; it is to the Lamb That was slain that we are to pay homage; it is to Him we are to turn in our quest of God. He is the glorious centre of the Christian life. Outside of Him there is neither Christian nor Christianity.

It has been no empty flourish to speak of Our Lord as the centre of the Christian life. In one of those expressions so common in the writings of St. Thomas, of which it might almost be said that they are overloaded with meaning, we find the following words: "totus autem ritus christianae religionis derivatur a sacerdotio Christi" (3a.Q63.a3)—"the whole rite of Christian Godwardness is derived from the priesthood of Christ." (There is no question in this context of the word "religio" being used in the narrow and exclusive sense of what we understand commonly by religious service and cult.) Christ sitting at the right hand of the Father is the source of a Godward and God-sent stream into which we, His subjects, must plunge. We must allow ourselves to be caught up by Christ. We must become as it were so many lips by which He may praise the Father, so many hands by which He may serve the Father, so many hearts by which He may love the Father. This stream which flows from the throne of the lamb, this mighty torrent which gushes from the right side of the temple (cf. Ezech. 47, 1-2), moves like the priesthood of Christ, with a double motion—from man to God, and from God to man. We are invited to allow ourselves to be caught up into the sacrifice of Christ, to offer Him—and ourselves in Him—to the Father, not by making an offering that will be entirely new, but by entering through Holy Mass into the one great offering that was His. This is the first aspect of the ritus christianae vitae: the sacrificial moment. It is Christ offering adoration and praise to the Father in us; Christ offer-

ing sacrifice in us; Christ praying in us and we in Him. Thi
is the gift of man to God in Christ; this is the Godwar
aspect of the Godsent current—Christ living in us, and turn
ing in us to the Father.

The second moment in the ritus christianae vitae is the
sacramental moment—the gift of God to man in Christ. This
we may say, is the Godsent aspect of the Godward current o
Christian life. For grace is the gift of God through which we
are enabled to turn to God, to converse with Him, to live
in the fellowship of the saints. In these two phases—the
sacrificial and the sacramental—is all our life summed up
We receive from God that we may turn to Him with all the
greater intensity; we turn to Him in Love and admiration
that we may be still more filled with Him. And it is Christ
Our King Who does all this in us. He found mankind out
side the current that swept to and from the throne of God
Man lay on the bank of the river of life, and, as with the
man at the pool of Bethsaida, there was no one found who
could lift him and bear him to those mighty waters that
rushed on their way to God. Christ has led us to the waters
that flow to the throne of God—and the waters are Christ.

From these considerations—and what human tongue can
be otherwise than all too inadequate in its effort to express
them—we get some idea of the place of the sacraments in
the Christian scheme of things. As we have so often said and
implied, the complete notion of sacrifice includes a double
offering: an offering of man and an offering of God. Sacrifice
in the usual and restricted sense is the offering of man; the
sacraments are the offering—or at least the channels of the
offering—of God to man. Christ is our priest in the full and
perfect sense of the term. To Him then belongs the principal
rôle in both these aspects of the priestly office. It is He Who

is the great Offerer of the Human race; it is even He Who is
What is offered. To Him belongs as well the principal part
in the offering that is made from heaven—to His Humanity
of course it belongs under the Divinity. That is to say, it is
He Who is the principal Cause in the administration of the
sacraments. The sacraments are His way of bringing to its
ultimate consummation the work begun on Calvary. Calvary
established peace between God and man; Calvary made of
Christ the Fount of grace That the Father had intended from
all eternity. But peace and grace were not as yet communicated to man. They were, if we may so speak, stored up for
us in Christ. He, the head of the Mystical Body was at peace
with the Father, He the Head was full of grace. But neither
grace nor peace had flowed as yet to us His members; and
until that would happen the work of our redemption would
be incomplete. Christ gives us grace and peace through the
sacraments. In them is His eternal priesthood realized. He
died but once on Calvary. That death can never be repeated
in His Body. But we can be drawn into it through Holy
Mass, we can reap the fruits of it through the Sacraments.
And so the Priesthood of Christ endures for ever, as long as
there shall be souls to turn to God, whether that be in the
fitful steps of the faltering wayfarers or in the steady march
of those who surround the Person of their King.

We asked in an earlier chapter should the Church alone of
the great social organizations of this world be deprived of the
glory of pageantry. We implied in the form of the question
that the answer could not be in the affirmative. We are now
in a position to see why this is so and what exactly the pageantry of the Church's life is. We have a King, One Who is
centre of authority and life. There are moments when we
come into the royal presence to pay our respects to our King;

moments when we come to protest our loyalty; moments when we declare our readiness to fight for our king; moments when we submit once more after a period of rebellion. These are the state functions of the Catholic Church; these are her sacraments. We are really in contact with our King at the moment when we receive His sacraments; lest we should falter in our realization of the reality that underlies our acts, these acts have been invested by Our King Himself with their wealth of striking symbolism. We do not see the throne, nor do we see the king, but our actions bear all the outward stamp of those of subjects in the presence of their liege and lord. We are not the subjects of a King of Whom we are ashamed. We do not come to Him as did Nicodemus; only by night and far from the eyes of men. We are content that men should know we have a King. We are content that they should know that He is a mighty King and that His subjects are faithful and true. This is our pageantry: the whole world as flung around the throne of Our King and the faithful few that form within the heaving mass of senseless man, press forward near the throne and ring it round, proud that they stand beneath the eye of their King, quickened and made strong by the miracle of His Life and His Presence.

But human life does not consist only in attending at the throne. There is the battle of life to be fought under the eye and the leadership of Our King. The opening of Our Lord's public life was signalized by His encounter with Satan, the king of the powers of darkness. Our Lord emerged victorious on Calvary. But His subjects must carry on the struggle in His name. For His victory becomes ours only to the extent to which we consent to fight under His leadership. Satan was defeated but not bound. He can harm still—but only those who come freely to him. He is already defeated if we remain true to our own King. This image of human life as a battle between warring kings and warring armies is no mere metaphor. Life is really a battle. We do not war with laws of nature or with blind forces and tendencies but with persons. To yield to sin and passion is to go over to the camp of Satan. He has a personal interest in seeing us desert Our Lord. Every sin is a triumph for Satan. He too has his throne —though it be a throne of torments—and from it he can view the world and see how his armies fight. He can see and glory in the faintheartedness of the children of light. There is another throne the majesty of which he cannot diminish. The King Who sits thereon has died once and dieth now no more. But Satan can still tear from Him His subjects; is it not no small joy to him if he can make the subjects of the Great King traffic with the King's enemies even if he does not persuade them sell their cause outright? The life of man is a warfare, and man does not realize that it cannot be waged by peacetime methods. This warfare has its sacramental side, as we see later in detail and as we may indicate briefly now.

There is a promise to those who battle, made in the Apocalypse, which one may interpret in the light of the sacramental system: "To him that overcometh, I will give the hidden manna" (Apoc. 2, 17). St. John refers, it is clear, to the fruit of final victory, the manna of the Beatific Vision. But are not his words applicable also to the Blessed Eucharist? We come to the throne of our King in Holy Communion to receive life and strength. But we come also to the same throne to receive our reward and consolation. Kings of this earth decorate their brave. Our King can do no less. The Blessed Eucharist is the food and consolation and strength of the Christian soldier. The fight waxes fierce. Our King sees us and singles us out, not just for a word of praise nor for a medal or a ribbon, but for a share in His own Royal Person and Strength. There are many states of soul that go to make up the attitude of him who approaches the Holy Table as he should. We must never forget that pride is one of them; pride in the King we serve; pride in the worth of His cause; pride in the Gift He makes to us. The soldier who goes to receive his decoration is proud of his cause. He may—but need not—be proud of himself; but it is imperative that he thrill at the thought that what he stood for was right and just and that to stand for it however unworthily is an honour. We come to the Blessed Eucharist clothed with the dignity of our cause. We in ourselves are nothing. Our King is all. But He is an All that is a Reality. His cause is worth while. His cause is no paltry one ragged though be His army. We adore Thee, O Christ and praise Thee. Make us conscious of our mission; of the justice and beauty of our cause; of the deep humanity of You, Our King.

6

THE GRACE AND CHARACTER
OF BAPTISM

OBJECTUM INTELLECTUS EST UNUM: intellect seeks or makes unity—a bald and technical statement but one that is fraught with meaning for the spiritual life. We tend naturally to simplify, to unite tangled threads, to weld facts and theories relating to one subject matter into a compact and jointed synthesis. Wherever the mind finds multiplicity it endeavours to make unity. When it understands anything thoroughly it finds that in doing so it has all unconsciously reduced the elements that went to make it up to one or a few basic principles. We may leave it to the philosopher to decide why this should be so. For us it is a fact, an inescapable law that conditions all intellectual activity. And being such a fact and such a law its workings may be traced in no uncertain manner in the soul's quest of God.

Life in its beginnings is often conceived in a manner at once too complex and too simple: too complex, for every day, every problem, every thought seems an experience that stands alone and tantalizingly new; too simple, for we think somehow that the answer to the world's questioning will be found in the world itself and that the things that are seen and heard and felt carry within themselves their full credentials. The soul's spiritual conversion is, among other things, a process of radical simplification of outlook. The soul awakes to the fact of God and accepts unhesitatingly and unreflectingly that God is the ultimate solution of all problems. Emphasis should be laid here on the word "unreflectingly." The soul accepts God as the answer to the riddle of the universe but it does not as yet work out the implications of that answer. Side by side with its newfound life of the spirit there remains a life of the unregenerated man, the same in almost every respect as before conversion, into which God does not penetrate; for no need is felt there for His Presence. The riddle of life is answered once again; but the answer is too simple to fit reality.

Conversion needs to be followed by the slow and arid process of subjecting body to spirit and spirit to God. After the happy days when the soul has thought that God could be loved as He desires and life lived at the same time as we desire, there come days of disillusionment which are also days of illumination. The soul sees that God must be worked into every detail of life. This truth considered as a speculative principle may have been admitted from the first day of conversion; in fact it is most natural that it should so be admitted. But its practical import is not grasped so soon. Either the absence of God from the details of life or the utter worldliness of the spirit which animates them or some such fact is not grasped, with the result that the soul, while admitting God as Master of its life and actions, really withdraws from Him more than it gives. There follows then a new stage in the spiritual life, this time one of complication. In place of the simple principle of the early days of its quest of God: "From this moment God will be all to me" there forms within the mind principle after principle: "I must love God in my work. I must love Him in my amusements. I must love Mary. I must be devout to the saints. I must give my daily Mass a big place in my life. I must often visit the Blessed Sacrament. I must become conscious of my membership of the Mystical Body"—and so on without end. Where will all this finish? Is the last state of the soul to be worse than the first? We know the answer and that it is a simple one. The final synthesis, in which the totality of the spiritual life—not fragments of it as is the case with the beginner—will be seen in one simple, though wonderfully rich, idea is the work of the Holy Ghost in the gift of Wisdom. That synthesis is one we cannot effect by thought or reading. It is the direct fruit of God's intervention. What we can do is to work for the multiplicity. We can strive to give Him every detail of our lives. We can strive to gather every thought, word, and deed, and set it face to face with God. But we must leave it to Him to unify. We can pray that He do so. More than that we cannot do.

So long an introduction as the one you have just read seems to demand an explanation. In fact, however, it is itself an explanation and an apology. For the sacrament of Baptism —and that of Confirmation, as we shall see later—refuses to allow its effects to be bundled into one compartment. Try though we may there will always remain a certain plurality of elements even after the most careful attempts at synthesis —unless of course our attempt consist in leaving out what will not fit in with our views. For the effects of Baptism group themselves around two principles, grace and the character. And since grace is not the character nor the character grace it follows that all attempts to find a created synthesis in which they will be one are doomed to failure. The soul is simply forced to face life now from the angle of grace, now from the angle of the character leaving it to God to show her how they are one in Him. There is no cruelty in this.

The spiritual life is something far above what man is fitted for by nature. It is then an act of mercy on God's part that He should, as it were, dole out to man its mystery in morsels that man can grasp. The spiritual life is the life of God in the soul. But God is so far above man. In One Simple Essence God contains all possible perfection. And we can understand all possible perfection only as being in some way the sum of all possible perfections. We are, as it were, items in a crowd, straining to glimpse a figure far beyond, and seeing it now from the right, now from the left, now in the act of turning towards us. And if the life of God that is in God be a mystery, the life of God that is in man is a mystery also. It is something essentially simple. But its sublimity raises it above the level of the things we can grasp in a single yea or nay. It is something we can only glimpse, perceive in stolen glances, and so we know it through many ideas, and otherwise than through many ideas it would not be possible for us to know it at all. The sacrament of Baptism must then remain a sacrament of a grace and a character. And as we know the life of God by splitting it up in the prism of the human mind, so also we receive it flowing through many channels and diversified into many streams.

When we consider the sacrament of Baptism as it is understood by the Church, we find that it involves a double consecration of the soul to the supernatural order. In the first place there is a consecration to the life of glory through the grace of Our Lord Jesus Christ. In the prayer at the exorcism performed in the Baptism of children the Church prays: "Lead him Lord, we beg, to the laver of regeneration, so that he may obtain with your faithful the eternal reward, through Christ Our Lord." This is the consecration, or setting apart, for the life of glory. The seal which marks the soul so set apart is grace. In the second place there is a consecration to Our Lord Himself. We read in the course of the same exorcism: "And thou, cursed spirit, never dare to violate this sign of the Holy Cross with which we sign his forehead." Baptism marks the soul as being in some way the possession of Our Lord; as belonging to Him in virtue of the power of His Cross. The seal of this consecration is what is known as the character. It is a consecration to Our Lord the great High Priest and a share in His Priesthood. All that we shall have to say concerning the sacrament of Baptism is summed up in these two consecrations.

The Grace of Baptism

The idea of finality is one with which we are all familiar. We readily admit that things of a certain kind are destined by their very nature for a proportionate activity. A pen is suited to act as a pen. A plant tends to grow, flower, and propagate its species. Finality is found in the spiritual order as well—in fact we may say that the whole essence of the spiritual order is unintelligible except in terms of finality. Grace has its tendency. It destines us for glory. The life of the face to face vision and unhampered love of God is the life proportioned to grace. To have grace is to be destined for that life. To have grace is to have received an intrinsic and vital impulse to God in Himself as final end. No matter what be the state of life or the occupation of the soul in the state of grace, that soul is at every instant fitted for one thing primarily and for other things only in so far as they lead to that one thing—the life of glory. No conditions of human existence are so mean as to exclude this plan. Grace is an eternal weight of glory—an "aeternum pondus gloriae"—drawn by its force to God as centre of attraction. This is the law of gravitation of grace. The child that comes to Baptism confesses to its truth through the lips of its sponsors. What do you ask of the Church of God? "Faith." What will faith bring you? "Eternal life." Faith and grace are sought as the germ that will grow into glory, as the life of God in the depth of the soul that will one day be the life of the soul in the bosom of the Trinity.

In giving the soul this impulse to the Trinity the grace of Baptism makes it child of God. And it is striking how literally the Church understands this matter of spiritual childhood. For we are given sponsors at Baptism precisely because we are children in the spiritual order and need instruction and care. The new-born babe needs a nurse, the child needs a teacher. The newly baptized needs tutors who will teach him what he should know about his Father in heaven and keep him safe from the dangers he does not understand. They receive him at the font, just born to the life of grace, not yet able to walk in the paths of justice, needing to be sustained and cherished, since being but a little one in the Lord.

We are children of God by grace, but adopted children. And adoption consists primarily, as is well known, in conferring a right to an inheritance. Grace makes us like God, it is true; and for this reason, which we have sufficiently considered on another occasion, it is said to make us God's children. But though it makes us like God, it does not make of us beings of exactly the same nature that God has. What it does however is to give us a right to a share in possession of the very Object that is God's great riches, namely His Own Essence, possessed through knowledge and love. We have seen that the soul in the state of grace is energized by a vital tendency to the Blessed Trinity. We may reaffirm the same truth now by stating that this tendency is to something That is our heritage, stored up for us in heaven until the day of our majority will have dawned. We are rich men, rich as is God Himself; we own all that is worth owning—but in spe, in hope. It is all ours; but we are asked to prove that we are worth the plans Our Father in heaven has in our regard.

There is then a striking appropriateness in the formula of Baptism: "I baptize thee in the name of the Father and of the Son and of the Holy Ghost." The operation is done in the power of Father, Son, and Holy Ghost. It is done as well in view of Them as end. It destines the recipient for the Father, the Son, and the Holy Ghost. Before Baptism there was the child, nothing more than a puny son of man and woman, tending by the whole force of all that was in it to the life of a stunted intellect and a weakened will. Now that same child has been set apart for the contemplation of the ever Glorious and Blessed Trinity. Possession is taken of it in the name of the Father, Son, and Holy Ghost. It is no longer just one more of the battered hulks that sag at the first strain of the waters of life. It is a new creation; a thing of exquisite beauty, with sails to spread when the great day of eternity will dawn and the wind will blow with steady strength along the path of Christ our Risen Sun. It has been given its first impulse along the way that leads to the Blessed Trinity. From the moment of Baptism it has no raison d'être other than to see God. The baptized is a wayfarer, a stranger in a far land; one who when asked who he is and what he seeks can answer only with the enigma and the boast: "I am one destined to see the face of God Almighty."

The doctrine of the Inhabitation of the Holy Ghost in the souls of the just assumes now a sublime significance in the light of this doctrine of the sacrament of Baptism. Baptism gives us a right to an eternal heritage. Here on earth how-

ever we receive a certain guarantee or foretaste of the inheritance we shall enjoy fully in heaven: ". . . you were signed
with the Holy Spirit of promise, Who is the pledge of our
inheritance" (Eph. 1, 13-14). The Holy Spirit inhabits our
souls by the fact that He is so present to us that we can, even
on earth, know Him in some way and cling to Him by
charity. We know Him as but in a glass, darkly. But we know
Him sufficiently well to realize that He is present to us as
the Guest of our souls and that He intends to remain with
us and be our joy and strength as long as we wish to have
Him. God is present in all things. But in us He is present as
a Friend to be appreciated and loved, a Friend in Whose
friendship we may grow up to the day of the indissoluble
union of eternity. As yet we do not know that Friend fully.
His full friendship is a reward that will be ours only hereafter. But we know enough of His loving interest in us
and abiding presence in us to be convinced that He is a Friend
Who will more than satisfy all our desires. The slight degree
of intimacy we have with Him on earth is at once an incentive
to search more ardently for Him, and a guarantee that He on
his side does not intend to withdraw Himself from us.

In coming to us as the Guest of our souls the Holy Spirit
opens our whole being to the influence of God. The soul
thirsts for God. By Baptism it is given it to drink great
draughts at the fount of the Godhead. This is the wonderful
symbolism of that ceremony of Baptism in which the organs
of the various senses and the principal members are signed
with the sign of the cross: "I sign thy ears with the sign of
the cross that thou may hear the divine lessons (praecepta);
I sign thy eyes that thou may see the brightness of God; I
sign thy nostrils that thou may perceive the sweetness of
Christ; I sign thy lips that thou may speak the words of

life. . . ." Every single organ is to become a channel by which God may enter the soul. "Lift up your gates, O ye princes, and be ye lifted up, O eternal gates: and the King of Glory shall enter in" (Ps. 23, 9). God will speak to us and our ears will be open to hear His voice. It may be that He will speak to us in prayer; it certainly will be that He will speak to us through the living voice of His Church. But we shall know that it is the Lord that speaks and His words will quicken and strengthen. Our eyes will see the glory of God in the heavens and in every thing that grows. Those eyes will waken one day to a more glorious sight still than God seen in His creation; for our eyes of flesh are destined to see God in His Incarnate Son and in the glory of His Mother and His saints. We shall breathe in the good odour of Christ. Christ will be the atmosphere we breathe; the pure invigorating air filling us with life and joy. Our words will be of God. We, creatures, sinners, members of a fallen race, will be able to speak of God and say things of Him that He will rejoice to hear. With God in our souls, in our minds and hearts, with God in every sense, the quest of God becomes the search of a child for the mother that but bides the moment when she may press her little one to her bosom.

We have referred thus far to certain of the rites instituted by the Church to make clear the reality of the interior transformation worked in the soul by Baptism; such are the exorcisms and the signing with the sign of the cross. The sacrament itself, instituted by Our Lord and Saviour does not consist in any of these signs but in the ablution with water made in the name of the Father, Son, and Holy Ghost, whether the ablution be by way of immersion, sprinkling, or pouring. In the early Church, and indeed up to the time of St. Thomas Aquinas, Baptism by immersion was the most common. The person to be baptized was literally plunged into the water. Does this rite, in which consists the essence of Baptism, imply anything in addition to the infusion of grace?

Immersion signifies that Baptism is a process of burial with Christ to the old life of unregenerated soul and body, succeeded by a rising with Him to the glory of a new life hid with Christ in God: "For we are buried together with Him by Baptism unto death; that as Christ is risen from the dead by the glory of the Father, so we also may walk in newness of life" (Rom. 6, 4). To receive the grace of Baptism is at once to die and to live: to die to all that we have from the corruption of our nature, to live to all that we hold from God. We are plunged totally into Christ that we may become new in Christ, and though this idea is seen clearest in Baptism by immersion it is really not hard to discover in any of the forms of Baptism. They all are a rite of cleansing; of making new what was old and defiled. Even in the case of Baptism as conferred in the Roman Rite of the present day the Baptized person is held under the flowing water: the idea is then not that of a partial cleansing but of a radical submission to the power of grace; we submit our heads to the water that they, summing up as they do all that we hold most dear in the matter of personal gifts and possessions, having been made clean, we may be totally and entirely clean.

The sacraments are signs which effect what they signify. The grace of Baptism is a consecration to the ends of the sacrament. Hence, since the thing signified by the Baptismal rite is death to sin and to all that leads to sin, wrought in us through life to grace, it follows that we are, by the very fact of having been baptized, consecrated in a special way to a mode of life which bears the imprint of these two tendencies. The life of the Baptized must be at once a life and a death.

In other words: Baptism gives us the power of uniting ourselves with God in this world, and consecrates us to the life of union with Him; but it consecrates us no less unambiguously to a life of mortification. We have been given the grace of death in Christ. Our life must be a constant death to all that is opposed to Christ. We have not received a grace which will grow and reach maturity by way of effortless progress. Our grace is one that grows on levelled ground, that walks by ways we must make smooth and paths we must prepare. It is a grace that thrives upon the cross. It is a grace that is most alive when the merely human in us is altogether dead. Baptism destines us for mortification. The baptized man who lives a life, good but self-indulgent, is a frustrated man. He is stunting the grace that is in him. It cannot develop unless through trials. Softness will stunt it; softness may destroy it. The intelligent man who tries to live without developing his intellect is admitted to be a fool. He is throwing away his chance of becoming something. To have the grace of Baptism and not to seek the Cross, is to be a far greater fool. It is to have a grace that can grow only on the hard and rocky soil of Calvary and to choke its roots with slime. In this matter of mortification there is one fact at least that the Christian should never forget: from the moment of Baptism mortification ceases to be optional; Baptism is a stamping and setting aside for the life of grace through the cross.

It would be tedious and out of place to explain in detail the nature of the mortification to which Baptism consecrates the soul. Those who need instruction on the point need only turn to any reliable book on mortification. The essential minimum is the amount of mortification included in the avoidance of mortal sin. Beyond that, is the unlimited sweep of total abnegation, to which also Baptism consecrates us; but this consecration is more a matter of honour and generosity. What is however relevant to our present purpose is to mention that mortification, as thus imposed upon us by the fact of Baptism, is not something purely negative. It is death. But it is also life. Baptism not merely removes stains; it makes us clean as well. Our Lord died on the Cross to all that was not God. But He lived, and lived most intensely to and in God, at the very moment that He hung in agony on the Cross.

One of the things that keep souls back in this way of mortification—apart from the terrible lack of generosity that is normal to man—is that the positive aspect of mortification is lost from sight, or never understood. When we endure hardship our whole horizon seems filled with pain; when we deny ourselves a legitimate pleasure, which is nothing more than a pleasure, we are aware only of the loss of an opportunity of experience which can never be recaptured. We do not see that to bear hardship is itself a form of life and that to shirk hardship is to refuse to live on the spiritual level. We do not see that to deny ourselves a pleasure is to perform an act which should be pleasurable beyond all imaginings. To bear pain or to refuse joy is to live the life of Faith, Hope, and Charity. It is Faith alone that tells us that there is a reason for acting so. It is Hope that sustains us with its promise of possessing God. It is Charity that urges us on with its consuming love of the Saviour. One cannot perform any single act of mortification in the way in which Baptism destines us for it without clinging to God at the same time, through the very act of mortification, in Faith, or Hope, or Charity, or all three. Mortification causes pain and grief. But we should experience joy and peace in clinging to God. We should keep this latter aspect before our mind's eye. Autosuggestion can be made an instrument of spiritual progress. I do not want to do what is hard; but I tell myself over and over—and this also is an act of Faith, Hope, and Charity—that to do what is hard should give pleasure because it is the unfolding of my true life. It does not follow that even after telling myself this a time will necessarily come in which each cross will be accompanied by a feeling of sense-perceptible joy. But there will be spiritual joy, spiritual peace; and the mind having once been drawn from the rut of whining complaint, there will be no obstacle to full and generous acceptance of all that the Divine Providence may send to try us.

Even when we say that this attitude of mind will not lead necessarily to a joy that the senses can perceive, there is no question of implying that the state of mind to be aimed at is one of cold, joyless, stoic endurance. St. Paul tells us to rejoice always; that he himself rejoices in his tribulations (Phil. 4, 4; Rom. 5, 3). He meant this to be taken literally. He did not mean, perhaps, that the joy he experienced was just the same as that of the man who has fallen in for a fortune or who has perfected an invention. But he did mean to say that he experienced genuine joy; genuine *spiritual* joy, not in the sense of shadowy or imagined joy, but in the sense of joy residing in the spirit. There is a peculiar pleasure and satisfaction in the unhindered working of any faculty. The man who has trained his mind to grasp the principles of mathematics is happy when he sets his mind to work on a mathematical problem. The man who is interested in historical research experiences a unique thrill in the presence of a newly discovered manuscript source. The soul endowed with the gifts of Faith, Hope, and Charity experiences a genuine joy every time it elicits an act of these virtues. The joy is there. It may not be experienced in all its purity, nor even to the full extent to which it is possible to experience it, while soul remains united to body. But this is not because it is not a real joy but because it is one that our coarse taste does not appreciate. Let us but wean ourselves from the desire of the happiness that this world can afford and we shall be given to taste and see that the Lord is sweet. Saints have felt in the midst of the most dreadful sufferings that their souls were at peace. We feel only the suffering because we are not saints. We see only death in mortification because we do not really want to live as God has prepared for us. St. Paul tells us to live "always bearing about in our body the mortification of Jesus, that the life also of Jesus may be made manifest in our mortal flesh" (2 Cor. 4, 10). Is it not a pity that men refuse to believe that an act of mortification represents a joy-value which has its roots in the thrill of the act of Charity in which Our Saviour offered Himself upon the hill of shame?

The grace of Baptism, then, is seen to be a résumé of the whole Christian life and a guide to the meaning of that life (this statement is of course strictly true if the grace be understood as implying in some way the character). It makes of us children of God, destined to see the Trinity in Heaven, destined to grow in grace here on earth through the avoidance of what is evil and enervating as well as by the pursuit of what is good. We find a striking confirmation of the acuteness of the Christian sense of the faithful in the importance they attach to the ceremony of the renewal of Baptismal vows. At the end of a mission the poor and ignorant gather together to renounce Satan with all his works and pomps and to promise to live as Baptism has mapped out life. They feel that in doing this they are making the supreme offering to God. And in this they are right. To be a saint is to be true to the grace of Baptism. It is to follow the bent given by that grace, to live up to the contract made with God when He poured grace into the soul. And what is of most immediate importance for us here and now is to realize that Baptism is a real contract and that to be untrue or even half-hearted in its regard is to frustrate one's life as well as to offend God. The ends of Baptism are not matters of choice for the baptized; they are the things for which he has been made.

THE CHARACTER OF BAPTISM

Our Lord Himself has been spoken of, and with truth, as the great Sacrament of the New Law. This idea, so fruitful for the spiritual life, if followed to its logical conclusion would lead us far beyond the limits that must be placed to the present book. But it serves as a most instructive introduction to the dogma of the sacramental character. For Our Lord demanded of all who approached Him, seeking life and grace in Him, one essential condition: that they have faith: "And he said to the woman: Thy faith hath made thee safe, go in peace" (Lk. 7, 50). Our Lord wished each approach to Him to be a protestation of faith in Him. Those who came to Him without faith may have been cured of their bodily ills; they were never cured of the ills of their souls. He demands the same condition of those who approach His sacraments that He did of those who approached Him in His role of first Sacrament of the New Law. Our approach to the sacraments must be a protestation of faith in the Person of Our Lord. There must of course be Hope and Love as well. But Faith is the directing principle. Faith shows us Our Lord as the source of life and the sacraments as His instruments; Love and Hope serve but to make us stride along the path that Faith has found. This, as we shall see when considering the character of Confirmation, is the key to the understanding of the sacramental character.

That certain of the sacraments confer a character is a matter of defined doctrine. We have the guarantee of the teaching authority of the Church with regard to the existence of the character. With regard to its nature there is room for diversity of opinion. The Church has not defined in what precisely it consists. The position taken up in the following section is, the author believes, that of St. Thomas Aquinas. It is then sure, and soul-satisfying. More than that cannot be claimed for it; but the claim that has just been put forward is no light one.

The sacraments of Baptism, Confirmation, and Orders give in addition to grace a spiritual reality termed a character. In general the character stamps the soul—and with a stamp that will last for all eternity, and is not lost as a result of any sin, however heinous—as being deputed for certain hierarchical functions. It is a sign, but a spiritual one, that the soul so stamped has a certain status in the priestly life that radiates from the throne of Our Saviour in heaven, and that it is consecrated to the exercise of duties in keeping with its state. Thus the soul bearing the character of Baptism is deputed to the reception of the sacraments and participation in sacrifice; the soul stamped with the character of Confirmation is deputed to the public profession of its faith; the soul stamped with the character of Orders is deputed to the ministration of the sacraments and to an active sharing in the transmission of the life of grace to mankind. In this section we shall deal with the character of Baptism.

We have seen in the previous section that the Sacrament of Baptism consecrates us, through the infusion of grace, to the life of children of God destined one day to live in perfect intimacy with their Father. It includes another consecration as well: our consecration to Christ the Great High Priest. This latter consecration is effected in us by the sacramental character.

Our Lord is the great High Priest and Mediator. It is His glory as King of the human race that men should enter into His Priesthood, be drawn into the Godward current that flows from His throne through the channels of Holy Mass and the sacraments. From time to time Our Lord lays hold, as it were, on a soul. Now this laying hold on, or taking possession of, a soul, implies two things. In the first place it implies that the soul in question is sent on its Godward way —and this is accounted for, as we have seen, by grace. But it implies as well that the soul has been drawn into the sphere of influence of Our Lord. The soul is now one in which He wishes to give full expression to His Priesthood. He wishes to make that soul recipient of the benefits stored up in Himself, Our High Priest. The soul has been captured for God, it is true. But it is a conquest of Christ's, to be led to God in and through Christ—to be presented to the Father as one of the conquests of the Most Precious Blood. The soul then needs a stamp other than the stamp of grace. It must be stamped as belonging to Our Lord. It must be stamped as a soul whose whole raison d'être is not only to belong to God, but to belong to Christ as well. The Christian soul is the soul whose life is hid in God—but hid in God through being hid in Christ. "For you are dead; and your life is hid with Christ in God" (Coloss. 3, 3).

St. Thomas has this in mind when he repeats again and again that the sacramental character is a "Participatio sacerdotii Christi"—a sharing in the priesthood of Our Lord. It is easy to see what this means when the character in question is that of Holy Orders, for the character of Orders is in a person who is a priest in the full sense of the term—though under Our Lord. What meaning can it have when applied to someone who is nothing more than a layman?

We encounter a similar problem when we read what St. Thomas has to say about the virtue of political prudence, that is to say, the virtue which renders a ruler fit to guide the state to its end. For this virtue is in the ruled as well as in the ruler, and is in the ruled in much the same way in which the priesthood of Our Lord is in the baptized. The prudence of the ruled consists in their capacity and willingness to follow the prudent directions of their ruler. It is in other words, a power of passivity with regard to rule—not of course a blind and unintelligent passivity, but one based upon an active appreciation of the nature and functions of government, and the obligation of the individual to submit to authority for the good of the body politic. Now, the baptized share in the priesthood of Our Lord in much the same way as the ruled share in the prudence of the ruler. Their share consists in a vital passivity with regard to His priesthood. They are given the capacity and the right to place themselves under His priestly rule and derive from it the benefits it is meant to confer. This capacity is, as we shall see later, and have implied already, a peculiar power of approach to Him through Faith. They obtain through their character the right and obligation to share, as official members of the Kingdom of Christ, in the offering the Father makes in return through Him to the human race. They become, as St. Peter so strikingly and authoritatively expresses it, members of a "spiritual house, a holy priesthood" (1 Peter 2, 5). The priesthood of Christ becomes something that is intended for them—and they become persons intended for the priesthood of Christ.

Two far-reaching conclusions follow from this fact of our

integration by Baptism into the priestly system of Our Saviour. The first is that through our Baptismal character we assist at Holy Mass in an official capacity. We do not come to Holy Mass as did the Scribes and Pharisees who were present on the hill of Calvary. They were bodily present at the offering of the Great High Priest. But He was not the priest of their choice and they willed no share in His sacrifice. They were ruled out of the number of those for whom the Sacrifice of the Cross was a vital reality, and this, not because Our Lord excluded them, but because they excluded themselves. Holy Mass, Calvary made approachable to us, may be offered up for the whole human race. But only those who bear the imprint of the character can unite in offering it. It is the sacrifice of all men in the sense that all men can derive benefit from it. But not all men can enter into the act of offering and make of it something which they have a right to present to the Father as theirs. This is the privilege of the baptized. Holy Mass is our Mass. The priest is not the only offerer. He offers in our name and we offer through him. An unbaptized person may have a Mass said for a certain intention and God will be pleased with what he has done. But he has not been an offerer in the sacrifice itself. He is not a member of Christ. He has no right of entry as offerer into Christ's sacrificial system. The Mass belongs to Christ and His Church. Only Christ and His Church can offer it in their own names and with authority. The poorest soul and the greatest sinner that is present at Holy Mass, provided only he be baptized, is present at a rite that belongs to himself. That Holy Mass is not just something offered for him; it is something he offers also. He is not as those who have no right to appear before their Father's face but must send others to plead for them; he has the right to come himself before his Father, covered with confusion, in fear and trembling it may be, but clothed with the person of his Great High Priest Who has entered into the Holy of Holies and lives for ever to make intercession for him. Holy Mass is my sacrifice. I have the right to approach God through Holy Mass.

The second conclusion is that we receive the sacraments also in an official capacity. The baptismal character marks us as beings destined to receive the sacraments, to grow in grace through the reception of the sacraments. We may go so far as to say that the whole proximate purpose of the soul stamped with the character is the sacraments. It is made for them. It cannot live without them. It is only when it is in contact with them that it is really alive. And this, as we shall see in a later chapter, is particularly true of the sacrament of the Blessed Eucharist, to the point that one may say that the Baptized soul is one that is intended to feed on the Body and Blood of Christ—that and nothing more.

Our supernatural earmarking for the sacraments through the character of Baptism is really admitted by all Catholics in an equivalent form though very few have analyzed the force of the equivalence. All Catholics admit that Baptism is the gate to the other sacraments and that this is so because of the character which it imprints. It is, in other words, commonly admitted that the baptismal character is something which entitles us to receive the other sacraments and something without which the others cannot be received. But it is entirely false to believe, as so many appear to believe, that this power of receiving the other sacraments can be a thing to be used at will. If God gives us the power of receiving sacraments He will mean that we should actually receive them; that in which the power of receiving them resides will be also the proximate foundation of the obligation to receive.

We have been given through our intellects the power of thinking. But in giving us an intellect God intended us to use it by thinking. The proximate foundation of the obligation to think is the intellect itself which by its whole nature demands to be allowed to manifest itself in acts of thought. It is just the same with the other powers that God has given. They are given for use. They are talents. We have not the right to wrap them up in a clean napkin and present them, unburnished by use, to the Master when He comes to make His reckoning with us. They belong to Him even before they belong to us. We have not the right to determine that what He made for use, and what He therefore made of such a kind as to demand use, should be diverted by us to the miserable end—if it may be called an end—of barren inactivity. Having through the baptismal character the power to receive the sacraments, we have thereby the obligation to make our lives sacramental.

CONCLUSION

Considering the sacrament of Baptism under this aspect of earmarking or setting apart we may say that in its totality it may be described as double "prise de possession" of, a double laying hold on, the soul. There is in the first place the sacramental grace which earmarks the soul for heaven and the life of the virtues and gifts, and among the virtues, for the life of those of Faith, Hope, and Charity, most especially; for these latter are the divinest of the virtues of the wayfarer. There is in the second place the character which earmarks us for a participation in the sacerdotal life of Our Lord; for union with His sacrifice through our participation in Holy Mass, and for union with the fruits of His Sacrifice through reception of the sacraments. Grace and the character, therefore, determine what our life must be. It must be a life wholly of God and wholly of Christ, it must be the life of God received in us through Christ, nourished and strengthened in us through Christ, returning with an irrepressible homeward urge to God through Christ. The Baptized Christian might be defined as a man set apart for God and for Christ. It is a simple definition; but it is one that should inspire.

Were we left to what reason can tell us about the things of God we should have no grounds for suspecting that the programme of life included in the sacrament of Baptism was not an entirely complete one. Faith tells us that there are other sacraments. Hence Baptism alone is not the whole way to God. But Baptism has this peculiarity, that it embraces the whole of life and needs not so much to be added to as to be intensified. The other sacraments do not confer on us something that is extrinsic to Baptism. Their grace and their character are foreshadowed and demanded by the grace and character of Baptism. In other words, the other sacraments do not enter into a section of our lives in which Baptism has had absolutely no part. What they do is to perfect a work of which Baptism provides the rough-draught. To derive then from the other sacraments the benefits they are capable of conferring on us we must first have submitted our whole lives to the control of the Baptismal grace and character. We must live as children of God, occupied with Our Father's business, serving and adoring Him in and through Our Great High Priest. This is not a matter of actions to be performed at stated times only. It is a programme of life. It means gathering up every stray thought, word, and deed, and submitting it to a new driving force and motive. It means whole-time Christianity without labour-shirking devices. But it means also to share in the greatness of God.

7

THE GRACE AND CHARACTER
OF CONFIRMATION

FROM TIME TO TIME the human mind comes to suspect that
there is a divine purpose in truths of religion which at first
sight seemed to be obvious even when weighed in a human
balance. Such a truth is that of the visible character of the
church established by Our Saviour. It is easy for the ordinary member of the church to say that it is quite clear why
Our Lord should have intended His Church to be visible;
that some kind of organization is necessary in any society;
that the Apostles were visible heads in their lifetime and that
the body of men that formed itself around them recognized
an authority which expressed itself on occasion in commands
and prohibitions to be executed before the face of the world.
All this is easy to admit until one comes to understand a
little better the primacy of the supernatural, the all-
conquering sufficiency of grace. If souls hidden away in mon-
asteries can change the face of the earth by prayer, and if
God in answer to their prayers will give the graces of conversion to souls that preaching failed to move, does it not
appear that true godliness is in the interior alone, in the work
done in secret between God and the individual soul, and that
the active life of a militant church is, at any rate when pushed
with vigour, the product of a gross and materialistic evalu-
ation of forces with a consequent lack of faith in grace as
weighed against words and deeds?

This is a new form of the old objection to ceremonial. It is sufficient to indicate where the answer lies. The life of grace is the life of elevated man. The power of grace is the power of God working through human hands. God means us to be divine in a human way, as this is the only way in which we can succeed. We become perfect as our heavenly Father is perfect by divinizing every thought, word, and deed, by serving in thought, word, and deed; we are invited to raise all that is in us to the level of Our Father, not to attempt to force heavenwards a spirit that has no wings. It is true that all depends ultimately on grace. But God deals with us in a human way and His normal mode of action is to give grace to those who have been prepared for it by the words of a fellow man. Even if the grace of conversion be merited in a monastery it will normally be given on the occasion of the ministry of someone engaged in the active life. God wishes us to busy ourselves with His interests. Some will be busy in prayer and theirs is the better part. Some will be busy in a purely material way, and theirs is a less perfect part. Some there will be who will be busy about the things of God, because filled with the love of God they feel the urge to spend themselves in every possible way in His service; such a soul was the great St. Teresa of Avila; such, we may say with all reverence, was Our Lord Himself—and theirs is the most perfect way of all, uniting as it does in one life all that is of value in activity and contemplation. In any case there must be some kind of social work in the Church. Grace is not diminished by the fact that it comes through the instrumentality of man. Rather, it stands out thereby in more striking relief as something that ennobles and elevates and makes gods out of stuff even such as we are.

When Our Lord ascended to heaven He left His apostles

behind to complete the work He had begun. But the first days of their ministry were days when the infant church was at a standstill. They remained in an upper room, fearful and timid. They had not deserted Our Lord. They remained united to Him in prayer: "All these were presevering with one mind in prayer with the women, and Mary the mother of Jesus, and with his brethren" (Acts 1, 14). They had the courage necessary to face the difficulties which they, as individuals, encountered in their relations with God. They struggled, we may believe, with interior temptation, they believed in God, they hoped in Him, and they loved Him; they were instant in prayer in spite of all desire to return to the life of the average Jew. But there was one thing lacking to them. They were afraid to live the Christian life in the full gaze of a hostile world. They wanted God, but they feared opposition. They were prepared to encounter any difficulty from any enemy within their own souls; but the enemy without, the world, its sneers, its opposition, and its disdain—that was more than they could bear. And so they fled the world and sought their God where there were none to raise a voice of protest when they bent their heads in prayer.

The Holy Ghost descended on them to prepare them to work in the open. They must continue to love God and to believe and hope in Him. But all this was to be done openly. They were men, social beings. If they had convictions they must be willing to admit them openly. They professed to believe in God. God asked of them the full homage of their belief—namely, that they be willing to allow others to see that they believed in Him. Man lives in society. He can know what regulates the actions of his fellow man, and his fellows can know what regulates his actions. If he knows that there is a Being greater than he and all his fellows, then he gives that Being all the homage of which he is capable only when he serves Him no matter what his fellows think— or better still, without reference to what they think. He must be willing to sink his social self in homage to such a Being; if other men can know that he serves an Ideal, then it is due to the Ideal that he allow other men to be conscious of his service.

If we consider for a moment the circumstances of the descent of the Holy Ghost on the first Pentecost we become at once aware of the fact that it took place for no other reason than that of the responsibilities that the Apostles were to face before the world. The Holy Ghost descended on them in the form of tongues of fire. He came upon them in the form of tongues: they were destined to preach, to communicate the good tidings to all mankind. He came upon them in the form of fire. Is this not an echo of those words of Our Saviour: "I am come to cast fire on the earth: and what will I, but that it be kindled?" (Lk. 12, 49). The news of the Kingdom was to consume the world as would a great fire, destroying all that dared oppose its path; in like manner the Apostles were to go among men, bearing, as it were, in their hands torches lit at the fire of the Saviour, kindling with their torches every soul that crossed their way. Fire and the word: with these two weapons they would engage the world; with these two weapons—which were also gentle healing—they would venture on the first crusade for souls, rejoicing when it happened that they were found worthy to suffer for the name of Christ.

What happened to the Apostles both before and after the day of Pentecost is an image of the progress of the soul from the grace of Baptism to that of Confirmation. Baptism makes us spiritual units. We receive in it the germ of a spiritual life. We receive the power to fight against the interior enemies of that life: sin and Satan. It places us on the path of union with God. The Baptized soul can think of and love God in a supernatural way; God inhabits it. Thus it is established in all that pertains to its own individual relations with the life of God within it and the enemies of that life which are also within. But it is none the less a child. It has no strict social obligations.

It is important to understand what we mean by a child in this context. The idea of childhood is one familiar to students of the spiritual life. We read of the way of spiritual childhood, of our being children of God through grace; Our Lord Himself tells us that unless we become as little children we cannot enter the kingdom of heaven. In each context the idea means something that is very simple, and easily understood on the analogy of human childhood. But human childhood is itself a matter of many phases and many motives. And so it is that childhood in the spiritual order refers at one time principally to one characteristic and again to another, each time with a perceptible shade of difference in meaning, though in every case in a way that can be readily understood by anyone who knows what a child is and what it is capable of doing.

When we speak of childhood as being something associated with Baptism which is corrected, as it were, in Confirmation, we refer to the fact that a child, as long as it remains a child, is free from the obligation to contribute immediately to the well-being of the community. The child's work consists in perfecting the life that is within it. It must go to school and acquire the knowledge it will need in later life. It must acquire virtue. It must learn to love and appreciate the principles that are of lasting value. It must make of body and soul an instrument under the control of an enlightened intellect and a resolute will. But with that its obligations cease. Provided the child does all that it can to bring out the best that is in it and—what is more important still—to acquire the good that is not in it, it has done its duty and its full duty. Anything else is accidental in its life.

With the man this is not so. The man is supposed to be perfect in himself and able to contribute to the good of society. The contribution expected of him may vary in form. Some men may be called to govern the state; others to execute measures demanded by the difficulties in which the state is placed; others are called upon to share in government by prudent use of the right to vote at stated times; others to teach and instruct; others to form public opinion; others engaged in agriculture and industry, to develop in the most advantageous way the resources of the country. But all render some social service, whether in their work or in their lives; at least—and this is a bare minimum—all are obliged to be ready to help the state when, without their assistance, it will find itself in a situation in which the common good will be unattainable.

Baptism gives us the germ of a supernatural life which God intends to grow within our souls. We are children as long as our relations are primarily those of soul with God, of soul with its own spiritual life. We become men the moment we are called to contribute to the life of the church as a visible body placed in full view of the world. This call comes through the sacrament of Confirmation; and that is why it is termed the sacrament of spiritual manhood. It is an error to suppose that the confirmed soul is necessarily in a higher state of grace than one not yet confirmed. The analogy between spiritual manhood and natural manhood does not consist at all in the relation in which both stand to the corresponding states of childhood considered from the point of view of growth in stature, strength, and wisdom. There may be far more grace in an unconfirmed soul than in a confirmed one. But only the latter has an official place in this social life of the church of which we speak; and the latter, with the little grace it has is equal to its duties, for the slightest degree of grace is able to overcome the greatest difficulties that may beset man.

We are led to see in a new and striking way the enormous difference between the spiritual and natural orders when we ask ourselves what exactly is the contribution expected of the spiritual man. He is expected to fight; to resist; to be intransigent. That of course is the ordinary attitude of men. But he is expected to fight, resist, and be intransigent because of a principle. Men will fight for gain; men will resist the attempts of others to get back what belongs to them; men will be intransigent in pressing the claims of national pride. But very few men go to extremes because of principles, because what they stand for is right. Yet this is what the spiritual man is asked to do when he is invited by confirmation to become the soldier of his faith. Baptism gives him a body of principles which he knows to be true and worth more than the whole world. Confirmation invites him to stand up for those principles against the world. Our faith is an offer made by God to man. It is a clear statement of how man can be saved. Confirmation asks us to do our part in keeping that offer open to mankind. The offer becomes paltry in human eyes if we are ashamed of it; it becomes just one more of the quack-remedies for all ills if we decide it is not worth dying for. In any case it is an offer made to mankind, and we, as members of a social group, with duties to the group, and with duties to God arising out of our membership of the group, are bound to keep the offer within the world's horizons, and keep it there as an offer made by no less a Person than God Himself, through no less a Person than the Incarnate Word. "For I am not ashamed of the gospel. For it is the power of God unto salvation to every one that believeth, to the Jew first, and to the Greek" (Rom. 1, 16).

The sacraments being, as we have said, signs of an interior grace, the rite of the sacrament of Confirmation gives us the key to the understanding of this change that it effects in the soul. The matter of the sacrament is Chrism, with imposition of the hands of the Bishop. Chrism contains oil of olives and balm. The oil signifies strength; the balm, being a sweet-smelling substance, signifies either the good name of the confirmed person or the fact that he is to be the good odour of Christ pervading the whole world. The form, which gives the ultimate signification to the matter, is quite clear in its implication. It consists of the words: "I sign thee with the sign of the cross, and I confirm thee with the Chrism of salvation, in the name of the Father and of the Son and of the Holy Ghost, Amen." To confirm with Chrism means to make one strong with Chrism. The rite is then one of anointing in view of a future combat, just as athletes were anointed with oil. The signing with the sign of the cross tells us what we are to fight for, and the standard under which we are to serve. We are to fight under the standard of the Cross for Him Who hung upon the cross. The imposition of hands signifies as ever a special donation of the Holy Ghost. In this sacrament the Holy Ghost is given as the Spirit of fortitude. "And when they shall bring you into the synagogues, and to the magistrates and powers, be not solicitous how or what you shall answer, or what you shall say; for the Holy Ghost shall teach you in that same hour what you must say" (Lk. 12, 11–12).

The sacramental grace of Confirmation is, then, in a special way a grace of strength. It is the Holy Ghost Who gives us strength to profess our faith. The promise made by Our Lord to His disciples during His lifetime, and which we have just quoted, was repeated in still more explicit terms during the days intervening between the Resurrection and the Ascension. He said: "But you shall receive the power of the Holy Ghost coming upon you, and you shall be witnesses to me in Jerusalem, and in all Judea and Samaria, and even to the uttermost part of the earth" (Acts 1, 8). The power of the Holy Ghost will be the secret of the Apostles' unfailing courage. That they and we should need courage follows upon the nature of the message of the Cross, "unto the Jews indeed a stumbling block, and unto the Gentiles foolishness" (1 Cor. 1, 23). The actual cross upon which Our Saviour died, with all its associations of shame, was the difficulty that weighed with Jews and Gentiles. The Apostles needed courage to preach that Cross. Today, the cross as instrument of torture of criminals of the worst type has ceased to mean anything to us. We do not find more difficulty in believing in a God Who died upon the Cross than in One Who should have died in any other way. In fact a certain imaginative glamour has attached itself to the Cross and hides its real repulsiveness from our eyes. It is not to confess to this Cross that we of today need courage, but to confess to the cross that is presented to each individual soul for its acceptance. The true Cross is for us a symbol as well as a reality. It was a thing of shame for Our Lord and that shame is something we cannot grasp with clear understanding. But it symbolizes annihilation of self, acceptance of injury, love of humiliation, preference for contempt. That is something we can understand. And to preach that that is desirable is to invite ridicule. Yet that is what we stand for. We stand for the apparent cowardice of forgiveness of enemies. We stand for the apparent silliness of not caring about money. We stand for the utter unreasonableness of insisting that it may be better to be thrown out of employment than to have a safe job, and that the day we have not got enough to eat is possibly the day we have really tasted life. Any one of these is enough to convict a man of lunacy. All taken together are just too funny for words. If we really were to try to stand up for our faith we should feel the need of the power of the Holy Ghost. As things are, many could pour their private philosophy of life into the ears of any atheist and hear in answer a sympathetic "Just so!"

We need strength because of the two things that hold us back from admitting the faith that is in us: fear and shame. We are afraid of the consequences. Yet we have been signed with the cross. And the cross is a guarantee of victory: "For which cause God also hath exalted Him, and hath given Him a name which is above all names" (Phil. 2, 9). We need have no fear; we are sure to win in the end; victory simply cannot be snatched from our grasp; the longer we have to fight the more glorious will be our triumph. The hour of death of the just will come, the hour of seeming defeat. But "then shall the just stand with great constancy against those that have afflicted them, and taken away their labours. These, seeing it shall be troubled with terrible fear, and shall be amazed at the suddenness of their unexpected salvation, saying within themselves, repenting, and groaning for anguish of spirit: These are they whom we held some time in derision, and for a parable of reproach. We fools esteemed their life madness and their end without honour. Behold how they are numbered among the children of God, and their lot is among the saints. Therefore we have erred from the way of truth, and the light of justice hath not shined unto us, and the sun of understanding hath not risen upon us. We wearied ourselves in the way of iniquity and destruction, and have walked through hard ways, but the way of the Lord we have not known. What hath pride profited us? Or what advantage hath the boasting of riches brought us? All these things are passed away like a shadow, and like a post that runneth on, and as a ship that passeth through the waves; whereof, when it is gone by, the trace cannot be found nor the path of its keel in the waters. . . . Such things as these the sinners said in hell" (Wisdom 5, 1–14).

The anointing with chrism is made on the forehead to warn us against allowing shame, the second cause of weakness, to lead to denial of our faith. A cross is traced with chrism on the forehead, where all may see it. St. Paul was conscious of the grace of his Confirmation. "I am not ashamed," he says, "of the gospel." And he tell why: "For it is the power of God unto salvation to every one that believeth, to the Jew first, and to the Greek" (Rom. 1, 16). We know that human life is a quest of God; that all men need God. We, and we alone, know where God is to be found: in the cross. We do not preach the cross or suffering because of themselves but because they contain God. God has revealed that to us. Not to know it is ignorance. Where is the shame in knowing what man could not know till God revealed it to him? Were the cross not the power of God I ought to detest it. But once it has been made the power of God there is no longer room for shame. God has offered Himself and that offer is made in the cross. Shame to embrace the cross is to refuse to believe that the possession of God counts more than the shortsighted bravado of doing without Him unless He suits our friends.

Such is the grace of Confirmation. It strengthens us to live the life of faith openly before the gaze of the world. It is union with God brought to the pitch of indifference to what men think about it. Still more, it is union with God brought to the pitch of believing that this union is the only thing we have that it is worth our while to communicate to our fellows. Hence it makes us men in grace: centres of spiritual strength, bulwarks of Christian belief, champions of the honour of God Himself. Wherever there is a grace there is an obligation. The obligation following upon Confirmation is contained in the idea of its character.

THE CHARACTER OF CONFIRMATION

We opened the section dealing with the character of Baptism with what must have seemed a puzzling reference to the need for faith in approaching Our Lord. It was not possible then to explain it any more fully than by noting that the Baptismal character, being the avenue to the other sacraments, must have something to do with Faith, the sine qua non condition for contact with Our Lord. It is only now, in speaking of the character of Confirmation, that it is possible to explain fully what was hinted at then. And this is only to be expected considering the close relationship which we have seen to exist between faith and the sacrament of Confirmation itself.

Faith in Our Lord is the indispensable condition of spiritual and vital contact with Him. There were some who met Him and whom He failed to heal because of their unbelief. There were others who, on His own admission, drew grace and healing from Him precisely because they had faith. The sacraments are the extension of Christ down the ages. We who wish to touch but the hem of His garment in order to be healed find Him in the sacraments. To come to Our Lord in His sacraments must then be an act of Faith in Him, a protestation of Faith in Him.

Let us recall once more that the sacraments are signs. They signify grace in our soul. But this is not all. They signify grace as produced in us through the merits and by the power of Christ. Thus, they are the expression of faith, not only in the reality of the interior change they work in us, but in the reality of the power of Christ as well. They are, in other words, a protestation of faith in Christ the Universal High Priest. No matter what be the sacrament in question, its reception is an act of faith in Christ. It follows then that the spiritual power of receiving sacraments—the baptismal character, in other words—must be a power of entering into such signs, of understanding them and accepting them, as one to whom they belong. They are Christ's own signs, instituted by Him while He was on earth. No one has a right to use them except he too be Christ's. The faith of him who is entitled to receive the sacraments must therefore have a peculiar quality: it must be a faith in Christ, endowed with a power, which is also a right, to express itself in signs that are the peculiar property of Christ.

This is expressed in the technical language of theology by saying that the character is a spiritual power which resides in the practical intellect. The practical intellect is that which guides us in our acts. Hence, the power of using spiritual signs—which are external things expressive of faith—must reside there where faith linked with works dwells, namely in the practical intellect.

We have seen in what sense it is true to say that this character (for the moment that of Baptism) is a share in the priesthood of Our Lord, namely, that it is a real, though passive power, of receiving its influence. To what extent may the same be said of the character of Confirmation? That it also is a share in Our Lord's priesthood is quite certain for St. Thomas. But it seems at first sight difficult to understand how this can be. For Confirmation is not a power of receiving new sacraments. Neither is it a new power of conferring sacraments. (The baptized can be ministers of Baptism and Matrimony and the confirmed have no greater power than that.) In what precisely does its sacerdotal nature consist? The profession of faith to which we are consecrated by Confirmation is a sacerdotal act in the first place since it involves bearing witness to the whole sacerdotal system of High Priest, sacrifice, and sacraments. Whoever professes one article of his faith professes the whole faith. It is impossible to die for any one article, precisely because it is an article of faith, without at the same time dying for every other article of the same faith. What counts primarily in faith is not what we believe but why we believe. Of course, it is impossible to believe what is wrong by the motive of true faith. But in believing what is right, it is only the "why," the motive, that is essentially divine. The thing believed is seen only in the mirror of creation. In professing our faith then what we do principally is to adhere to the motive of faith; and so, in professing any one article we adhere to every other article in so far as it falls under the motive, and in the order in which it falls under the motive. Now, after the Blessed Trinity, it is Our Lord and His sacramental and sacrificial system that comes first among the things to be believed. As we saw when speaking of the matter of Confirmation, the cross is really the substance of our faith. Profession of faith in no matter what revealed by God is, in other words, principally a profession of faith in the Crucified and in the Cross. The whole reason of belief in things is that they have been sanctified by the Death of the Incarnate Word. It may be the Immaculate Conception of Our Lady that is called in question. But what does the Immaculate Conception mean apart from the Incarnation and the Redemption? Take an even less obvious example. Take the case of any Christian virtue at all. Virgins have died in defense of their virginity. But what does virginity mean without Christ? Young lads refuse to tell a lie. Is not a lie an offense against Eternal Truth hanging on the Cross? In fact, that is just what any sin is; and any virtue—it does not make the slightest difference which one you may choose—has Christian meaning, and falls under faith, only in so far as it is a manifestation of the life of Our High Priest on the Day of Calvary, and of the life which He pours from His throne in Heaven into the souls of them that love Him.

Few would care to deny categorically that the priest who dies at the foot of the altar in defense of the honour of God, performs by his death a truly sacerdotal act. Every profession of faith is sacerdotal in the same way. Every public act of faith is a defense of the catholic sacerdotal system, and of the honour due to God and to our great High Priest. Public profession of faith is then no small matter. It is not a question of standing for an isolated item of belief. Each time the stand is made for the whole of our faith. The priesthood of Our Lord is at stake each time. Man needs to come to the great High Priest and his approach must be through faith. Every public profession of faith is then an invitation to man to come to Jesus, a publication of the fact that Jesus is High Priest, an indication of where true priesthood may be found.

It is a priestly act, made in the strength and in the name of Him Who thirsts to see all mankind gathered at the founts of His priestly ministry.

There is a second way in which we may detect a sacerdotal element in public profession of faith—though it must be understood that this second way cannot be entirely divorced from the first—and this is by considering it as the communication of a gift of God to man: The priest is the mediator who offers the gifts of man to God and the gifts of God to man. It follows that wherever we can find a person destined in virtue of an official commission to perform both or either of these offices we may speak of his being a priest in the respectively full or partial meaning of the term. The sacrament of orders gives the full priestly power. The ordained priest offers sacrifice—the gift of man to God—and dispenses the sacraments—the gifts of God to man. Baptism gives the Christian the right and commission to share in the offering of the gift of man to God—namely Holy Mass—and to benefit by the offering of God to man by the reception of the sacraments. It makes thus of the Baptized a kingly priesthood, whose priesthood is at once passive and active; though in so far as it is active it is necessarily subordinated to that of the priest as offerer of the sacrifice of the Mass. The sacrament of Confirmation, in its turn, gives a right to share in a new way in the gift of God to men—and hence a new title to the priestly dignity. It commissions the faithful to communicate their faith—which is itself a gift of God to men—to their fellows. Notice that it has been said that it "commissions" them to communicate their faith. A person who has been baptized but has never received any other sacrament can lead others to the faith. But he has not been commissioned to do so. Hence his act lacks the official priestly nature. But the confirmed has been commissioned. He has been set apart for the public profession of his faith. He has advanced a stage in participation in the priestly life of Our Lord. He is now not only one who benefits and one who shares in the offering of sacrifice, but he is one whom Our Lord intends to use to communicate divine life to the world. He is active. He is, it is true, in the lowest grade of the active priesthood; above him are the ordained priests and the bishops. But he is really one on whom Our Lord counts now for the spread of His Church. He is called to be a burning and a shining light that will flash upon eyes of flesh and light them up with questioning. He is called to be a voice crying in the wilderness of a world that knows not God, to waken there echoes that will ring when the voice itself is passed. He is called to dwell in a city built on a mountain top at which the curious and the hostile will stare, and to venture down to the steaming stuffy plain, a stranger with a strange exalted look, to whisper to drowsy louts that air can be pure. He is a full-grown member of the Church of Christ. There is man's work for him to do.

These two reasons indicate why St. Thomas could assert that the character even of Confirmation was something priestly. From the second, the one we have just considered, there follows another consideration which is traditional in the teaching of the Church, namely that Confirmation makes of one a soldier of Christ.

The life of Our Lord on earth was a warfare with Satan and sin. Satan and sin are still in our midst and they have found agents to aid them in their work. Their work is the destruction of what Our Lord came to establish—His Church, namely. They are arrayed against it as an army. There was left to Our Lord no alternative but to make of His Church an army as well. He had been a great commander; his followers must be soldiers. He had fought to establish His Church; the members of His Church must fight that it exist and spread. He had triumphed on the Cross; His soldiers must fight under the Cross as standard. Every soldier of His may be known by the fact that he was marked on the forehead with the Cross.

Our Lord did not establish a leaderless army. He constituted some soldiers, and some captains. The captains are the Bishops. Their duty is to lead and to command in His army. The soldiers are the faithful, enrolled by Confirmation. Their duty is to follow their leaders and to fight under their guidance. We may sum up the effects of the sacramental character of Confirmation in this connection in three points: it imposes a duty not implied in the Baptismal character; the duty is to fight; the fighting must be done under a leader.

Every spiritual power implies a duty. If then the character of Confirmation is a power of professing faith in the name and person of Christ, there lies upon the confirmed the solemn duty of doing so when conditions demand it. This is the basis of Our Holy Father's right to call the laity to Catholic Action. It is the duty of the laity to serve the Church. They have not the right to be merely passive. They are soldiers of Christ and must serve when He needs them. The obligation to Catholic Action does not arise solely from the fact that Our Holy Father has sent forth the call. What I mean to say is that the call to Catholic Action is not a call to something to which we are not already obliged. One may turn to a neighbour for help that could and should be given by some state official such as a policeman. The neighbour is not obliged to help—if equivalent help is obtainable from the official in question. If he does help he does something which rested entirely with himself. But it does not rest with us whether or not we shall answer the call to Catholic Action. It is our duty to answer it. We have been set apart for Catholic Action by Confirmation. The moment the call goes forth we are bound to obey. And to obey is no burden; for it is the glory and pride of a soldier to fight for his country.

In the second place, the duty which the character of Confirmation imposes on us is one of fighting. It is not possible for the earnest Catholic to be at peace with the world. Consciously or unconsciously we all tend to look on days undisturbed by conflict or the rumble of approaching forces as days to be cherished in memory, as days of which all life should be made were it not for unfortunate and pointless accidents. There is nothing at all accidental in Christian striving. It is not accidental that we should feel opposition rising within us to the life of grace and that we should experience pain in beating that opposition down. Grace cannot tolerate sin; and where grace finds sin it must strive or succumb. This is the warfare to which we are consecrated by Baptism. Neither is it accidental that we should meet opposition from without. "If the world hate you, know ye, that it hath hated me before you. If you had been of the world, the world would love its own: but because you are not of the world, but I have chosen you out of the world, therefore the world hateth you" (Jn. 15, 18–19). The Church stands for what is foolishness in the world's eyes. What is still more, the Church stands for the destruction of the supremacy of the world in the world. The world might tolerate foolishness—though in point of fact human pride does not allow what differs from its point of view to escape unscathed—but there can never be question of its tolerating organized opposition. The Church is organized opposition to the world; and this not merely to the world as an abstract notion, but to every institution of this world in which the interests of the world are supreme so as to exclude, or diminish, or disregard, the interests of God. Say if you wish that the Church aims not at destroying but at saving: the inevitability of armed conflict is not made less clear. The world does not want to be saved in the Church's way. The world is more than content to be master in its own house. Whoever comes to save the world must come as the strong man armed.

Far be it from us to understand this conflict in terms of idealized heroics. Very few in any age are called on to die for their faith. The duty of the average man is to live his faith publicly and to let the world see that he is not ashamed of it. There may arise from time to time circumstances in which even that will excite some opposition. A family moving into a new neighbourhood will excite unfavourable comment if it appears to deviate in any way from the crooked line of what is accepted. Sometimes, too, saying grace before and after meals and suchlike practices meet with a certain mild, but unequivocal opposition. But though the combat be but a series of skirmishes, or even nothing more than unopposed reconnaissance flights, there is everything to be gained by feeling the full beauty of it all. Any skirmish, however slight, is really making contact with enemy forces. It is not a thing that does not matter. The confirmed Christian is at that moment really a soldier. He wears his uniform—the sacramental character. What he encounters is a real enemy, out to serve the enemy cause. How then can the skirmish not matter? In warfare, reconnaissance groups do not chat with their opponents. They fight. The fight may result in nothing more serious than a slight flesh wound on one side or the other and a great all-round loss of breath. But the principle is clear; the enemy is the enemy, and no issue is slight when it is a question of soldiers in the service of their country.

In the third and last place, Confirmation engages us to fight under a leader. This follows from the fact that the confirmed is a soldier. The duty of a soldier is to follow his captain. He does not take the initiative himself. What distinguishes an army from a rabble is discipline. The soldier who fights just how and when he wishes, serves not his country but his own whims. The soldier awaits the word of command, and when it is given there never arises in his mind any trace whatever of questioning or hesitation. His duty is to obey. Should the venture fail, his obedience will be none the less glorious. The really great man is willing to lose his life in a really great cause.

The captains in the army of Christ are the Bishops. And at once we see the notion of the Church as an army going over into that of the laity as destined for Catholic Action. For our late Holy Father, in calling the faithful to Catholic Action, stressed the point that the call was an invitation to follow the lead given by the Bishops. The laity were to share in achieving the destiny of the Church under the guidance of their Bishops. With this idea the notion of the duty imposed on us by Confirmation is complete. It is a call to fight, but as a simple soldier; a consecration to active service, but as one destined to obey rather than to command.

It is not necessary to analyze here in detail what we mean by Catholic Action. As a matter of fact all that can be said about it either follows from or is closely linked up with the few principles we have just noted. It is however not out of place to stress again the idea of serving as a common soldier in the army of the Church. There will always be Catholics who will refuse to accept Catholic Action as it has been proposed to them by the Church and as it is imposed on them by Confirmation. Some will refuse to do their part. They will refuse to fight. These are the cowards, the traitors, the half-Christians who think that their faith is not worth an allegiance as full as that they owe to the state. But there will be others too who will miss the mark through lack of military discipline. They are all athirst for activity, but they want to lead themselves. Whatever appeals to them is what the Church needs; they have no hesitation about leading private crusades, and no lack of obstinacy in persisting in them even when their misguided zeal has led them to extremes. These—though they will refuse to admit it—are the plunderers and booty-hunters that come in the wake of any great army. The Church is for them a glorious opportunity of growing in power, fame, and importance. Under the cloak of enthusiasm for some good principle or other they give free rein to their own personal ambition—though it may sometimes be a question of giving rein to nothing more than ignorance—and the time may come when they will dictate to their Bishops and even to the Holy See what it is that Our Lord wants of His Church. This is not Catholic Action. It is the misguided action of erring Catholics who are too blind to see that their greatest glory is to obey, as to the Lord, and their greatest shame to make of the army of their King an undisciplined marauding expedition.

To be a soldier of Christ demands readiness to sink one's individuality in the interests of the Mystical Body. The soldier of Christ—the confirmed—must then be a man of mortification, an ascetic, a man dead to the ruling motive of self-interest. There must be about him a certain other-worldness, a certain spiritual atmosphere. "For we are the good odour

of Christ . . ." (2 Cor. 2, 15). St. Thomas makes one striking statement in this connection, with which we may very
aptly conclude: the confirmed is to be, as it were, one brought
up from the furthest regions of the Church to fight in its
defense. We must be utterly unlike those whom we combat.
We may well imagine the terror inspired in armies in days
gone by when an invaded country called to its defense those
of its inhabitants who lived in the very heart of its territory,
or on its most inaccessible mountains. These were soldiers
steeped in the traditions of their country, soldiers for whom
their country meant everything, soldiers who looked strange
and uncompromising to the invader. Our Lord asks His
soldiers to be strange and uncompromising in the world's
eyes. He has marked them and set them apart for holiness by
the character of Baptism. He brings them now by Confirmation from the inner regions of His Church to fight in its
defense. They should look strange; because they are holy.
They should be uncompromising; for their cause is too
precious to be sold or bartered. He relies upon them, upon
their courage and their discipline. God relies on man to lead
man to union with God.

8

THE BLESSED EUCHARIST

"I am the bread of life: he that cometh to me shall not hunger."
(JO. 6, 35)

THERE ARE MYSTERIES in the natural as well as in the super-natural order—inescapable truths or facts which we cannot explain without diminishing their profundity, nor ignore without missing much of the sense of life. Free will is such a mystery. To explain it fully is to become determinist or to rule out the Divine foreknowledge of every thought and act. To ignore or disregard free will is to miss the experience of life as a noble adventure, to remain for ever without the vision of the world as a thing to be shaped by the hand of man, and the hand of man as a thing that determines destinies. There are lesser mysteries too, not quite so profound as the mystery of created freedom, but full of vital import for the finer shades of the meaning of life. Among these we may class the mystery of the power of personality.

It is an undoubted fact that the more subtle lessons of life are never understood until they be revealed through immediate contact with a person. The broad outlines of life can be detected in everyday experience. That there be a God, that there be a Church, that there be sacraments—all these central truths may be understood in essentials without the strictly personal touch of a loved teacher being required. They will be learned in sermons from priests we hardly know; they will be learned at school from teachers we never see once school hours are over. But it is hardly possible that they will ever be grasped as vital if communicated to us in this way only. Normally they first dawn upon us as matters that count when some one we know and love—a mother, a father, a friend—communicates to us some little of his or her enthusiasm for them. A living person has this mysterious power of warming and enlightening that words and reasons have not. And going still further in our analysis of the need for contact with persons as distinct from mere ideas, we may say that there can be no really deep appreciation whatever of the nature of Catholicism which has not originated in contact with some person—human or Divine—and which has not reached its consummation in contact with a Divine Person, That namely, of Our Lord and Saviour.

The superiority of personal contact over words is a mystery. Inadequate explanations can be given of it. But after such explanations there always remains something to be still accounted for. A professor in the lecture hall may express himself in words less happily chosen than those he would use in a communication to a scientific body. And yet the lecture will give a far deeper insight into his thought than the communication could ever do. A child reads, with great wealth of detailed elaboration in the written page, that it should be truthful. It never really sees the guilt of a lie till the day when its mother will look at it in a pained and quiet way and say how disappointed she is that her little boy or girl should tell lies. We may of course try to explain all this by referring to the fact that the spoken word appeals to more emotions than does the written word; that in the spoken word there is the tone of the voice, there is the sight of him who speaks. But there is more than this, more than an appeal to sight and hearing. There is some contact of person with person, some subtle communication of soul with soul, some transfer of light to the intellect and strength to the will, that cannot be explained as due to mere faculties and forces. The words of a living man are more than just words, the voice of a living man is more than a sound. The living man has what words and sounds lack: the force and magic of personality.

Almighty God—as He has always done—made allowance for this psychological law in the institution of the sacraments. In Baptism and Confirmation—and in all sacraments except the Blessed Eucharist—the recipient is in immediate contact with only the sanctifying power of Christ, Who is both God and man. Now it is true that there is no real difference in God between Power and Substance. Wherever God's Power is God is. But it is not so with Our Lord as Man. His power may be operative in us while He himself is distant from us. On earth He worked miracles while at a distance from those upon whom He worked them. Still His human intellect and will concurred in the performance of these miracles. It is in somewhat similar manner that He sanctifies us in the sacraments we have considered up to this. He Himself in His Person is distant from us. He sits throned in glory at the right hand of the Father. He is united to us by His power and operation only. It is His power that washes us from the stain of original sin; it is again His power that strengthens us to profess our faith without fear or shame. But we miss the thrill of contact with His Person: there remains after the reception of Baptism and Confirmation a still unexplored way of grafting the Divine onto the human, the way of immediate contact with a Person, with a Man Who is anointed with the unction of the Godhead. In the other sacraments God comes to us through the channel of the power of Christ; in the Blessed Eucharist He comes to us through the channel of Christ's Person and Substance.

It was therefore supremely appropriate that a sacrament should be instituted in which would be contained the Substance and Person of the Incarnate Word. Once established, however, the place of such a sacrament is not a matter of mere appropriateness; It becomes necessarily the end and perfection of all the others.

The Blessed Eucharist is the end of Baptism. We are baptized that we may grow up in Christ: that we may put on Christ. It is also the end of Confirmation. For the whole purpose of profession of faith is to draw our fellow men to Christ, and it is in the Blessed Eucharist that they will find Him. The full force of the dual consecration of Baptism and Confirmation may be summed up by saying that these sacraments consecrate us to the Blessed Eucharist. It is around the Blessed Eucharist that our whole lives should centre. The Blessed Eucharist is not a sacrament to be received from time to time and then forgotten. There may be a deeper meaning in those words of St. Augustine "So live that you may be worthy to communicate daily" than is commonly recognized. They may mean—and even if they do not mean it, it remains none the less true—that the whole of our daily life should be in view of, or as result of, our reception of the Body and Blood of the Lord. To live so as to be worthy to receive is to live under the motive of reception. This then is the meaning of the Blessed Eucharist: to be the end of the sacramental system. Having said that, all is said. But to understand what has been said more must still be added.

It is well for us to recall once more at this point what has been the central doctrine of the last few chapters: the fact that Our Lord is King. He is now really King of Glory.

He has His throne in heaven. He has His court there—His Queen and His angels and saints. He has also His earthly subjects, poor wayfarers, poor soldiers, members of the Church Militant, but proud and eager to serve so great a King. This doctrine has been for us the key to the sacramental system.

Now we have seen that man is not fully satisfied until he comes into contact with the person of whomsoever it may be that is his guide. Words, forces, cannot get down to real depths of the soul. We are then not satisfied with serving under the orders of the great King, nor with feeling that His strength supports us. (It should of course be understood that we do not speak here of a natural desire of human nature as such for the Blessed Eucharist. The desire of which we speak here is based rather on God's power to elevate than on man's power to achieve.) We wish to meet our King in Person, to know by experience Who it is we fight for, to draw enthusiasm and strength from contact with Him in Whom our cause is made concrete, with Him, in fact Who is our Cause.

There is on the other hand our great weakness and sinfulness. We should never dare to enter into the audience chamber of the King of Glory even if we had the power of doing so. It is vain to speak of the mercy and compassion of Our Lord while on earth, so great indeed that sinners did not hesitate to approach Him. He was then clothed in mortal flesh; He is now clothed in immortality. There was one occasion during His life on earth when He revealed to three of His disciples the glory of His Kingly Person. That was on Thabor. And the Apostle Peter who was there could find no words but foolish ones to express his terror: "For he knew not what he said; for they were struck with fear" (Mk. 9, 5).

Our approach to Our King must be made possible by some veiling of His awful Majesty. This does not mean that we may not approach His Person in all its truth and reality. It means simply that whereas it will be the Great King in Person Who will visit us, He will come incognito. There will be the Person of the King, but the trappings of a subject. In other words, our desire of union with the very Person of Jesus will have as answer a sacrament. Just as His Power is present in Baptism under a sign which indicates its presence, so also His Person will be present in another sacrament, and nothing will meet our eyes of flesh but a quiet shining as of a thing of sense.

The Divine Wisdom saw that it was good that the sign of the Person and Substance of the King should be bread and wine, that is to say, food of the body. Our Lord willed to hide His glory from our eyes under the veils of the outward appearance of bread and wine. In doing this He instituted a true sacrament or sign. Hence the very way He chose to veil His Majesty was intended by Him to be a revelation of the inner meaning of His coming to us in Person. What He meant to convey to us by offering Himself to us under the appearance of bread was that His coming effected in us something akin to what bread effects in our bodily organism; in other words that He, hidden beneath the appearances of bread and wine, comes to us to be the spiritual food of our souls. The mystery of the Blessed Eucharist is then a mystery of spiritual food.

Were we to ask in what it is that spiritual food differs from material food we find that there is one answer which is traditional in the mind of the Church: material food is converted into the substance of him who eats, spiritual food converts into the substance of Him Who is eaten. "As the living Father hath sent me and I live by the Father; so he that eateth me, the same also shall live by me" (Jo. 6, 58). Our Lord was sent into the world by the Father and seemed thereby to eyes of flesh to have lost that marvellous unity with Him which unites Divine Persons the One to the Other. But this loss of unity was only apparent. The Incarnate Word still lived by the Father. We who receive Our Lord in Holy Communion will live by Him in a way that bears some resemblance to this. We shall live by Him because we shall have been transformed into Him. We shall have eaten His Flesh and drunk His Blood not that They might be made into our flesh and our blood, but that we might become other Christs, that Christ in all the truth of His real Person might abide in us and we in Him.

The effect of Holy Communion is union with and transformation into Christ. We may express the same truth in a somewhat different way by saying that Its effect is charity. St. Paul tells us that charity is the bond of perfection (Col. 3, 14). Charity it is that brings the spiritual life to its final fulfillment here on earth. Our union with Our Lord is realized in its highest manifestation through charity. By charity we not only have Him present in our souls, but we are united to Him by a bond of love. He comes to us that we may love Him. He does not come to find within us an as yet unoccupied space, a place that He may occupy. He comes to us that we may love Him, that we may occupy ourselves with Him, and so the natural effect of His coming is an increase in our power of loving, an increase, that is to say, in the infused gift of charity. What is still more, His coming effects an increase in the fervour of our acts of charity and excites us to elicit such acts. Our Lord does not come merely that we may have the power of loving Him. He comes that we may actually love Him. Hence the effect of His coming is a powerful attraction to acts of love, and even sensible fervour and devotion in producing these acts. It is true that all the sacraments increase our charity. But all except the Blessed Eucharist do this, we may say, secondarily. Their primary effect is to produce the grace peculiar to the end of the sacrament in question. But the end of the Blessed Eucharist is union with Our Lord in charity. Hence union and charity are its primary effects—as indeed we might have deduced from the simple consideration with which we opened this chapter: for the peculiar effect of contact with a person as distinguished from contact with his written word is a deep enthusiasm for and an intimate affective appreciation of him—love, in other words, or charity. To come to Holy Communion is to receive Our Lord in Person. There is something in even the thought of this privilege that should make the most tepid Christian warm with a glow of generous feeling.

If the effect of Holy Communion be transformation into Our Saviour and unrestrained love of Him, the state of mind in which we should approach the Blessed Sacrament can be no ordinary one. It is not my intention to speak here of what is sufficient to constitute a good intention. I am speaking now to souls who aim at perfection, and speaking rather of the intention which they should strive to have than of that which they are bound under pain of sin to have. With this proviso we may say that the disposition to bring to the reception of Holy Communion is a complete and total donation of self to Our Lord. There must be absolutely no reserve whatever. The condition for the ideal reception of material food is the power of assimilating it perfectly into our organism. The corresponding condition for the reception of spiritual food is that there be absolutely no obstacle whatever to its transforming us into itself. We must come to Holy Communion ready to sink our own petty views, to abandon our own hopes and desires, to make frank and candid surrender to Him Who comes within us. This is what is meant by being willing to be transformed into Jesus. It is what is meant also by receiving a sacrament that has as direct end to make us love Him. For love knows no bounds. To expose ourselves to the risk of being led to love Our Lord without measure, is to submit entirely to Him. And to receive Holy Communion is to expose ourselves to this risk: for the peculiar end of Holy Communion is love, and those who come to it should come desiring to be infected with the folly of love.

It is profitable to examine what is the condition (understanding the term in the sense we have just indicated above) for the reception of the two sacraments we have studied and then see in what it differs from that for the reception of the Blessed Eucharist. This condition, as we now take it, is the full acceptance of the end of the sacrament. For Baptism it is, then, the willingness to become a child of God. That is the whole immediate end. Nothing more than that is asked. In Confirmation it is to be willing to be the soldier of Christ. That again is all. In Holy Communion it is to be willing to be transformed totally into Christ. That is all; but there is nothing else left to give. Every sacrament implies a donation of self to God and to the ends of the sacrament. But the Blessed Eucharist is the only one which demands immediately that the donation be radical and entirely without reserve. The other sacraments are as it were so many stages in the tardy offering we make of self to God, and find their completion and full meaning in the unreserved donation which the Blessed Eucharist signifies and demands.

The Blessed Eucharist is the great sacrament of union

with God in Christ. It is the answer to the soul's search for where God may be found. All the other sacraments point to the Blessed Eucharist. It sums up all that they have to give; it is a total expression of our laying hold on the Divine. But there are two phases in our ascent to God. There is the phase of sacrifice and the phase of sacrament; there is the humble turning of the creature to the Creator crowned by the all-merciful turning of the Father to His child. If then the place of the Blessed Eucharist in the scheme of man's intercourse with God be so utterly unique and complete, It must be both sacrifice and sacrament; It must be such that without going outside It, man can find an adequate expression of the relation in which he stands to God, and God can find an adequate expression of the good-pleasure He wills to manifest to man. It is thus that the Blessed Eucharist has been instituted. Our Lord instituted It as sacrifice as well as sacrament. Not only did He say "This is my body" and "This is my blood," but He added those other words "Do this for a commemoration of me."

It follows from this that the reception of the Blessed Eucharist has a double meaning: it is at once an expression of entry into a sacrificial process and submission to an act of Divine Power operative in a sacrament. That these two meanings integrate themselves into one will be seen shortly. Just now, however, we may with profit consider them separately.

St. Thomas tells us (IIIa Q82 a4) what the reception of the Blessed Eucharist means in the sacrificial act: ". . . Whoever offers a sacrifice should become a sharer in it, because the exterior sacrifice which is offered is the sign of the interior sacrifice by which a person offers himself to God; hence, by participating in the sacrifice, the offerer shows that the interior sacrifice really affects him" (the participation in question in the context is that which consists in eating some portion of the thing offered). At Holy Mass we offer, through the hands of the priest, the same Victim Who offered Himself in a bloody manner on Calvary. The Mass is one and the same sacrifice as Calvary. All that differs is the manner of offering: for the Victim Who then offered Himself in mortal and suffering flesh on the hard wood of the Cross now offers Himself in an unbloody manner on the altar of His Church, as the Offering of His Church, through the hands of the ministers of His Church. Let us just think what this implies, without burdening our minds with abstract theological speculation concerning how all this can be. What it implies for us here and now is that the offering of Holy Mass is the Offering of Calvary. Hence our reception of Holy Communion at Mass signifies nothing less than our interior adherence to Calvary itself.

It is possible to confuse this simple statement very much by unnecessary subtleties. But it is also possible to leave the matter too vague through omitting those distinctions that lead to clarity and precision. Let us then make a few distinctions, but let them be as few and as fundamental as possible. The meaning of Holy Mass should emerge from the process.

We may distinguish in the sacrifice of Calvary an exterior sign and an interior act. The exterior sign was the death of Our Saviour; the interior act was the acceptance or willing of that death as expression of an attitude of soul. Both elements go to make up the sacrifice. The death alone was not a sacrifice. If that were so we could say that Our Lord's crucifixion by the Jews was an act pleasing to God the Father. It is only when death becomes a sign by its willed reference to an interior attitude that it is a sacrifice. The interior attitude is one of love and submission: submission to God Who is Lord and Master of all things; love of Him Who is Our Father and Whose rights we are ready to admit. The interior act in the sacrifice of Calvary was then one proceeding from the virtues of charity and religion—we may say either that it consisted in charity offering religion, or religion offering charity, though the first form is the more exact. And this interior act expressed itself in the visible offering of the Cross. Our Lord offered His life to the Father in token of the love and submission that were His. This is something before which we can only pause in reverent silence. The Love of Our Lord for the Father—the Love of the Incarnate Word for the Father—this is something altogether sublime. And then His spirit of submission, His clear midday grasp of the inviolability of the Father's rights—could we have ever thought that a human nature would be found to bear the strain of such a vision? Two mighty acts welled up within the soul of Christ, and joined their steady streams into one grand sweep of sacrificial enthusiasm. It was this that made of the death of Our Saviour something holy and pleasing to the Father. It is only in relation to this that His death is a sacrifice. This is the interior act, the interior sacrifice, which gives meaning to what eye and ear may perceive, which makes a sacrifice out of what was else unrelieved blasphemy.

When we come now to consider the sacrifice of the Mass we must remember that it is the same sacrifice as that of Calvary. There is the same Victim and the same High Priest really offering the Victim, though allowing man to enter into the offering. The exterior sacrifice is then the same as on Calvary: the Victim offered is the Same. What of the interior sacrifice? Is it too the same? It is clear that, if by the interior sacrifice we mean that of Our Lord and Saviour, it is the same in the Mass as on Calvary. In Holy Mass Our Lord does not offer Himself to His Father in virtue of new dispositions and as the expression of a new state of love and reverence. If this were the case we could no longer speak of the Mass as being the same as the sacrifice of the Cross unless in a very loose and inexact sense. But if we mean by the interior sacrifice the interior act of the man who offers the Divine Victim with the priest at the altar we find ourselves in face of something that is altogether unique in sacrifice: for in the case of Holy Mass and in this case alone the exterior sacrifice—meaning the Victim and the dispositions of the Victim—has priority over the interior sacrifice and determines its nature.

This, we have said, is something unique in the idea of sacrifice. In every other sacrifice the interior sacrifice is prior to and determines the meaning and value of what is exterior. An offering made to God in the spirit of sacrifice by someone outside the true fold is of value only in so far as it is the expression of an interior attitude. If the thing offered happens to be of great value as a thing, it may excite a more intense act of intellect and will than would a thing of little worth. But its value as a sacrifice is not its value as a thing. And if it should happen to have more value as a sacrifice than something else, this will be only if and when it is offered in response to a greater interior sacrificial urge. Now it is true that the meritorious value of our sharing in the sacrifice of the Mass depends not immediately on the Victim offered—for the Victim is the same no matter who offers, or with what dispositions he offers—but on our interior dispositions. But this does not give our dispositions absolute priority. For it is the exterior sacrifice which in this case determines what our interior sacrifice should be and not vice versa as is the case in every other sacrifice. Our Lord's interior dispositions were such that only by His death upon the cross could He give them adequate expression. On Calvary then the interior sacrifice dictated the nature of the exterior one. But our sacrifice—that of the Mass—is not something that it is left to us to determine for ourselves. It is the same sacrifice as that of Calvary. What we must do then is to enter into the sacrifice of Calvary. Our interior sacrifice must be an entering into the sacrifice of Calvary. In other words, our interior sacrifice must conform itself to the sacrifice of the Cross in its interior aspect. Our Holy Mass will be of value for us only to the extent to which our interior acts reproduce those of Our Saviour.

We are now in a position to grasp the meaning of Communion at Holy Mass. It is the expression of our interior conformity with the great sacrifice of Calvary. It is a protestation that we desire to have the sentiments Our Lord had when He hung upon the Cross. It is a declaration that the offering we make is no mere external rite without echo in our souls. There is within a sacrifice; there is within an offering of ourselves to God: this offering is a renewal of the interior offering of Jesus. It is some little participation in the intense sincerity of His great offering. It is—for this is the only way we could share in His interior sacrifice—something wrought in us by Him: it is He offering Himself once more through us, and us with Him. Our Lord is Eternal Priest, not only as Victim but as Offerer. Our offering of Him in Holy Mass is His offering of Himself through us. His interior dispositions will therefore be the norm of ours: our interior sacrifice will be a sharing in His. Our Communion is the expression of the reality of this in our interior. We partake of the Victim to show that we wish to be fully one with Him; and this in the case of the sacrifice of the Mass necessitates oneness with Him in His rôle of Victim and Offerer. Communion at Holy Mass is, in fine, our ultimate expression of conformity in interior dispositions with the Great High Priest of Calvary.

We have already drawn attention to the fact that our Saviour's death on the Cross was to all appearances a death of shame. His acceptance of that death was an act of utter submission to the Divine Majesty. This is what we are invited to reproduce in ourselves each time we assist at Holy Mass. We are invited to fall down in adoration; to confess that we are nothing; that we are sinners, which is worse than being nothing; that we depend entirely upon God; that the existence we have, and of which we are so proud, is something we receive at every instant from the hand of God; that without Him we can neither think nor speak nor act; and we are invited to confess all this in a burst of rapturous enthusiasm, with love and alacrity. Our Saviour humbled Himself becoming obedient to the death of the Cross, for which reason God exalted Him (Phil. 2, 9). Our Saviour was made King and Lord and this by the very fact of His acceptance of a shameful death. Now, it has pleased the Divine Goodness to reproduce this mystery in a most wonderful way in our souls. For Communion in the Mass considered as sacrifice is the act by which we declare our union with Christ in His self-abasement; but this same Communion, considered as reception of a sacrament, is a sharing in His exaltation. For us also the very act by which we declare our utter nothingness in the sight of God is that by which God has chosen to raise us above the whole creation and has made us "sit together in the heavenly places, through Christ Jesus"

(Eph. 2, 6). The condition of our sharing in the glory of Our Saviour is willingness to be partaker of His shame.

We saw in an early chapter that the process of our deification might be summed up as a gift of man to God and a gift of God to man. The gift of man to God is sacrifice; the gift of God to man is the sacrament. This is a new revelation of the meaning of the Blessed Eucharist. At Holy Mass we make to God the Father the greatest offering that can be made to Him—His own Divine Son. This is an offering that pleases the Father. It is an offering that pleases Him not only because of its own intrinsic worth, but because it implies as well an interior state that is itself most pleasing. God now makes His offer to us. What He offers is His Divine Son, this time not as Victim, but as Fount of Grace and life, as King. To receive Holy Communion then is to receive our King. Holy Communion is in an especial way the sacrament of the Kingship of Christ.

This wonderful identification of the gift of man to God and the gift of God to man in one Person is part of the mystery of Our Lord's mediatorship. He is Mediator in an altogether complete sense. He is at once the expression of what should be man's attitude to God, and of what is God's attitude to man. Whether man wish to communicate with God or God with man, the communication is already made in Christ Jesus. He is the incarnation of all we have to say to Our Father, He is an unceasing prayer for all that we need from the Father—"always living to make intercession for us" (Hebr. 7, 25)—just as He is the One in Whom are stored up all the treasures that the Father wills to bestow upon us. He is thus Mediator. He links up in His Person the needs of man and the riches of God, the prayers of man and the good-pleasure of God. He stands between God and man, "For He is our peace, who hath made both one" (Eph. 2, 14). In Him, dying on the cross, man was reconciled with God, and God was given to man.

Now we know in what the gift of God to man consisted: it was the gift of a new Head to the human race, the gift of a King. This gift, the completion of sacrifice, is made to us individually in Holy Communion. In receiving Holy Communion we accept, for our part, the donation made to the whole human race on Calvary. This means that each Holy Communion is an acceptance of the full Kingship of Our Saviour. There is no escaping this. The gift of God to us is the gift of a King. We cannot receive God unless in our King. And we cannot receive Our King unless on His own terms. He is a real King Who has won us as His subjects. We belong altogether to Him. His glory is to exercise His kingly power—that is to say to rule souls, to fill souls with the life that is in Himself, to uproot souls and draw them into the Godward current of which He is the source. Holy Communion is an act of complete surrender to Our King. Love for Him should bring us to Holy Communion. He is really King; we should desire to see His rule spread in all souls—first of all in our own; we should wish Him to reign in us without restraint. We come to Him asking Him to exercise over us all His rights. He is our gift our food; but He is a spiritual food that will transform us entirely into Itself, that will bring death to all that is opposed to It, that the life of which It is the source may be the only life by which we live. If then we come to Holy Communion as to the completion of our sacrifice—as to the reception of a gift from the hand of God—we should be under no delusion as to the nature or the worth of the gift. The gift is God Himself, given to us in our King on condi-

tion that we accept His Kingship. To accept His Kingship
is to be made Godlike, for His rule is to lead us to God. But
is there not a special beauty in that other aspect of our King's
long waiting for His subjects? He is King. But He can rule
as He wills to rule, only over those who come to Him and
accept Him. Holy Communion is such a coming and such an
acceptance. Our prayer at Holy Communion should then be:
"Lord I am Thy subject; come, reign in me, and be glorified in me."

If we approach Holy Communion in this spirit we shall
experience within ourselves a feeling of pride that is not at
first easy to analyze, but which is altogether appropriate to
the act we are performing. Now, in saying that the moment
of reception of Holy Communion is a moment for pride, it is
not intended to run in any way counter to the tradition of
the Church Who puts on our lips at that moment the beautiful and humble "Lord I am not worthy that Thou shouldst
enter under my roof." This act of humility is altogether
fundamental. We can hope for no grace unless in the measure
in which we are empty of self. But there is more than self
in Holy Communion. It is a "communion," it is a union
between two, between the King and the subject. And even if
the subject have no reason for pride at the sight of his own
unworthiness he has every reason for pride in his King. Our
"Lord I am not worthy" leaves room for a "The lamb that
was slain is worthy to receive power, and divinity, and wisdom, and strength, and honour, and glory, and benediction"
(Apoc. 5, 12). We should be proud of Our Lord when we
come to receive Him; we are not subjects of a petty human
princelet; we are not the slaves of a tyrant weaker in spiritual
fibre than we. We are the subjects, the members and brothers,
of Him Who has a Name that is above every name. When

we come to receive His Body and Blood we know that They are meat and drink in very truth, that They can strengthen and elevate us and that there is no prince of earth that can do this. Is not this cause for pride? Is it a mean or contemptible thing to have such a King? Every man feels a thrill of pride when his king calls him to his presence to reward him or speak a word of praise. It is something of moment to come into contact with a person as great as a king is. Holy Communion is our reward and encouragement. It is the hidden manna promised to him that is victorious (Apoc. 2, 17), consolation for all that labour and are burdened. It is our entry to the throne-room of Our King. We should enter with head erect.

There is of course, nothing very new in this combination of pride and humility which we consider so fitting. It is but a continuation of the paradox of the "Agnosce Christiane dignitatem tuam"—"Christian, be conscious of your worth"—as applied to followers of Him Who was meek and humble of heart. Though there be a paradox there is no contradiction. For the worth of the Christian is something which fosters his humility, and his humility is the condition of the revelation of his worth. What we are worth is Christ's; what we have reason to be humble for is our own. We are proud of what Christ can do—even in us; we are abashed at what we can do and are, even in spite of Christ. Our divinity belongs to Him; our misery is our own. Christianity does not consist in rooting out our natural powers. It consists often in redirecting them. We have a power of appreciation and praise of what is noble. This is natural to us. But if we concentrate it upon what is not noble—upon ourselves considered just for what we are worth in ourselves—then we misuse it. It must be given an object worthy of its exercise

When exercised on self it is sinful pride. When exercised on Our Saviour or in what in us belongs to Him, it is essentially Christian and ennobling. We should appreciate and praise Our Lord and His works. It is blindness, obtuseness, stockishness, not to do so. We should even be proud of Him and His works; since pride adds to appreciation and praise, the elusive touch of possession. Pride is appreciation and praise of something as belonging somehow to us. But Our Lord does belong to us. He is Our King. Granted, we are unworthy. But our unworthiness does not make Him cease to be Ours. On the contrary, it makes the fact of His being Ours, and His Own intrinsic nobility, all the more worthy of our admiration. He is a King Who can bend to earth while remaining essentially of Heaven.

The whole essence of the Blessed Eucharist seems to be summed up in the three ideas we have just exposed: it is contact with the Person and Substance of Our Lord; it is union with Him as our Spiritual Food; it is full and entire submission to the exercise of His Kingship—acceptance of the Gift of Christ the King. These ideas are of course fundamentally all the same. They are different ways of expressing the same truth. One will appeal at one time, another will appeal later; one will appeal to one soul, another to a soul whose temperament and outlook lead it to relish something else. It is more than possible however that the idea of spiritual food is the one richest in suggestiveness and most suited to the understanding of the average man. It is the one preferred of Our Lord Himself. It is the one suggested most clearly by the symbolism of the sacrament. But any idea of the three will lead to all the consequences that may be deduced from either of the two others. However, for the sake of avoiding unpleasant repetitions, we shall confine ourselves

to showing very briefly how the Blessed Sacrament considered just as our Spiritual Food produces certain minor effects
—if the term be permitted—in the spiritual life.

The first effect is spiritual joy and gladness. Gladness is
an effect of material food. Spiritual gladness is an effect of
spiritual food. We say in the prayers of Benediction: "Thou
didst give them bread from heaven having in itself all sweetness." Earth is a vale of tears. There is much that is bitter
to be swallowed down; there is much that is hard and that
must be borne. Almighty God's normal way of dealing with
men is not to force them to overcome their distates for what
is hard by mere fortitude. He wishes to give them encouragement; He wishes to mark the road they must travel with
milestones of pure spiritual joy. Holy Communion is the
source of this joy. Not every Holy Communion will bring
as much joy as every other one. But Holy Communion can
and does bring joy, and the joy it brings even once in a lifetime is more than enough to sweeten life's bitterest chalice.

Though we may often fail to perceive the spiritual joy
which Holy Communion brings, we can be sure that it never
fails to strengthen us. This also is an effect of food. Food
strengthens the body. Spiritual food strengthens the soul.
We read in the third Book of Kings of how the Prophet
Elias was fed in the desert by an angel and how "he walked
in the strength of that food forty days and forty nights unto
the mount of God, Horeb" (3 Kgs. 19, 8). We find in
Holy Communion the strength to struggle on to God's dwelling place—which is also our own—to heaven, namely. What
is still more, Holy Communion is a foretaste and guarantee
of the possession of eternal bliss: "Pignus aeternae gloriae."
In Heaven we shall see God face to face. Through Holy
Communion God is really present within us. We do not see

Him, it is true. But He is there within us, and there to prepare us to see Him hereafter. By Holy Communion we become, as it were, accustomed to intercourse with God, so that when the great day of revelation of the Godhead comes, we may be at our ease, seeing God as He is because made like unto Him.

Holy Communion not only gives strength, it makes good the loss of strength sustained in daily skirmishing with evil. Forgiveness of mortal sin is not the direct or normal effect of Holy Communion. But it does forgive venial sin. The harm done to the soul by venial sin corresponds roughly to the effects of the wear and tear of life on bodily organisms. Since it is material food that makes good this daily loss of physical strength, it is fitting that the loss of spiritual strength should be made good by spiritual food. This same truth follows if we consider that the primary effect of Holy Communion is charity. It causes charity not only as a virtue—all the sacraments if fruitfully received cause the virtue—but even excites us to the act of charity. Now charity is sufficient to drive out venial sin. Hence, Holy Communion, by increasing our charity, necessarily remits venial sin also.

There is much more that could be said about the Sacrament of the Body and Blood of Our Saviour. Yet it is well to pause here, leaving the treatment unfinished, perhaps, but adding nothing that would obscure the clear outline of the substance of its truth. We are not in need of teaching. What we do need is a few lessons in emphasis. We know all, or most, of the doctrine of the Christian life. We do not see what are the central ideas about which the main body of truths is grouped. For the Blessed Eucharist there are at least four possible focal points: the Sacrament of the Kingship of Our Lord; the Sacrament of spiritual food; the sacrament of personal contact with Our Saviour; the Sacrament which is the completion of a sacrifice. Any one of these ideas will give order to all the others. Any one of them should make us long for Our Lord.

And after all, is not the test of our understanding of a sacrament whose sign is the appearance of bread and wine, hunger for that Substance Which underlies?

9

THE SACRAMENTS AND THE MYSTICAL BODY

"For we, being many, are one bread, one body, all that partake of one bread." (1 COR. 10, 17)

RECENT YEARS HAVE WITNESSED an extraordinary reawakening of interest in the doctrine of the Church as the Mystical Body of Christ. The word "reawakening" has been used advisedly, for the doctrine is in itself nothing new, nor is it even a new thing that it should be taught as an integral and central part of Christianity. The doctrine itself is as old as Christianity. Our Lord told His disciples that He was the True Vine and that they were the branches; St. Paul insists upon it also, and this under the explicit image of a body of which Our Lord is Head. Neither is it a new thing that the doctrine should come once more into prominence. It was never forgotten, though it may have been neglected in great part for some time, or taught only in equivalent forms, such as the social character of the Church and the unique and universal Mediatorship of Our Saviour. But then it is nothing new in the history of the Church for a point of her teaching to recede into the background of the popular consciousness—though its substance can never recede into a background of the Church's official teaching—and to be brought to the focus of attention in a providential way at the time God sees most fitting.

Now it is of faith that the Church is a society. It is not an arbitrary grouping of individuals. Study of the doctrine of the Mystical Body leads to a better understanding of the social nature of the Church, and of the essentially social nature of membership in the Church. We have already seen some slight indication of this in our treatment of the sacrament of Confirmation. The confirmed appeared to us to act in some way in a social capacity. We did not analyse in detail the specifically social aspect of their work. That was taken to a certain extent for granted. But the very fact that such a thing can be taken for granted indicates that even yet the full significance of membership of a Church which is also a society is far from being understood. For it would be altogether false to believe that it is only with the sacrament of Confirmation that the Christian begins to act as a member of a society. In fact we may say—and this will probably appear to be a striking overstatement—that from the organically social point of view the importance of the sacrament of Confirmation is far less than that of Baptism or the Blessed Eucharist. Confirmation does not make us members of the social group. We are that already by Baptism and Holy Communion. What it does is to make us active members of the group. It delegates us to defend and spread the social system of which we are members. But it presupposes that we are members. It is the very fact of being members that makes us eligible to be raised by Confirmation to the dignity of becoming active agents in the service of the Church. To express this truth in technical language: Confirmation is the sacrament of the ad extra social life of the simple member of the Church; the Church's intimate social life has its source in Baptism and the Blessed Eucharist. Thus far has been anticipation of our main thesis. Let us now take it point by point.

Our first incorporation into the Mystical Body of Our Lord comes with the reception of the Baptismal character.

This reception is first of all union with the Head of the Body. The character of Baptism sets us apart, as we have seen, as being the property of Our Lord. It is His first laying hold on us. It grafts us on to Him. It unites us to Him in such a way that He can now communicate life to us through the sacraments and we can receive from the sacraments the life they have to communicate to us. We commonly regard a person's property as being an extension of his person, and this is one sense in which the soul marked with the character of Baptism is an extension or member of Christ the Head. Baptism makes souls belong to Him to use for the ends He has proposed to Himself. Others must respect such souls in so far as they are His property. They may not be a very valuable possession. They may even be absolutely dead to the life of grace. But at least they belong to Our Lord, and while they are as yet in the state of wayfarers they can always hope to draw life at some time from Him, the source of life. It is only after death that the Baptismal character can become for a soul a cause of remorse, a sign rather of wilful rejection of union with Christ than a possibility of complete identification with Him.

Nor is the character of Baptism without significance for the social life of member with member within the unity of the Church. It is, we have seen, the doorway to participation in the sacraments and sacrifice of the Church. But the reception of the sacraments is a social action. The sacraments are conferred by ministers, men like ourselves, members of our social group. The great sacrifice of the Mass is offered up by a minister in the name of the whole Church. Hence, when we receive the sacraments we receive something that comes to us through the ministration of a visible body acting through its delegates; when we assist at Holy Mass we assist not as individuals offering up their private homage to God, as individual to Individual, but as members of a visible Church, offering up in union with that Church and through the hands of her minister the sacrifice which belongs to the whole Church and which is ours only in so far as we are united to her. All this is social, organic. We simply cannot have a religion which will be nothing more than a matter between God and ourselves, for however easily we, on our side, can concentrate our interests upon what concerns us immediately and us alone, God has wider interests than our sole welfare and God will have us accept Him as He is, wide interests and all.

Baptism is said to be the sacrament of faith, since faith is the beginning of our justification. But faith itself is something social in character. We believe by faith what the Church proposes to us for our belief. The act of faith is made with the help of a divine interior grace. It accepts what is proposed to it on the authority of God Himself. Under these two aspects it is a matter between God and the individual soul. But though God gives directly the power to believe, and though His truth is the reason for believing, it is the Church Who indicates what is to be believed. Every act of faith puts us therefore in the Church's debt. The Church has contributed to our act of faith. We believe as members of an organism in which there are other members whose function it is to direct and safeguard the workings of inferior powers.

Our integration into the Mystical Body by the character of Baptism is not however in any sense a final stage, nor is it even a degree of integration complete in itself. For a branch is grafted onto a tree that it may draw sap from it; we are grafted onto Christ by the character of Baptism that we may draw from Him the sap of sanctifying grace. "I am the vine;

you the branches: he that abideth in me, and I in him, the same beareth much fruit" (Jo. 15, 5). Our Lord is the True Vine. In Him is all the fulness of grace. It is to His glory that mankind should draw life from Him. Man can become like God only by being established in vital and organic union with Christ. Life flows from Him to us as it does from the trunk of a tree to the branches. The moment the sap ceases to flow to the branches they die. They may still be united to the parent trunk—and it is in much this way that the baptized who have lost sanctifying grace are united to Christ—but they are useless members, fated, unless the sap can be brought to flow once more in them, to be cut down and cast into the fire. We who have received grace live by Christ. It is only through what we receive from Him that we can act in a spiritual way. It is from Him we draw grace and with it Faith, Hope, Charity and all the virtues—all those different mouths by which we drink in God, all those different nostrils by which we inhale the pure air of eternity. This life is the purpose of our engrafting on Christ. We become His members that we may live by Him: the character of Baptism is incomplete until it be accompanied in the soul by grace.

It is not a little puzzling to learn that the Blessed Eucharist is the sacrament which perfects the unity of the Church. The average soul, in its moments of devotion after Holy Communion, finds itself lost in Our Lord and in Him alone, or at least tries to lose itself in Him. It would seem then that the Blessed Eucharist should be, to the exclusion of everything else, the sacrament of union of the individual soul with Our Lord. Yet St. Paul is explicit in his linking of Holy Communion with the mystery of the unity of the Church: "For we, being many, are one bread, one body, all that partake of one bread" (1 Cor. 10, 17). And the Church in the secret of the Mass of the Feast of Corpus Christi is no less insistent on this point: "Grant mercifully to Thy Church, we beseech Thee O Lord, the gift of peace and the gift of unity, which are mystically represented in the gifts we offer." What is the mystery hidden in this association of Holy Communion with unity?

To understand how Holy Communion can be, more than any other sacrament, the sacrament of the unity of the Church we need but recall that Holy Communion effects our complete transformation into Christ. But Christ, as He really is, is Head of a Mystical Body. Hence it will be the same sacrament which will integrate us most fully into Christ, and which will effect our most complete identification with His Mystical Body. To be united to Our Lord at all is to be united to Him as Head of a Body. But to be united to Him as Head of a Body means nothing other than to become a member of that Body. Since then it is Holy Communion which perfects our union with Christ Our Head it will then be It also Which will perfect our union with the members of His Mystical Body initiated in the sacrament of Baptism.

This is not a truth that is without importance for indicating the dispositions we should endeavour to have when approaching the Holy Table. We come to receive Our Lord. But we come to receive Him as Head of a Mystical Body. We must therefore come willing to be members of the same organic unity as all our fellow-men. We cannot nourish resentment against a fellow-man and still dare approach the Holy Table. We must be willing to accept all men as our brothers—if not for their own sakes, at least for the sake of Christ. And after all it is that that counts—to love Our Lord so much as to be willing that all men should come beneath His rule and that we should be united with them in the kingdom which is also

His Body. This is a wonderful bond of union between the members of the Church. All are one body, for all are united in the same Christ, and He is One Who is a Head. As there are many grains of wheat and one bread, as there are many grapes and one wine, so there are many who eat the same Bread and drink of the same Chalice, and all are one in Him Who has made Himself our Food and Drink. He is the Bread of Life; we are the scattered grains made one with Him, and made one, the one with the other.

Clearly therefore the Blessed Eucharist is not the Sacrament of the unity of the Church solely in that filling us as It does with Divine Charity it leads to our loving all men in Christ and so being united with them in affection. It has this effect, and this is the union which It most immediately causes. But It presupposes an existing organic union between member and member, and between member and Head. We come to It as already members of one body, seeking in It the perfection of our membership. We come to It that our membership of the Mystical Body may be a real driving force in our lives, that united already to our fellow men by the physical bond of drawing grace from the same Source as they we may be further united to them as to those we love. It is then the sacrament of the unity of the Church in that It intensifies the existing physical unity and makes it issue in unity of love and interests. We are not members who have no power of initiative independently of the Body to which we belong. We are members in a unique sense, for we can, if we will, refuse to contribute to the well-being of the Body, or contribute to it only half-heartedly. We can, if we will, regard our fellow-members with indifference, refusing to admit that, since we are all members of a greater unity, their good is our good. Holy Communion wards off this selfishness. It fills us with love of Our Head, and leads us through love of Him to cherish His members, our fellow men. We become thus one with them in aims as well as structure, one in love as well as life. No man hateth his own body; neither can we hate anyone whom we know to be united to us as member is to member.

The two sacraments we have so far considered are concerned in the main with the life of the Mystical Body considered as something that manifests itself within the Mystical Body, perfecting It and making It a thing of beauty. But the Mystical Body has a life of contact with the outer world as well. There are enemies that threaten its life and there are possibilities of extension. The sacrament which perfects the Mystical Body in its contact with what is of this world and of this world only is Confirmation.

In speaking some few pages back of the sacrament of Confirmation it was altogether inevitable that the precise social nature of the work to which it consecrates the soul should have been left obscure. It was possible to indicate then in a general way that the work was a social one and that it was distinguished by something connected with its social character from the work mapped out for us by the sacrament of Baptism. But we have now seen that Baptism is itself a social sacrament: that men are built up into a social organism by the sacrament of Baptism and that this organism reaches its perfection through the Blessed Eucharist. Is there then any sense in which Confirmation is social in a way that does not hold with equal truth for the two other sacraments? Is nothing more than convenient parcelling up of doctrine at the back of the common idea that it is Confirmation that makes of a man a Christian in the fully social sense, that it was Pentecost that made the Apostles conscious of a social task?

The answer to this question cannot come as something new to those who have followed our line of reasoning thus far. Confirmation does not make of the Christian a member of a society for the first time. It is a sacrament conferred on someone who has already been incorporated into a social group. But this is not equivalent to saying that the common idea that Confirmation has some definite social implications is altogether false. For it has social implications, though they are such as to presuppose the existence of the society. It makes the member of that society zealous for the spread of the society; it gives him what we might term class-consciousness; it makes him realize that the group to which he belongs has a right to a full allegiance; that he must live for it, fight for it, and if necessary die for it. The end of Confirmation is to make man face the world as a member of a society, not as an individual. Baptism, and to some extent the Blessed Eucharist, make him member of a society rather in the eyes of God: Confirmation makes him member of a society in the eyes of men and gives him the strength to live up to the traditions of his society no matter what be the opposition.

We can now see that bearing witness to the faith is more than a matter of loyalty to Our Lord considered as an historical Person, or even as one single Being reigning now in heaven. It is an act of loyalty to Christ Our Head—that is to say to the whole Christ, members as well as Head. It is thus an act of loyalty to the Church, an act of solidarity with every member of the Church. We know that if we deny the faith we shall merit eternal damnation. To deny the faith is to incur the risk of loss to self. But the doctrine of the Mystical Body teaches us that denial of the faith by any single member of the Church is a loss to the whole Church, Head and members. He who denies the faith declares himself ashamed of the Body to which He belongs; he declares himself ashamed of His Head. He who professes his faith declares his pride in Christ and in His Church. And if one should be lost through denial of faith he is lost to the whole Church. He is a limb cut off from the Mystical Body of Christ. His loss is not merely his own. It has affected the whole Mystical Body.

There is no contradiction in regarding the Church at one time as an army, or society, or something of that kind, and at another as a Mystical Body. Both are partial expressions of the one great mystery: the union of Christ with those who are saved by Him. When we say that the Church is the Body of Christ we do not mean to exclude the fact that the members of the Body fight for their Head. In fact this is a phenomenon that may be observed in any living body, that any member, say the hand or the arm, is willing to expose itself to danger, if only in doing so it can safeguard the head. Neither is the idea of an army incompatible with that of union in one body; on the contrary, it finds in it a new wealth of meaning. For the union between the soldiers of an army under their leader is after all an accidental one. Soldiers and leaders form one moral body, but there is no physical union between them. They depend the one on the other for the end they have in view in engaging in battle. Neither the leader alone nor the soldiers alone can be victorious; victory is the fruit of their cooperation. But there are so many other things in which they are absolutely independent units; their family life, their intellectual life, their hobbies. The union between Christ and us is a physical one. We are not independent spiritual units who have come together for the sake of some common, but accidental, end. All our spiritual life comes from Christ. We have no private life, no family life, no hobbies, which do not depend on Him. When then we fight for Him and for His body, we fight for something to which we belong entirely; we fight as does a hand for the head or for another hand. There can be no respect under which it is for us a matter of indifference how the struggle may turn, there can be no hope of any spiritual existence whatever if our army be defeated, for the struggle is one for the life of the Vine on Which we have been grafted, and the existence that will be ours if the Vine die is the existence of the twig that falls to the ground with the trunk and withers in a day.

Such is the sacramental process of the building up of the Mystical Body of Christ. We are grafted on to Him by the character of Baptism; there then flows into our souls the sap of sanctifying grace. Holy Communion strengthens the bond of union, makes the sap flow more freely. Confirmation strengthens us to resist assaults from without—from the world, the enemy of the Body of Christ. To explain this we have been forced to confuse our metaphors, to speak at times as if the Church were a body, at other times as if it were the branches of a vine. It would be well now to consider briefly how much of this imagery is metaphor and how much of it is fact, linking the treatment up the while with the doctrine of the sacraments. We shall confine ourselves here to an analysis of the Church under the aspect of Body of Christ.

It is clear from the Epistles of St. Paul that to speak of the Church as the Body of Christ is to use an image. The Church is not the physical body of flesh and blood that Our Lord had and has, nor is it a body in any sense of the same kind as that was. Our Lord has not two bodies of flesh and blood. But it is clear also that St. Paul was aware that the union existing between Christ and His Church was of a peculiarly intimate nature. And to convey some idea of its intimacy he could find no image more apt than that of the union between head and members of the same physical body. We may then speak of the Church as being the body of Christ: but what we mean is that it stands in a relation to Christ similar to that in which a body stands to its head and nothing more. The precise force of the term "Body of Christ" is to be gathered therefor not from a minute analysis of human bodies, but from an analysis of the relations in which we stand to Christ. There will be things that will be true for physical bodies and which will have no application to the Church. The Church is, in other words, a Mystical Body. That is not to say that there is no real interplay of vital forces between Christ and His Church. But it does mean that they are not strictly those of a physical body, but that they bear them sufficient resemblance to be designated by the same words.

Now Christ is first among His brethren in power, perfection and dignity, while still remaining our Brother. This is why we speak of Him as being our Head.

He is first in power.

From Him flows all the grace we have. Grace comes to us principally in the sacraments, and we have seen that in them He is Ultimate Source—Ultimate Source under God, if we speak of His Sacred Humanity. There can, as well, be a transfer of life from one soul to another. We can pray for others and merit for them. But all that depends ultimately on Him, for it is through Him that our prayers are heard and it is through Him that we can merit. It is under Him that Our Blessed Lady and the saints have power to help us. He is the unique Mediator between God and man in the sense that there can be no mediation which ultimately does not depend on His. He holds thus first place among men in power of

sanctification. He supports by His power the grace which we
receive from Him in the sacraments. Thus our whole life is a
continuation of the state of dependence on Him which is so
evident at the moment of actual reception of grace.

He is first also in perfection.

He is full of grace and truth. His is a Humanity hypo-
statically united to the Godhead. In Him, in One Person,
are the Divine and the Human; and the One Person in
Whom are the Divine and the Human is also Divine. Were
we to meet Our Lord on earth we could point to Him and
say "That man is God." This is an amazing interpenetration
of what is human by what is Divine. Other men may be *like*
God; but only He *is* God. And then, He is full of created
grace: full of it, not merely in the sense that He has more
of it than any man ever will have or has had, but in the
sense that He has all that there can be of grace in the present
order and that all others, no matter who they be, no matter
how near they be to God, can have grace only by sharing in
the grace that is in Him. No thing of earth can shine with
a brighter light than that of the sun, for it is from the sun
that it will necessarily draw the light that is in it: no man can
be more just than Our Saviour, for He is the Sun of Justice
that enlightens every man that comes into the world.

He is first in dignity.

It is true that Our Lord came on earth to save us, that had
man never fallen Our Lord would probably never have
become man. And yet—even if it be true that He is in this
sense "for" man—man is also "for" Him, for He is greater
than man and man must contribute to His Glory: He is "the
first-born of every creature: For in Him were all things
created in heaven and on earth, visible and invisible, whether
thrones or dominations, or principalities, or powers: all things

were created by Him and in Him. And He is before all, and by Him all things consist. And He is the head of His body, the church, Who is the beginning, the first-born from the dead; that in all things He may hold the primacy (Coloss. 1, 15–18). He is God as well as man. As God He is Creator from all eternity, Model after Whose Likeness all things were made. As Man He is Redeemer, making mankind holy after the likeness of the holiness that is in Himself, making of the holiness of mankind a triumph for Himself and for the Father.

There is one thing more wanting to make Him Head, and that is that He be like those who are to be termed His members. For head and body are always of one kind: the head of man is found on the body of man, and the head of beast on the body of beast. Christ is like His members: ". . . one tempted in all things like as we are, without sin" (Hebr. 4, 15). His created grace is like ours; His human nature was like ours; He felt pain as we do; He died as we shall. He became in all things like to us, except in sin and its consequences. And so He can be Our Head, for He is really One of ourselves. The Three Divine Persons have pre-eminence over man in power and perfection and dignity. But the Three Divine Persons are not man. Their relation to us then, no matter how intimate it may be, is not one that we can term the relation of head to body. That is the title of the Incarnate Word, precisely because He combines in Himself with all these other notes the additional one of being like us in a human nature. He is our Head because being One of us He has saved us and guides us.

These four notes are the reasons for speaking of Our Lord as Head of the Mystical Body. In any body the head is the member that is most noble, and perfect, and which controls and moves the others. This is what Our Lord does for His Church. Hence He may be termed the Head of the Church, His Body. We are now entitled to add to the general considerations with which this chapter opened that the Church is not only a society of the common type under a leader, but that it may aptly be spoken of in its relations to Our Lord as a Body, and that He stands to that Body in the place of Head.

Let us note now in this precise context the place of the sacraments in our relations with Christ Our Head. He is Head because of the life He pours into our souls: but this, as we have so often seen, is the work He performs normally through the channel of the sacraments, and which He never performs without an implicit reference to them. Under this aspect then it is primarily because of what He does for us in the sacraments that Our Lord is Our Head. He is Head also because of His infinite perfection. In Him is the plenitude of the Priesthood: but we share in His Priesthood through our sacramental character. In Him is the fulness of grace: it is in the sacraments that we receive grace. Hence, when we speak of Our Lord as having in Himself the full perfection of what is in us in part—whether it be grace or priestly rank—we consider Him under an aspect suggested by the sacraments and hence under this aspect also it is primarily because of the sacraments that it is relevant to speak of Him as Head. Finally there is His priority over man in dignity. This is a point which we have endeavoured to emphasize throughout this work as being at the basis of all sacramental teaching. The sacraments are a hymn of praise to Our Lord; they are a public profession of faith in His Worth; they are the process of our consecration to His use and to His glory. Here then do we see once more that it is principally through His sacraments that Our Lord is Head.

They are the nerve-fibres through which movement is communicated by the Head to the members; they are the instruments He uses to give us a share in His perfection; they are the ways by which we express our acceptance of His great dignity.

When we come to consider the final point essential in speaking of a head, that there be similarity between head and members, we cannot but be filled with the conviction that this is a matter in which the Blessed Sacrament plays a preponderant part. This is not equivalent to stating that the part of the Blessed Eucharist in realizing the other three conditions of headship just considered is minor. That cannot be. Even in their regard the Blessed Sacrament continues to be, as ever, the first of the sacraments, the end and completion of all the others. But it is the precise end of the Blessed Eucharist to transform us entirely into Our Lord, to make us like Him as far as that is possible. If then similarity with the members be a condition of headship, that sacrament which has as its peculiar end to make members like unto their head must hold a place apart in the process of the building up of the Mystical Body.

And yet, we see at once that even if the Blessed Sacrament perfect the Mystical Body by establishing similarity of Head and members It does this in the way that is peculiarly its own: It does this rather by making the members like their Head than by making the Head like His members. Our Lord is like us in that He is Man. But He is more than mere man, and even as Man He is full of grace and truth. The perfection of the harmony between head and members in a body demands therefore that within the framework of the Mystical Body there be some means of elevating souls to the likeness of Christ their Head. All that can be done to draw Him down to the level of human stature was done at the moment of His Incarnation; it remains that man be raised somehow to the level of Christ. Now the Blessed Eucharist is the sacrament of our transformation into Christ. It is spiritual food which makes of all who receive it other Christs. It is then this same sacrament which makes of the Mystical Body something that we may term homogeneous—something in which Head and members harmonize in scale and proportion. Without the Blessed Eucharist the members would never be fully one with their Head; all grace of transformation into Christ implies the reception of the Blessed Sacrament in fact or in desire. A perfect head on a deformed body, or even a body which falls short of the perfection of the head, loses half its beauty. The whole Christ, Head and members, must be a Thing of exquisite beauty for It is God's masterpiece. Not only the Head must be all fair, but the members must be worthy of the Head. This is the sight that enthralls the piercing eyes of angels, that God Himself sees to be all fair—Head and members jointed into a wonderful whole by the sacramental character, lit up with the same loveliness by the sacrament of the Blessed Eucharist. The Mystical Body of Christ is His Sacramental Body; the sacraments are our ways of becoming more worthy members of our Head.

Thus far we have seen that it is possible to speak of the Church as being a Mystical Body in that it has a Head and that it stands in much the same relation to that Head as do members in a body to the head of the same body. But there are also relations between member and member in every body. Are there any parallels to these relations in those existing between member and member in the Church, and do the sacraments contribute in any profound way to calling them into being?

The members of every body are related the one to the other by a relationship of subordination of higher to lower, and by one of mutual communication of life. These relations are found to subsist between the members of the Church and they are due to the sacraments.

In every body there is subordination of member to member. Heart, lungs, and such organs, have a more responsible part to play than, say, arms or legs. The eyes seem more worthy than the hands; for a man will expose a hand to a danger which threatens his eyes. Now the beauty of the body consists in the harmonious combination of different organs, the one subordinated to the other in view of a common end, the well-being of the whole body. Hence the subordination of member to member is not something accidental. It must be that certain members fill more lowly places, for without them the more worthy members would fail to function. The scheme of things, within the body as within the structure of the world, demands diversity as well as unity, and the purpose of diversity is to make possible what defective created unity falls short of.

This hierarchical subordination of member to member is found in the Church and there it is due to the sacramental character. Recall what was said about the sacramental character and the Priesthood of Our Lord. Our Lord's Priesthood is His power of communicating the gift of God to man and of offering the gift of man to God. Now men share in this Priesthood in different ways according as they have received the character of Baptism only, or of Confirmation, or of Holy Orders.

He who has received the character of Orders has full power (in so far as a man can have it) of giving grace to his fellow men through the channel of the sacraments, and of offering on their behalf the Sacrifice of the Mass. He is on that account a member of the first importance. Other members depend on him for their life and activity. His office makes him of more dignity than they. And this first diversity of dignity between the members—that between priest and layman—is willed by God and contributes to the beauty and harmony of the Mystical Body, for in it we see for the first time diversity of members leading to the end of the whole unit—the restoration of all things in Christ.

The character of Confirmation makes of one a member of less dignity than the priest, but nevertheless an active sharer in the Priesthood of the Head. The confirmed are, as it were, the strong arm of the Church. The arm is not the most noble of the members; but there are times when it is a necessary one. The arm should not envy the arteries—the priests being instruments of our sanctification may be compared to the arteries which carry the life stream to the body—but should rejoice in that it is privileged to receive from them. It can even serve them on occasion. Though more lowly it is no less necessary for the perfection of the whole, and to contribute to the perfection of such a whole is an honour of which no member taken in isolation is worthy.

There is finally the character of Baptism, which makes of one a member of least dignity; one who receives in the sacraments, who offers sacrifice only through the priest, who is supposed as yet unable to defend the Body in time of danger; one who must submit to authority and recognize that guidance is a good, that there is no shame attached to being led if one is led to a perfection that else eludes one's grasp.

Now this diversity of priestly functions is willed by God. It contributes to the beauty of the Mystical Body. But there is another diversity which is not willed by God but rather permitted by Him, and that is diversity in grace or in perfection of life. God wills that Our Lord be full of grace and truth and that after Him Our Lady come next in perfection; but with these two exceptions. Whom no man can equal we cannot say with certainty that He sets a limit to the perfection to which any man may aspire with the help of grace. He who is lowest in hierarchical dignity may be highest in grace. There is no reason why he should not at least be the equal in grace of the highest in dignity. In fact an all-round equality of life in the members is one of the characteristics of a perfect body. If the lowest member be lacking in vigour it takes from the life of the whole body. It has no right to refuse to remain low in dignity, but it has every reason to strive to be on the same level as every other member in intensity of life. The stream of life must flow equally to all the members. It will enable them to perform functions of varying importance—but it is one, equal in all.

The sacramental character, as we have said, is the jointing of the Mystical Body. It makes of many members one Body, that One Life, the Life of the Head, may be in all. It matters little whether we be jointed into a place of honour or one of obscurity; what does matter is that we receive the Life. God has willed that layfolk be subject to priests, priests to bishops, and all to Our Holy Father in what concerns the priestly office—and this is no great burden, for the priestly office is there to lead us to God. But He does not will that we be less than any in grace, in union with Himself. Our Lord is Our King. Now a king gives the highest posts to those who are best fitted to fill them; but he gives his friendship most of all to those who are most loyal to him no matter what be their post. What we really value is

Our Lord's friendship, not honours. Let others rule in His Church, what does it matter if only we know and love Him to the limit of our capacity. We wish to contribute to the beauty of His Mystical Body. There are two ways in which we may do so: by respecting its diversity of functions; by striving after equality of distribution of its life. One should not be more dear to us than the other: one is not even possible without the other; for life comes to us through the ministration of orders, and orders cannot be without a greater and a less.

There is, in the second and last place, in every body a mutual communication of life between members. This must be present in the Church also if we be entitled to speak of it as a Body.

There is such a communication of life between the members of a physical body. If one member be exuberantly healthy it provides a reservoir of strength upon which others may draw in time of sickness. We often hear it said of a sick man that he would have died were it not for his wonderful heart. It is also true that a weak member weakens the whole organism. If heart or lungs or stomach be delicate the life of the whole body is endangered. Now there is a somewhat similar phenomenon in the spiritual order and it is known to all the faithful under the name of the Communion of Saints. We are concerned with it here only in so far as it affects the members of the Church Militant in their relations the one with the other.

There is in the first place the fact—to which we referred a short while ago—that the ministration of the sacraments, which are the channels of grace, has been confided to members of the Church—those usually who have the character of Orders. I wonder do we realize how unutterably sacred is the office of the priest. He is there to give us life. No matter what may be his defects, no matter how useless he may seem from the point of view of civilized society, no matter how great an obstacle he may appear to the enlightenment of the masses, he, and he only, has the power of giving us God in the sacraments. Whether he be good or bad he can do this. He should of course be good. But even if he be bad he is entitled to a share in the respect we have for God Himself because of the dignity of his office. He is the normal channel of our sanctification. To will to be holy without the priest is to refuse to be holy. God works through him—that entitles him to respect. He is the ambassador of our King. We respect him for Our King's sake. If Our King, through love of man, suffer the indignity of being forced to see the men whom He has made His ambassadors treat their position lightly, must we add to this the insult of refusing to accept them for His sake?

There is, as well, the fact that one soul can help another outside the way of administration of the sacraments by meriting grace. This is something which depends not on priestly dignity but on personal sanctity. The soul in the state of grace can obtain certain graces for others by way of merit and prayer. Grace comes to mankind normally through the sacraments; but it is received in proportion to the dispositions which are the recipient's at the moment of approaching them. Now one man may merit for another the dispositions required for fruitful reception of the sacraments. One friend is always willing to lend an ear to the request of another friend. God is the friend of the soul in the state of grace and in answer to its prayers He will Himself prepare other souls to receive grace through the sacraments. This is a way in which every member of the Mystical Body can be of assistance to every other member. We should each live so that the holiness of our lives may be a continual prayer to God to lead all men to Himself and to unite more closely to Him those who are already members of the Church. One earnest soul doing its daily work for God, living in union with Him, thirsting that His Kingdom come, and adding to its quota of work and suffering just that it may come, can save souls and strengthen the whole Mystical Body in a way we shall understand only in the Beatific Vision. The Little Flower could never have been made Patroness of the Missions were not the daily Christian life an infallible means of persuading God to spread His Kingdom in souls we have never seen and never will see on earth. The more we draw of grace from the sacraments the more we are able to contribute in this way of merit to the growth of the Mystical Body. We can all be missionaries and apostles if only the holiness of our lives be a treasure house upon which our active missionaries and apostles can draw for the success of their work.

Let us note in conclusion that this way of spreading the life of Christ in His members and of bringing new members into His Body which is open to every soul redounds necessarily, unlike the way of priestly ministry, to the eternal glory of those who walk it. A priest cannot glory in the souls made holy through him, solely by the fact that he, and not another, happens to have administered the sacraments to them. In that he has been only the instrument of Our Lord and it is to Our Lord that the glory is due. But he who by the sincerity of his life and sacrifices has merited grace for others has given to them something of his own and will have glory in heaven in that he will be regarded there as in some small way a saviour of souls. It is true that he can merit only through Our Lord, and that Our Lord will have had more to do with the conversion worked in answer to his prayers than he will have had. But unlike the case of him who contributes nothing more to a conversion than what is the working of his priestly character he will have given of what is really his own, though it be Our Lord's as well. Even in this world credit is given not to the man who in virtue of his office can do what others cannot but to him who puts something of himself into what he can do, to him whose work is not the work of an official only but of a living and self-sacrificing personality as well. It is a consoling thought that at no time in a person's life does he become a useless member of the Body of Christ. As long as he can remain in the state of grace and advance in love of God—and this means as long as he may live—he is a centre of life to the whole Body. Others draw on him without his or their being aware of it. The knowledge of what he will have done in years of apparent helplessness is one of the great surprises that awaits the Christian when he goes to meet his God.

The first plan of this book included after the chapter on the Blessed Eucharist another entitled "The Blessed Eucharist and Daily Life." This chapter under its original title has been omitted. But it is still to be found in substance and in the place originally reserved for it. For the Blessed Eucharist in our daily lives is the doctrine of the Mystical Body. We feed all on One Bread that we may all be built into One Body, members united to Head and member united to member. Our daily life should be lived in the full consciousness that no matter what be its prosaic outline it is the life of one who is a member of a Body of which Christ Himself is Head; that it is a life to be lived under the influence of the grace flowing to us from Our Head and with a view to the perfection of the whole Body. No action of ours will then be trivial. Every deliberate action involves the life of Christ in us and its extension in His members. Our devotion to the Blessed Eucharist will not be a mere matter of a few visits to the Blessed Eucharist in the course of the day nor even of efforts to excite within us the desire to receive it frequently and well. It will include all this. But there will be more still. Devotion to the Blessed Eucharist in daily life will mean living our daily lives in the spirit of men who have been transformed into Him who is both King and Head of a Body. Our lives should consequently be stamped with the consciousness of our union with Him and with His members; for the aim of receiving the Blessed Eucharist is to make the Whole Christ one in life and love.

Every man has within him the secret ambition to be a force in the world. He will find its realization in the life of the Mystical Body.

10

THE SACRAMENT OF PENANCE

*"Father I have sinned against heaven and before thee; I
am not worthy to be called thy son."*

(LK. 15, 18–19)

IN THE CHAPTER on the sacrament of Baptism we had occasion to refer to the psychological fact that man tends to
systematize knowledge and that systematization involves
reduction of the many to unity. We were forced to recognize
on that occasion that the concept of Baptism involved two
mutually irreducible realities: character and grace. We have
since seen that though they cannot be united in any one
thing they are really united in one Person; for sacramental
character and sacramental grace are both participations in
the fulness of Christ Our King. He is the synthesis which
mind could never make. But there are more pointed an-
titheses in the spiritual life than those of character and grace.
There is the antithesis of sin and grace. Can the mind effect
unity between things so opposed as these, or must their
obstinate opposition force us to renounce forever the hope
of arriving at a logical and compact spiritual doctrine?

The use of the word logical in the question just formulated
seems to give a clue to the answering of our problem. Is not
life commonly said to be something more than logic, and is it
then to be wondered at if the boundless expanse of life
at its highest—life understood as embracing the process of
man's acceptance and rejection of God—should refuse to
be limited by a horizon that ends where the full glory of God
has not as yet begun? If our spirituality must contain such

opposing elements as sin and grace is it not because our logic is at fault rather than that these elements cannot be reconciled?

This is the type of remark one might allow to pass uncontradicted were it not that it becomes very frequently the justification of most irrational judgements and conduct. If we understand the word logic in its strict sense it is quite false to say that the world is wider than logic: or, better, it is quite false to say that judgements can be true and conduct moral if they refuse to fit into the framework of logic. But what is true in this context—and it is made without cause the basis for a stupid attack on logic—is that life is wider than our premisses. We do not know enough about life to be able to work out its every mystery with the aid of our logic. What is at fault is not our logical method but our insufficient data. And is not this in itself a triumphant vindication of logic, for to argue from insufficient data is itself a sin against logic?

There have been and will be, cases of men who have ridden a principle to death, have ended in failure, and have heard their tragedy summed up as being the fruit of excess of logic. It may be that they were men who looked on sham of all kinds as being contemptible and proceeded invariably to show up the shammer at no matter what cost to themselves or to others. Their error was said to lie in their logic. They should have been content to believe that sham was mean and leave the matter at that—believe in their minds that it was mean, and act as if they held it was not. This so highly recommended course of action lays, needless to say, no claim to being logical: but it is supposed in some mysterious way to be equated to life. No matter what is objectively right the super-logic of life does not demand that we pay it the tribute of suffering for its sake.

Now the precise fault in riding a principle to death is not that it is too logical a course, but that to do so is to ignore the fact that life involves always an interplay of conflicting principles and that no one principle represents the whole issue at stake. Sham is bad; but in real life we meet not sham but shammers and the first thing to do is to weigh the shammer against the amount of sham that is in him—throwing into the scale on the side of the shammer all the good that is in him and the ignorance that is in him and the harmlessness of his petty display—and then draw a strictly logical conclusion from the result. But when once we are in possession of all the data bearing on a case we are not free to act illogically. Logic is not too narrow to fit life; because logic is not a principle but the rule of harmony of all principles.

It is painful to be reminded by daily experience that there are many souls who refuse to submit to God just on the plea that life does not demand actions which follow rigorously from judgements about what is right and wrong. If a thing is right, and right for me here and now, I should do it, cost what the effort may. If a thing is wrong, I simply may not do it. If it happens on occasion that I am sure God is calling me to do something that others are not doing, then I should obey God's call. The fact that others seem to read a different message into life from what appears to me to be the true one—and which I may know on reliable external authority to be the true one for me—is no reason why I should hold back. I am bound to lead my life in logical dependence on the premises that are valid for me. Others lead their lives in accordance with the demands made upon them and the graces given them. What these demands and these graces are I can never know. The premises from which the life of my neighbour sets out are hidden from me. I can know those which are relevant to my own life. I must accept them and work them out to the bitter end.

If then we dismiss the possibility of a system of spirituality in which all truths would follow with mathematical rigour from one single principle, this is not because we wish to belittle logic but because the spiritual life represents not so much a plan as a plan that has been frustrated and restated. The spiritual life is not just the progress of a creature to intimacy with its Creator: it is the progress of a fallen creature, and the progress of a creature that having fallen first of all in the head of the human race is liable to fall once more through its lack of personal effort. It is impossible to start from the soul's thirst for God and to deduce therefrom all that the soul must do. Sin, for example, is not implied in the concept of a soul thirsting for God. It is impossible to make this deduction even if we start from the revealed truth of our destination for glory through grace. For each article of our faith is itself a first principle not necessarily implied in any other, and unless we take explicit account of all, we fall short of the understanding of the least of the problems of life. We cannot have the whole truth unless we have made room for sin in our synthesis; we do not understand Our Lord unless we see that He is a Redeemer. We cannot fit life under one heading, not because our logic is defective, but because our life being divinized can enter the prism of the human mind only on the condition of being split into a thousand hues.

Our first contact with the mystery of sin was made when treating of the sacrament of Baptism. We saw then that the grace of Baptism is a grace of healing and salvation. We are made by it not just children of God, but children of wrath become children of God. And there remains even after Baptism the wound of our nature and the need of struggling against the law of our members, so that our life becomes a living death, a life-giving death. Baptism is a resurrection from sin, but to a life that is lived within the shadow of the tomb.

The life of grace poured into the soul by Baptism is not given us as something that is irrevocably ours. We are given it, it is true; and on the side of God there is no absolute intention of retracting the gift. But though God does not will to take His gift away we may always lose it through our own fault. For we remain men even when we are divinized men, and the life of man is a thing to be shaped and reshaped while life lasts. For the angels there was no question of receiving a grace that they could lose and regain. The angelic will, so strong and resolute, never wavers when once it has chosen. But man is weak. He can revalue life. He can err and correct himself. He can be right and go astray. He can cling to the good and then adhere more closely to it, or reject it as of less worth than the delusion of easeful peace. In any case, short of a miracle, the free will of man can always intensify its first clinging to God—in fact the only way it can ever arrive at close union with Him is by the way of gradual progress—so that we see that the grace of Baptism is a grace that man may lose, not in order that man may lose it, but because otherwise he could not grow in it. Were God to give man a stable grace at Baptism He would by that very fact deprive him of all hope of intense union with Him. Without changing the nature of man, He could not give him a grace which would not be intrinsically conditioned in its growth by the exercise of a free (and for man, defectible) will.

Seeing then that we are such poor creatures that God's mercy was forced to provide a space of time for us in which we might learn to know and love Him—just as the mercy of the Redeemer showed the blind man at first trees, as it were walking, lest the unwonted glory of the midday sun should destroy the eyes that use would render strong—there followed a second double consequence: that being free we could fail to profit by the time allotted us for growth, and that God should provide a remedy for our possible failure, the sacrament of Penance. Penance, we may say, is a sacrament which does not lie upon the straight line of spiritual growth. It is there to be used in an emergency. It is our spiritual first-aid equipment. It would not be needed were there no possibility of our falling by the wayside. But we can and do fall, and for those who fall it is the normal means of rising and pursuing their way anew. Since therefore it follows from and is conditioned by sin it can hardly be understood without understanding first of all what sin is. And if we speak in this context of "understanding" let the word be excused; for who can dare to speak of giving men to understand the depths of the mystery of iniquity?

ACTUAL SIN

The life of man is intended to be a conscious quest of God. Actual sin in its most complete form is the conscious abandonment of this quest in the pursuit of some apparently desirable object. Actual sin is sin strictly so called. It is the work of the free-will of the individual, the work of his deliberate choice.

We may refer to it in the following pages as sin without further qualification. In general also there will be question most particularly of what is known as mortal sin.

Sin consists first of all in turning away from God Who is desirable above all that the heart of man can desire. God offers us His friendship. We turn aside. We tell Him that His friendship is not a matter we can rate very highly. He offers us, as it were on terms of equality, the right to share in His life for all eternity. We reject the offer as being not just what we want. God really loves us. He wishes us to return that love by allowing our hearts to be caught up in the current of child-like devotion that flows Godwards from the throne of the Lamb. We treat His love for us as a thing of little moment, as a thing worthy of no particular notice, and we declare in effect that the needs of our souls can be more fittingly met outside of God than within the warmth of His friendship. There is no person like to God; but we pass Him over in favour of some paltry rival.

St. Paul in words of immeasurable appositeness has labelled this Frenzy of human folly when he described to his dear Timothy the qualities that should be sought in a bishop. In the middle of his list we find the words: "Not a neophyte, lest being puffed up with pride, he fall into the judgement of the devil" (I Tim. 3, 6). We are all neophytes in the things of God. We cannot evaluate them at their true value for we have no deep experience of what their real value is. And being blind to what is of worth, and of greater worth than we are, we are exposed to those moments of self-conceit when nothing seems to count but ourselves, and puffed up with pride we barter what is of ultimate worth as though it were a straw. Every mortal sin implies a sin of pride. It implies the power to reject God. It implies that a sinner looks on himself as one who may dare to reject God. Neophytes that we are, we dare to believe that the things of God have been given us as playthings, that the friendship of the Most High may be turned down by us in a moment of tumorous conceit. Man's petty arrogance is never seen with more tragic clearness than when he elects to smother in a hole of his own making rather than to be indebted to God's air.

There is in sin, as well as this rejection of God, an election or choosing of something in the place of God. In turning from God we turn elsewhere: in turning to a being other than God we turn necessarily away from God Himself. We have not been forbidden to turn our wills at any time to creatures. But we may turn to them only as creatures, that is to say, as God's handiwork and worthy of our wills only in so far as they reflect the beauty of Him Who made them. To make of a creature an object of desire while abstracting from its relation to its Maker is to snatch it from the hand of God. The creature is His. All that is in it is His. He made it for His glory and has the right that it be used for His glory. By constituting it our end we make it the instrument of our rejection of God. We snatch from His hand the thing He made to lead men to praise and love Him, and use it as a motive of treating Him with contempt. We set up as end what should be a means to arriving at our true end, and we make of God, the end of all that is, a means to the gratification of our blind passion for drug and heady poison.

Our self-conceit has led us to determine life independently of God, and in doing so it maims and cripples us. Sin is really the frustration of life. It is in God that we live, move, and have our being. When we cut adrift from God we lose life—totally, if we refer to our supernatural life; in part, if we refer to our natural life. By willing to become independent of God we condemn ourselves to perish. We simply cannot *be* independently of God. He is the source of all being, of all life. There is no being or life outside of Him. To turn to something other than God as to the fulfillment of desire is to make deliberate choice of death. By wishing to become autonomous we become impotent. The very act which claimed to be a supreme manifestation of the power to create a destiny is the act which flings us headlong into powerless misery. And all this happens, we may say, without the machinery of divine vengeance being moved to unseemly haste. We have chosen to be without God and God simply allows us to have our way.

Sin is an offence against the love we should bear our Father in heaven; it is as well an offence against the debt owed to the Lord of the universe. God has a right to our service. He has made us. We belong entirely to Him. We are bound in justice to yield to Him the fruits of what He has planted. We ourselves are His husbandry. He has planted us that we might bring forth fruit in due season. The fruit belongs to Him. We have not the right to refuse to bear fruit, or to yield the fruit we have borne to one other than our true Lord and Master. All belongs to God. And then, the created thing that we make the object of our sin—it also belongs to God and was made by Him that it might excite us to know Him and love Him. He has the right that His handiwork be used to that end and to that end exclusively. It is unjust to use what is entirely His for an end that is entirely opposed to His interests. He has a right to determine the end of the use of what He made. We can determine the end of nothing in the universe, for there is nothing in it that we have made in its entirety.

Sin is finally an offence against Christ the King and Redeemer. It is a rejection of His friendship, contempt of His sacrifice. It means that we go over ostentatiously to the side of those who put Jesus to death. The world is really a battlefield. There is no sin which is just a standing aloof from the battle. Sin is active service on the side of the enemies of Christ, just as virtue is active service on the side of His Mystical Body. In addition, sin is injustice in regard to Our King. We really belong to Him. He has a right to rule in us, to direct us. When we sin we violate that right. We who belong to Him as His subjects—and the subjects He has won at the price of his most precious Blood—refuse to be loyal to Him, refuse to recognize his Kingship. This is treachery and injustice. It adds to violation of the rights of friendship the new crimes of treason and plunder.

When Our Lord instituted a sacrament for the forgiveness of personal sin He conceived it as an effective retractation of the disorder of sin itself. It would include a return to God as corrective of our abandonment of Him; it would include renunciation of the creature which we had made the cause of our abandonment of God; it would include restoration of the supernatural life lost by our wilful separation from the Fount of Life; it would include the idea of making good the injustice done to God; and in the last place, it would be an act of recognition of the rights of Christ the King. We may begin our consideration of the sacrament most conveniently with this last point.

Sin is an offence against Our Lord's right to our love and homage. The effective destruction of sin in our souls demands that we accept this right through the sacrament of Penance.

The priest who hears our confession is the representative of Our Lord Who died on the Cross for us. It is not possible for us living in the twentieth century to go to the foot of the Cross erected on the Hill of Calvary and tell Our Lord hanging on it that we are sorry for having treated His friendship so lightly, and that we are determined to try to be more worthy of His love and sacrifice in the future. But Our Lord foresaw this incapacity and He provided for it by appointing representatives who, invested with His commission, accept our profession of repentance in His name. In this sense our confession is made to Our Lord, though in the person of another and not in His own Person. But it is a test of the sincerity of your repentance that we be invited to deal with Him thus at second hand. And do we not know that He, even in the hour of His hanging on the Cross, saw us as we kneel now at the feet of His representative, and accepted then as offered to Him in Person what we now offer to Him in His minister the priest?

The sacrament of Penance is, as well, an acceptation of the Kingship of Our Lord. Since it is sacramental forgiveness it is forgiveness through the power of Christ. To go to confession is to submit oneself to the power of Christ. But that is to accept His Kingship, to admit that He is the source of spiritual life, and that life once lost can be regained only through Him. It is to come to the throne of His glory, not as one who has been faithful but as one who has been a traitor and can find no better form of condemnation of his treachery than the admission that treachery has led to impotence and that outside the Kingdom of his Lord there is but pain and chaos.

This submission to the Kingship of Our Lord is submission to His power to sanctify. But this power really proceeds from the throne of Christ—even though it passes by the hands of the priest—so that under this aspect our confession is a personal contact with Our Saviour. It is really He Who forgives our sin, Who pours into our souls the grace that makes them once more live and pleasing in the sight of God. And —what is more—it is He in His character of the Lamb Who was slain Who so sanctifies us. It is really the Chirst Who hung on the Cross Who washes away our sins, and He does this as eternal High Priest completing through His sacraments the work of salvation begun in His great sacrifice. Though we cannot approach the historical Calvary precisely in so far as it is an historical event, it may be said that the historical event of Calvary can enter into contact with us, because each sacramental forgiveness of sin is the completion and continuation of Calvary's sin-offering. We cannot turn now to Our Saviour on the Cross. But Our Saviour Who hung on the Cross can apply now to us what He merited for us at the moment of His death. The grace that comes to us in confession is therefore the grace of our dying Saviour. It is a small thing to have stood in the spatial neighbourhood of the Cross. It is a great thing—and it is what Our Lord died for—to have submitted to the power of the Cross. We can make that act of submission. That is detestation of sin, that is atoning for sin. Submit to Our Lord, give Him free play in your soul; remember that the grace He pours into you is a grace you have despised, though a grace He died to win for you: that is the sacrament of Penance.

Penance destroys sin also in so far as sin includes aversion from the Divine goodness. Penance is a reentering upon the road that leads to God. Sin interrupts our quest of God; by Penance we set out once more in search of Him—chastened and humbled, it is to be supposed, less full of ourselves, more willing to turn to God our only hope. It is through Our Saviour that we return to God. He is there to lead us to the

Father. In refusing to submit to the Kingship of Our Saviour we lose the power of moving Godwards. When we submit to Our Saviour His first action upon our soul is to lay hold on it for His Father, to destine it by grace for the eternal possession of the Ever Blessed Trinity. There is no question of a delay between the moment of forgiveness of sin and the fresh conferring of the right to the face-to-face vision of God.

The repentant sinner must detest his past sin. He must regard it as an evil, that is to say as something that of itself is unworthy ever to be the object of choice. It is a mistake to associate the word "evil" with bodily harm and nothing else. Things that harm us are evil under the respect of their harmfulness. But there may be other respects under which they could be desired—just as the loss of a limb is harmful in itself but may be desirable if the life of the whole body depend upon the amputation. Now sin is an evil in the sense that it can never be desired either for itself or because of something else. Penance involves admitting that it is such an evil. And this admission is the destruction of sin in us, because sin was the admission that the object of our sin was desirable. By Penance we retrace our steps. We return to God and declare to Him that the thing which had led us away was not worthy of our attention, that it was not something in which the will could rest. To detest sin in this way is to assert God's unique place in the universe. He alone can be the ultimate object of desire. To repent of sin is to admit this truth as the fruit of bitter experience.

By detesting sin we reject creatures as ultimate ends of activity and thereby restore the divine plan in which all things are subjected to God. We had snatched a work of God's hands from His grasp and set it up as our god. We return the creature to its rightful place when we detest sin. Detestation of sin is not detestation of creatures. Creatures are good and we should love them. But they are to be loved as means not as ends, as God's property not as His rivals. The sinner introduces disarray into creation; the penitent put things back in their proper place.

The sincere penitent is filled with the desire to make good his offence. He is not content with loving God once more and with treating God's handiwork with respect for the future, but he feels that having outraged the divine justice he should offer something additional in the spirit of restitution. He feels called upon to make satisfaction. This idea of restitution or satisfaction at once distinguishes the spirit of penance from charity or love. Love of itself does not imply previous faithlessness. Something more than love will therefore be demanded of one who has been faithless. A true friend who has never failed in friendship lives his part by his continued friendship. Love is the totality of his obligations. But one who has failed has a past to wipe out. Even if in point of fact there is nothing he can do over and above making an offer of renewed love, this love will necessarily take on a new character. It will be repentant love, chastened and fervent. The love of Mary Magdalen was not quite that of St. Teresa of the Child Jesus. And St. Teresa recognized that this could not be otherwise, that forgiven love has a character all its own, and she endeavoured to work into her life and love that note of gratitude for pardon which she felt was the ultimate perfection of created human charity.

The satisfaction God imposes upon those who come to Him in the sacrament of Penance is usually light. But what is of the essence of the sacrament is not the performance of the satisfaction itself but the interior readiness to make amends which is ours at the moment of receiving absolution.

This is a point to be carefully noted. We shall see its full significance when we speak of the spirit of Penance in daily life.

Let us note in conclusion to this section that forgiveness of sin starts on the side of God. It is not so much we who come to Him to be forgiven as He Who draws us to Himself by actual grace to seek forgiveness. This is because of the complete spiritual impotence to which sin reduces us. We become through it utterly incapable of taking the initiative in any act whatever that leads to our eternal good. Eternal life is the peculiar property of God. It belongs entirely to Him. We cannot thrust ourselves into eternal life. He must draw us thither. And though we can follow His guiding once He has set us on the path that leads to Himself, there can be no question of our first entry on that path being our unaided work. The dispositions of faith and hope and fear with which we approach confession are aroused in us by God. Though it is He Who is the offended party it is really He Who makes the first move to restore us to His friendship. Here on earth it is usual for the offended to await some sign of repentance before making any move on his side. With God it is never so. He is always the first to move. The very grace of shame which should arise so spontaneously in a generous heart comes from God. Sin reduces the soul to utter helplessness in God's eyes. Thus the ultimate reason for the forgiveness of all sin is Mercy.

Sin injures the Mystical Body of Christ. That is why it is forgiven through the ministry of a priest, member of the Mystical Body, and in a rite which may be seen and understood by our fellow-members as an external confession of guilt. We have been integrated into a spiritual organism. Life comes to us through that organism, and restoration of life as well. There would be a certain incompleteness in the divine plan as it now exists if sin were to be forgiven normally on an interior confession of guilt to God. We cannot say that we have sinned only against heaven and before God. We have sinned against Christ and against our fellow-members as well. Forgiveness will come then to us from God through Christ and our fellow-members. We should try to realize when confessing our sins that confession to a priest implies that we have failed mankind. There were souls who would have benefited by our resistance to sin. We have refused to help them. Confession includes pardon of our social fault. Hence it presupposes admission of our social guilt.

We have considered sin and its undoing hitherto from a mainly static standpoint; we have seen the elements that go to make up sin and the elements that make up its undoing. There still remains the actual process of forgiveness of sin and the stages through which the soul passes before receiving absolution. St. Thomas has treated this question in his own way—characteristically concise and full—in the third part of the Summa, Question 85, article 5. His doctrine has received the highest confirmation in that it has been received by the Council of Trent and used as the groundwork for its treatment of justification (Chapter 6 of the Decree of Justification).

The first stage in the conversion of a sinner is due entirely to the action of divine grace. God moves the sinner to return to Him. The sinner loses by his sin the power of reentering on his own initiative into the state of friendship with God. Grace, which makes one a friend of God, is a gift due in its totality to God's free act. God, Who wills not the death of the sinner but that he be converted and live, gives the first grace to the sinner. The first grace cannot be merited. The soul, even if it be the soul of a grown man, does nothing to merit the grace of conversion. If it loses grace through sin it can do nothing which will entitle it to receive grace once more. For grace is entirely beyond the capacity of nature, and to merit grace in strict justice would demand to exist already in the state of grace. Once established by the liberality of Our Father in heaven in the state of grace we can merit to grow in His love and friendship. But to be established thus is His gift and cannot be won otherwise than as an undeserved honour.

God in His unscrutable wisdom, having mercy on him on whom He will have mercy, sees the sinner chained by sin and elects to free him. He sends forth His Spirit, not yet to inhabit the defiled heart, but to touch and soften it. It was the Spirit Who drew order out of the chaos of primal matter, for God loves all He has made and wills that it enjoy the peace of inner harmony; and the same Spirit—now more than ever the spirit of Love—touches lightly and tenderly the wreck that was once a compact and jointed soul, and under His touch the frozen hardness of pride and obstinacy in sin begins to melt. The sinner raises his eyes to God in faith. God touches the soul and the soul awakens to faith. "Enlighten my eyes that I never sleep in death: lest at any time my enemy say: I have prevailed against him" (Ps. 12, 4-5). Every sin involves a greater or less willed blindness to reality. God shatters that sought-out sleep of death, so sadly like the real death of damnation, and the eye of faith is blinded by a revelation of the Majesty of Him we have offended, of the punishment we have merited—an eternal punishment, a supernatural evil; or it may be that we see Our Saviour on His Cross, and that we stand there too with the spear that will transfix Him in our hands. This is the message of faith. We are free to accept it or to reject it. It is a grace that can be ignored, or we can choose to sleep on in death. But we can accept it, submit to it; and in this we begin already to undo the evil of sin.

Faith will lead to fear. We see that we have offended God, that we have crucified the King of Glory, and we know that there awaits us a punishment, which, though it cannot equal our guilt, surpasses infinitely our human powers of endurance. There is a hell. God is just: God is not mocked; we have tried to be without Him: we have succeeded merely in opposing ourselves to Him. Pain awaits us—endless pain. And then the eating desire, the gnawing need of God, unable to forget Him and unable to rest without Him: tortured in that we cannot see Him and tortured in that we cannot but think of Him. Never an end to our unrest, never an end to our agony. Pain, pain—and all for one sin, for the pleasure of one instant, for the thrill of one moment of uneasy glory. There is need to fear. Our little all, our ego—treasure above all treasures—is about to be engulfed and overwhelmed in the irresistible surge of an unending destruction and a perpetual rebirth to pain.

Were the soul to remain at this stage it would despair. Judas reached thus far. He saw the enormity of his sin and the punishment that awaited it, and hardening his heart to grace—for to go still further demands humility and trust—he hanged himself with a halter. But in the truly repentant sinner fear will be succeeded by hope. "My God is my helper and in Him will I put my trust . . . Praising I will call upon the Lord: and I shall be saved from my enemies" (Ps. 17, 3-4). "Hope confoundeth not" (Rom. 5, 5). The Lord God is merciful and patient. He wills not the death of the sinner but that he be converted and live again in grace. The sinner cannot of himself rise from sin. Left alone he will inevitably fall headlong into the depths of hell. But there is the mighty arm of the Lord to snatch him from the jaws of death. He knows he can trust in his Father and that his Father is able to help. His Father in heaven is not like fathers of earth who stand by impotently while their children are rushed to the tomb, or who can oppose but weak words to stem the rising tide of temptation, though they cannot spare themselves the pain of foreseeing the ruin it will work. God is omnipotent. There is an evil—the evil of eternal damnation—which awaits the sinner. His own strength cannot avert it. But he can count on the strength of God. Grace urges him to do so. He accepts to follow grace if he submits to the rule of hope. But, note that it is, once more, an act of submission that is asked of him: he who wished to be a power in the universe and arbiter of right and wrong in his own sphere, is bade rely on the power of God, confessing thereby that of himself he is but a broken reed. If he obeys the order and submits to the majesty of the power of God he breaks one more of the many chains that have bound him to his sin.

We have now reached the moment of the reception of the sacrament. The penitent is on his knees before the priest. Faith, fear, and hope, have done their work in his soul. They have led up to that state of sorrow for sin known as contrition.[1]

Faith revealed the enormity of sin. The sinner now hates his sin. He is sorry for having sinned. He would, if it were possible for him to do so, wipe out the past. His sin, which before seemed so attractive, is now a thing of loathing in his eyes. He turns from it—not necessarily with sense and feel-

[1] The term "contrition" is used here in its wide sense, embracing imperfect as well as perfect contrition.

ing—with his will. In spite of all that sin may offer, and in spite of what past sin procured, the sinner regrets his sin because he can now see a repulsiveness, a source of harmfulness, in it which makes it impossible for it to be his final choice. His will refuses to rest undisturbed in sin. It may answer to the mood of the moment, but reflection shows that it is the denial and negation of all happiness and that it bars the road to what the soul most intensely desires.

There is sorrow for sin in the heart of the penitent who kneels at the priest's feet. There may be no tears, but the sorrow is true and heartfelt. It is more than the sorrow which wells up in the soul that regrets a foolish or unworthy act, for it is a sorrow which comes from God's grace touching the heart. No mortal sin is excluded from this sorrow since all such sins unite in a common guilt and shame. And it has filled the heart with the determination to avoid sin for the future; and even to do what is more—to make amends for past sin, to make satisfaction to Our offended Father. Sorrow and satisfaction are in the heart; they bring confession to the lips. We tell the priest in sorrow that we have sinned, and we are resolved to make the slight compensation he will demand of us in proof of our sincerity. Then he absolves us in the name of the Father, Son, and Holy Ghost. For there remains nothing more that we can do. We have undone sin, as far as in us lay, in its every toil. Now, last of all, we have come in humble submission to the sacramental throne of Christ and have submitted to the power He confided to the ministers of His Church. The forgiveness of sin is complete. On our side, sorrow, satisfaction, and confession of guilt; on the side of God, and Christ, and His Church, absolution— these are the sacrament of Penance and the instruments of victory over sin.

A point of capital importance was made in an earlier chapter when a distinction was made between grace as such and sacramental grace. The grace given in the sacrament of Penance is a sacramental grace. It is not a grace of mere friendship with God: it is a grace of restored friendship. The forgiven soul lives by the grace of Penance, for every grace is a principle of life. Would it not then seem that the life of one who relives through Penance should bear a stamp not imprinted on the life of one who has never offended God? If this be so, we find that Penance ranges itself side by side with the three great sacraments of Baptism, Confirmation, and Holy Eucharist, in that it moulds and determines the whole of life. It would appear not so much a point in the genesis of life as a factor in its ultimate constitution.

The sacraments are signs of the grace they produce. The nature of every sacramental grace is revealed on a consideration of the essential rite of the sacrament. Now the essential rite of the sacrament of Penance is the absolution of the contrite sinner. The reality it signifies is God's conferring of grace on a soul that stands before Him in penitent love. The grace itself of the sacrament will be what we may term the perpetuation of this scene: it will be the expression in terms of being—what are called ontological terms—of the sorrowful love of the penitent and the merciful love of the Father. It will be—and this is exactly the same thing—the transformation into terms of life of the anguish of one who has crucified and the gentle indulgence of Him Who was crucified. The sacrament of birth makes us children; the sacrament of maturity makes us soldiers; the sacrament of Christ's Body makes us one body; the sacrament of forgiveness makes us forgiven souls. The moment of absolution remains for ever in the grace of the sacrament. What was for us a psychological phase becomes a principle of life. Even on God's side the moment of absolution is perpetuated. What sustains our grace is the loving mercy that conferred it upon us. God does not give grace to the sinner in mercy and then preserve it in love alone. His attitude in regard to the forgiven sinner will always be one of mercy as well as love. There is no question of His friendship being now of a fragile and undependable kind; but it is different from what it was before sin, for it has now a new character of forgiving tenderness. Sin is a reality; sin really has taken place. Things can never be as if there had been no sin, no estrangement between God and the sinner. They will be friends once more, and friends whose friendship knows neither doubt nor shadow, but friends as Jesus and the Magdalen were and Jesus and Martha could never be.

The saints taught this in their amazing perception of the unique character of the grace of Baptism. They felt rather than knew that the grace of Baptism once lost returns normally accompanied by the grace of Penance, and that there is a difference in spiritual structure between the soul that has never sinned mortally and the soul that has been made live again by the grace of this second sacrament. They rated their baptismal robe highly. They knew that in the clear light of eternity their grace would be seen to be the grace of Penance or Baptism as the case might be. One grace would be distinguishable from the other. And this distinction which becomes so apparent to all souls in heaven, and which is sensed by the saints on earth, is real even here on earth, though perceived by so few. A penitent has a spiritual stamp all his own. He will have therefore obligations which are not those of other souls: the life that is in him will demand an expression which would be forced if it were imposed upon one of another spirit. Penance received through inner necessity becomes a principle of life.

This is what is meant by the distinction made commonly

between interior and exterior penance. Exterior penance is activity of an essentially expiatory kind such as fasting or the use of the discipline. Interior penance is rather an attitude of mind, a detestation of sin. It will of course influence activity, but it does not consist essentially in this activity, nor does it dictate activity of any very defined type. Any act at all which is morally good may be performed under the guidance of interior penance: it receives thereby an added intensity and godwardness, but for the rest is unchanged. Now it is the teaching of St. Thomas—and in this he merely echoes the Christian tradition—that interior penance should characterize the whole subsequent life of the penitent. In other words, the grace of the penitent is not the grace of the newly baptized, and demands that it be allowed to issue in the life peculiar to it, namely that lived under the guidance of the spirit of penance. He tells us that interior penance is sorrow for past sin and that this sorrow should remain till the end of life. He does not intend that it should remain a mere unit in a spiritual mosaic. It is to be a force in life. Sorrow for past sin should colour every action, every thought, every prayer. It will even prompt action—generous action: for it is becoming that one who has been forgiven should be generous in all that he does. Others may presume to believe that they are entitled to measure out what is due to God. But the forgiven sinner may never dare to do so. Interior penance will prompt acts of exterior penance. But these latter will be made from time to time only, whereas interior penance must be ever operative. In fact St. Thomas tells us that exterior penance will find an ever decreasing place in life according as one advances in grace and the love of God, but that interior penance will never decrease. God wishes from the forgiven sinner the perpetual tribute of a contrite and humble heart, and the sinner can pay no other tribute to God without being false to the urge of the grace that is in him.

Interior penance is the soul's great protection against future sin as well as its fitting attitude in the face of past sin. It is under the aspect of strength to avoid future sin that we speak commonly of the sacramental grace of Penance. We can see now in what this strength consists. It consists in that interior penance which prompts us to fly sin in the future. The fact of having sinned and having been forgiven is a motive for avoiding sin in the future, and the lived conviction that one has sinned induces a state of mental balance which the idea of fresh sin will jolt and shock. That grace of Penance which is the grace of one who has sinned is of its very nature the grace of one who has forever renounced sin.

Baptism and Confirmation are sacraments which consecrate the soul to a definite type of life. Penance also consecrates. Its consecration is to the life of interior penance. The sacrament of Penance is received in love and shame at the foot of the Cross. It consecrates us to live in love and shame at the foot of the Cross. The forgiven sinner may never stray in mind from the presence of Him Whom he rejected and put to death. If not more than is expected from others, at least something different is expected of him. The Cross must be the background to his life. He should be incapable of judging or willing otherwise than as against that background. He knelt once for pardon; in spirit he should remain on bended knees.

Tradition tells us that tears furrowed their way down Peter's cheeks. Few receive the favour that Peter did. There is however a spirit of tears which issues in devoted service. It is refused to none.

11

OUR BLESSED LADY: QUEEN OF THE SACRAMENTS

"A Woman clothed with the sun, and the moon under her feet." (APOC. 12, 1)

IN THE OPENING CHAPTER of this book we considered three of man's attempts to find happiness outside of God: the pursuit of riches, the pursuit of power, and the pursuit of friendship. Though these attempts were necessarily doomed to failure, the soul of man being simply too great to rest in anything less than God, they contained a lesson: they indicated certain of the lines upon which natural striving runs, and so mapped out in their own way the path that leads to God. We come to God as the great Riches: and this is approach to Him in faith. He who wishes to possess God one day in clear vision must be baptized, receiving that faith which is the guarantee and foretaste of eternal life. We come to God as the Fount of all power: and this is approach to Him in hope, by which we receive Omnipotence to work out our salvation. Integration into the Mystical Body of Our Saviour is also union with the God of power, for this membership makes of us centres of force and sanctification for the whole human race: it enables us to influence other men for all eternity. There is finally our approach to God Our Friend: and this is to approach in charity. God gives Himself to us through grace that we may love Him, that we may abide with Him in reverent familiarity. Riches, power, and friendship,—we find them all in God through grace, and we find grace in the sacraments.

Now it is of primary importance to understand that this union with God which is effected by the sacraments is union with God in Christ and His Mystical Body. The sacraments unite us to God by intergrating us into the Mystical Body. There is no sacramental union which is not membership of Christ and fellowship with His members. It follows from this that union with God through the sacraments is also union with Our Blessed Lady and the Saints, and it will be through this union with Her and them that She and they will be enabled to enter into vital relation with our lives— just as it is by integration into Christ by the sacrament of Baptism that we are caught up in the current of life which is His to give us. To speak then at this point of Our Lady and the sacraments is no artificial observance of what might be termed the proprieties of ascetical writing. The sacraments set us in quite a definite relationship to Our Lady. They could not do otherwise. And there can be no question of any treatment of the sacraments laying claim to even schematic completeness if it does not indicate the place filled in them by Our Lady.

In spite of the danger of becoming to some degree irrelevant it is well to point out now in passing that Our Lady fills a wonderful place in the matter of union with God as Our Friend. Our Lady is, after Our Lord, the great revelation of God's friendship to men: we may even say that She is for many a still greater revelation than Our Lord is, not that She is more than He but that She is more accessible to many than He is; for there are many who fail to see the beauty of a King and who can readily submit to the charm of a Mother. They have in Mary someone they think they can understand and they see that She is all love and compassion. They have found a genuine friend—one too who can give direction and support to life—and they are lifted up to the supernatural by their devotion to Her who is the Mother of its Author.

But if we consider the matter absolutely—that is to say, asking ourselves no longer what are the thoughts and attractions of particular souls but what are the essential functions of Those on whom thoughts and attractions are centred—we find that Our Lady is ultimately not so much a self-contained embodiment of motherhood of souls as an expression of the Divine friendship for man. All that Mary has comes from God. All her tenderness, all her patience, all her preoccupation with love and apparent impatience with justice—all these have been given her by God. There is not a feeling of mercy that she has ever experienced that He did not pour into her heart. And if we see that her Mother-love triumphs over bare equity it is because God wills that it should be so. Mary can save sinners from the divine wrath because the divine wrath is willing to be swayed by the divine love and mercy.

If we consider Our Lady in this light we see that her person is a blinding revelation of God. She tells us that God is a mother to us. God—He Who sits throned in light inaccessible, He Who made me out of nothing and to Whose essential happiness I can contribute nothing, just as my sin can in no way take from it, He Who sends the thunder and the earthquake and Who allows nations to be engulfed in war—He cares for me as does a mother. It is a great thing to be told that the Lord God of Hosts wills to be my friend. And yet it is so easy to whittle down the sense of friendship, to admit that God is a friend without thanking Him or the gift of relative equality with Him which is the basis of that friendship, and so without realizing the full extent of what His friendship has done for us. We can whittle down too—for there is no ingratitude of which the heart of man is not capable—the meaning of the Incarnation and Death of Our Saviour. They mean that God loves us to a point which should cause our hearts to burst with love. But we can harden our hearts and retain the ungenerous suspicion that Our Saviour did not after all feel what He did for us, that there was some unreality about His adorable Humanity. And if we descend to this depth what will remain of our conviction that God is truly a friend? Now it is hard for the mind to accept the fact of Our Lady and still to deny her character. One can equivalently deny that God gave her to us as Our Mother. But if one accepts the fact of her motherhood one will necessarily accept the fact of her caring for us as a mother does. A mother who does not care for her children is too great a contradiction for even a human mind to admit. Our Lady is then God's final attempt to convince us of the fact that He is our Friend. She has nothing but what He gives her. He is the source of all her love and care of us. He is therefore a friend who loves not only as Father, as Brother, and as King, but as Mother also. His friendship for us is so real that He cares for us through Mary as a mother cares for her children. To stand aloof from Mary on the plea that only God matters is really a refusal to love God. We do not know God as He is in relation to us till we know Mary. We cannot have the full sense of fellowship with God that is possible for us unless we see Him in Our Mother. Without Mary He will appear just, merciful even, fatherly even. But He will never appear as full of mother-love for His men-children. Mary is the setting in which He has placed this divine jewel of blind and tender love. And the knowledge of God in Mary is the last element in the vision of the saint on earth, no less than the last hope of the sinner who has refused to submit to the attractiveness of the transcendant Godhead.

This union with God through Mary as the incarnation of God's tender love for us, real though it be and necessary in some degree for every human soul, is not that which is peculiar to the sacraments. It would have existed had there never been sacraments if only God had determined to become Man for our redemption and to take unto Himself a Mother who would be in some way worthy of Him and sharer in His work of redemption. Sacramental union with Our King is a matter of entering into His Mystical Body and drawing through it on the life stored up in the Head. Sacramental union with Our Lady will also be a matter of union with her in the Mystical Body and through the sacramental system. We can arrive at some understanding of it by applying what we have already said about union between member and member to the particular case in which one of the members will be Our Blessed Lady. This latter particularity will introduce certain new elements into the problem. But they will not be of an entirely novel type. They will differ rather in degree than in kind from those which go to make up the relation between any one member and any other. This difference in degree will be sufficient to show that Mary's place is one apart; but yet not so far apart as to mar the sweet humanity of her motherhood.

One member of the Mystical Body can influence another by way of priestly ministry. In this way the priest who confers a sacrament is united to the person who receives it. Mary is not united to us in this way at the moment of our reception of the sacraments. Though it would be rash to say that the term "priest" may never be applied to her except in an altogether metaphorical sense it is still true that she is not an ordained priest. She has not the power of Orders that the priest has. She cannot hear confessions nor confirm. Nor is she a high-priest in the way in which Our Lord is one. If this were so she could be said to confer the sacraments in a priestly way in the person of the ordained priest just as Our Lord is First Minister in every act of priestly ministry performed on earth. It remains then to see if our union with Our Lady in the sacraments can be explained by way of her merits and intercession since these form the second bond between members of the Mystical Body. We shall find that this way is the true explanation and that it links up in a most unexpected manner with that of priestly ministry.

There are two aspects of the relationship in which Our Lady stands to Our Saviour which should be carefully distinguished the one from the other: her physical motherhood of the Son of God and her sharing with Him in the work of redemption. It is true that untheological piety feels little need to make any distinction at this point. For most people, all that can be said about Our Lady has been said when she is termed "Mother of Christ." This attitude of mind should not be rashly classified as error. The early Fathers frequently see Our Lady principally in the light of her physical donation of the Saviour to the human race by the fact of the Incarnation. What saves this position from error is that it really implies something more than the physical act: it implies a certain union of will and purpose in Our Saviour and Our Lady. She gave with her heart Him Whom she gave by her womb. She brought Him forth in His specific character of Redeemer and willed His birth as an element in the scheme of redemption. This implication of the supernatural in the physical (or of what some have termed the mystical in the physical) is present in the thoughts of the simple faithful of today. If for them Our Lady is principally she who brought forth God made man they understand her as giving birth to Him in view of our salvation and as co-operating in that way with Him in His glorious work.

It is useful however to separate these two aspects—the physical and the mystical—in a more formal treatment such as the present one. Each has its own application to the doctrine of the sacraments.

If we consider Our Lady as physically Mother of the Lord we are reminded at once that it is her Child Whom we receive and Who works upon us in the sacraments. "Ave verum corpus natum de Maria Virgine" sings the Church in one of her well known hymns: "Hail true Body, born of Mary." The Saviour and King Who comes to us in Holy Communion is He Whose Humanity was formed in the womb of Mary. We cannot forget this in receiving Holy Communion. Christ has only one true Body. In receiving it we are placed in Our Mother's—and His Mother's—debt. It can hardly be irrelevant to think of the Mother when the Son is our Meat and Drink.

Though it is only in Holy Communion that we receive Our Lord, He acts on us and unites us to Himself in the unity of His Mystical Body in every sacrament. In Baptism we are cleansed from sin by the Son of Mary and made brothers of the Son of Mary. In Confirmation we are enrolled under the standard of the Son of Mary. In Penance we are reunited to the Son of Mary. If Mary was ever, at any point of time, Mother of Our Lord, she remains His Mother in that same way up to and beyond the end of time. She remains always His Mother. He remains always her Son. It is her Son Who is King and Centre of the sacraments, and He in His sacramental life has not grown ashamed of His Mother.

To have been predestined to be the physical Mother of the Redeemer was a glorious privilege. But God had predestined Our Lady for something more glorious still: He had predestined her to share in a unique way in her Son's work of redemption and sanctification. This is what we mean by the mystical Motherhood of Our Lady. God deigned to have need of her not only for the Body of her Son but for His work as well. It is by sharing in His work that she enters most intimately into the sacramental system. Sacrifice and sacrament are supplementary in His work. Mary will then take part in the sacrifice of her Divine Son and in His communication of the fruits of His sacrifice. It is in this way that she will be entitled to be regarded as in some way a central figure in the plan of Redemption.

There is no evident impossibility in the idea that Christ could have had a mother who would have given Him His Body and then entered no more deeply into the work for which He needed a body. History can surely tell us of mothers of great men who were mothers to their greatness only in the accidental respect of being mothers to their manhood. It is not however hard to see that there was a special congruity in associating Mary as fully as possible with her Son's work. She came very near to Him physically; she lived in His company for the greater part of His life. It would appear to follow that this physical contact called out in some way for spiritual contact. If Christ came that we might have life, she who was nearest to Him ought to have most life. If He came to save souls, she who was nearest to Him ought to be like Him in that also. We can see that this was fitting and we believe that this is what God decreed to be. The woman as well as her seed unite to the destruction of the serpent. Freedom from sin and the life of grace come to us through Mary as well as Jesus.

The Cross was the chosen instrument of our redemption. It was at the foot of the Cross that Mary offered her great sacrifice and prayer for man. All that had preceded in her life was a preparation for this moment. Her free and meritorious acceptance of the duty of Mother of God, her Presentation of her Child to His eternal Father—these and the other acts of hers which were so many renewed gifts of Jesus to His Father and to mankind were completed and formally accepted on the day of Calvary.

Calvary was Our Saviour's great offering. Only He—for only He was God and Man—could redeem mankind by an act worthy of the Father and offered by the Head of the human race. He was the Head of the human race. Hence His act had value for all. Only He was Head. The act of another, however good it might be in itself, could not claim to be an act of satisfaction offered on behalf of the whole of sinful mankind. He was the second Adam and like the first bore in His person the whole human race so that as all could sin in the one so all might make amends in the Other. None other, not even Mary, could act in this way on behalf of sinners.

Only He, too, could offer to the Father an act of satisfaction which required nothing more than the Father's acceptance to make it fully redemptive. The satisfactory act must be one of infinite worth, for sin was an offense against the infinite. Christ alone of the sons of men was of infinite worth in Himself. He was a Divine Person. Every act of that Person—even when performed by His human powers—

was the act of a Divine Person and therefore of infinite worth. Christ could therefore in virtue of His own inner constitution make full reparation for sin. His acts were infinite because of what He was, not because of what might be added unto them. This can be said of no act of mere man— nor even those of Mary.

From this double fact—that Our Lord is official Head of the human race and that He alone has within Himself the sources of an act worthy of the Father's acceptance—it follows that all others, if there be any such, who offer satisfaction to God for sinners, do so through Our Lord and in dependence on Him. If He is the source of all grace and there is no grace which does not come from Him, there can be no act pleasing to the Father which does not spring from His grace received into the soul. We readily admit all this when it be a case of one man meriting for another. We say that he who merits must be a member of the Mystical Body animated by the grace of the great Redeemer. But we must say as well that Our Lady's way of merit differs only in degree from that of other men. And the difference consists in this: that whereas they can merit for some of their fellows and some of the graces they need, she merited for all mankind and all graces. Yet she as well as they merited under Our Lord and in dependence on Him.

We understand the preeminence of Mary's merit when we think of her at Calvary. Our Lady standing at the foot of the Cross was united more closely than man will ever be to her Divine Son. She was full of grace at that moment: full of His grace, for it was He hanging on the Cross Who was the source of the grace then filling her soul. His grace made her like Him, made her think as He did, made her love as He did. Her thoughts and desires were His thoughts and desires expressing themselves in her mind and heart. He was doing what those around the Cross could see Him do, that the world might know that He loved the Father—and that the world might also know that He loved His errant sheep. His love of God and man reechoed in Mary's soul. In love He offered Himself upon the Cross: in love she offered Him too. And her offering was just His offering renewed in her—the torrent of His love bursting through a new channel.

What Mary did then was pleasing to the Father. She was not our head: neither was her act independent of her Son's: hence what she did did not constitute a new redemption. But it constituted, so far as that was possible, complete identification of her soul with Our Lord's in His redeeming act, and had as its reward a corresponding share in the effecting of redemption. What Jesus did for us Mary did. But whereas He redeemed us of Himself, she redeemed us through Him and in Him; He, by His offering satisfied the Divine Justice; she by sharing in His offering appealed rather to the Divine love and mercy. Jesus and Mary both merited our salvation but by different titles: He as satisfying to the full, she as united to Him in a way that the Divine Goodness did not reject.

Theologians sum this up by saying that Our Lady merited our redemption de congruo whereas Our Lord merited it de condigno. Mary's participation in the offering of Calvary was not of itself sufficient to be entitled to acceptance by God. If God accepted her offering as really contributing to our salvation—and we believe that He did—He did so in mercy. He could without injustice have refused to allow what she did to count for us. But He has not elected that course. He willed to associate Our Lady to the fullest degree possible

with her Son. He accepted her offering, and to that extent
Mary's share in our redemption is an effective one.

There follows from this a conclusion of deep value for our
understanding of the sacraments. Our Lady merited our redemption de congruo, that is to say, she merited for us, de
congruo, every grace ever poured into our hearts. And having merited grace she is allowed to share in its distribution—
once more under her Son. For just as He ever makes intercession for us, so does she also through Him, and God
bestows none of the graces she has merited except in answer
to her prayers. The graces of the sacraments pass then
through her hands. They are graces she has merited for us
on Calvary and now distributes to us from her throne in
heaven. Her merit and mediation are both universal through
the loving kindness of God: they extend to every grace we
receive no matter what be its proximate channel. Even the
graces of the sacraments come to us through Mary's intercession and merits. The sacraments are now seen to be her
motherly devices for nourishing and caring for her children.
There is no possibility of divorcing sacramental justification
from Mary. Neither then can her presence in our thoughts
at the moments of receiving the sacraments be an intrusion.
Grace—the gift of God—is the gift of Jesus and Mary. It
may take years to synthesize ideas apparently so diverse—
God, Jesus, and Mary. But the embarrassment we feel as
we turn to one or the other in our preparation and thanks-
giving is not necessarily a sign that God will have us adhere
by force to a single idea, as poor as it is simple in content.
It is rather a sign that our synthesis, like every spiritual
reality, must be built up in sorrow and patience—and that
ultimately the building is a work of the Holy Ghost to which
we can contribute but our pain.

Both the dispositions for the worthy reception of the sacraments and the sacramental graces come to us through the merits and intercession of Our Lady—for the dispositions are themselves graces and she is Mediatrix of all graces. We ruled out some little while ago the possibility of her communicating grace to us directly by way of priestly ministry: and in this there is nothing to be retracted. But if we consider the point raised just now—that Mary is Mediatrix of all graces—we see at once that even the priestly ministry cannot be wholly independent of her; for it too is a grace in the sense of being necessarily knit up with our sanctification. Is it therefore necessary to clarify our first position in any way?

Let us abstract once more from the fact that Mary having been Mother of Jesus in the physical sense is Mother of the High Priest, and so in some way Mother of all who derive their priesthood from Him. We are not concerned here with connections that are primarily physical. Let us abstract too from what may be very real for some of us one day but which is hardly the rule for all—that Mary may intervene either by way of manifestation of herself or by interior impulse to send priests to those who, being in sin or in danger of death, are in need of the sacraments. Let us abstract finally—and this is the hardest yet—from her undoubted intervention in the confessional when she inspires the priest with the words which are needed to touch the sinner's heart or when she gives him in the administration of any sacrament that reverence and zeal which dispose souls so wonderfully for the infusion of grace. Let us abstract from all these and think simply of this: that it is Mary who gives priests to the Church.

The vocation to the priesthood, considered in its sense of

fitness of the candidate, is a grace. This grace has come from Mary. She sees the need that the Church has of good priests. She sees that the harvest is great and that the labourers are few. She sees also that it is by priests like to her Divine Son, not only in the character of Orders but also in the plenitude of grace, that souls will be saved. She determines then to provide the Church with such priests. Whenever a lad feels drawn to God, Mary has been generous in her inspirations. She will give him piety, moral fibre, generosity, love of God and of souls. One day the idea will come to him to become a priest just in order to serve God and his fellow men: Mary will have mediated that grace for him. He will make little sacrifices to prepare himself for his task: they will have been prompted by her. He will fight against fear and cowardice, against lowering the standard he first set himself: that is her work. He will prepare himself in the seminary by years of study and prayer and finally will go to receive the priestly commission from the hands of his bishop: but Mary has merited that that commission might be given to men, and she has prepared him to receive it as a holy thing. He will go into the world and his consecrated hands will be the instruments of salvation and those who are saved by him will remember that he has been mothered by her who formed the priestly mind of Christ.

If we consider now the different sacraments individually we shall learn something more about Our Lady's place in our sanctification.

Baptism, which makes us children of God, makes us as well children of Mary. We are said to be children of God from the moment that the reception of sanctifying grace makes us like to God. We do not mean by this statement that God has no interest in us whatever till we receive Baptism. What we do mean is that His first interest in us is to have us baptized and made like unto Himself. Similarly, in saying that Baptism makes us children of Our Lady we do not mean that she has no interest in the countless pagan souls that have never been baptized. What we mean is that it is through her intercession we receive the sacrament of Baptism imparting to us the life stored up for us in her merits, so that we may be said to be born then of her, that is to say, born to a new life which is like hers and which is hers to give us.

Baptism now becomes the ground of a new duty: that of regarding Mary as a mother. The grace of Baptism is one that comes through Mary. It implies therefore obligations to Mary, although their binding force falls far short of those it imposes on us in regard to Our Father in heaven. But however far she be below God, she is really our Mother. For Baptism adopts us into the family of the children of God and this family has a real mother through God's mercy and loving kindness. We should then act in dependence on Mary, seek her advice, turn to her in time of need. Acceptance of Mary's motherhood is part of the perfection of our acceptance of God's Fatherhood. We must become as little children if we wish to enter into the kingdom of heaven, and we are fully children when we accept, with all its implications, the fact that we have one to mother our spiritual lives. This demands extraordinary humility. It is utterly opposed to the spirit of the world—to the pride of life—to depend on others and to admit that their support is necessary. But God demands that His Baptized be empty of pride, and submission to a Mother is an easy way of satisfying His demands.

Confirmation is the sacrament of the soldier of Christ. Mary is the virgin most powerful: she it is who received the commission to crush the head of the serpent: it is under her that Christ's soldiers serve. Mary is a tender Mother. She is no less the valiant woman of the scriptures. She is the inspiration of the army of Christ. She cares for the wounded. She has words of consolation for the fearful. She thinks out plans of campaign for those who must lead. And there is nothing harsh in her valour. She is mother of both them who fight for Christ and of them—deluded men—who fight against Him. She wills to crush not the human enemy but Satan. She will spare the vanquished, even enlisting them when possible on her side. The Church is not a thundering car of war that crushes and lays waste. Its leader is a mother whose children are engaged on either side—some, children that are, some, children that yet may be, but all in some sense children.

It does sometimes happen—though, thank God it happens but rarely—that public champions of the Catholic Faith forget that, whether their dispute be with other Catholics in view of purity of doctrine or with non-Catholics in view of the essentials of truth, they enter the lists as confirmed soldiers of Christ. Their method of warfare should be dictated to them by their sacramental character. If they adopt another method their struggle becomes to that extent a private one. Now it is essential to their warfare that it be waged under the standard and leadership of Mary. This is because the war is a war for the faith and it is Mary who has ever banished heresy from the earth: "Quae cunctas haereses sola interemisti." But Mary will always lead her troops to fight with charity. She will tell them to establish the truth without wounding feelings; to avoid attributing interested motives; to avoid presupposing that the opponent is an ignoramus; to avoid captious insistence on minor points that afford an opening for an easy but barren victory; to leave men free to accept or reject what her Son has left open, since she is fighting only for what He stood for; and finally to pray much, for prayer is a greater weapon than speech.

Mary gave the Incarnate Word to mankind on the first Christmas. The confirmed give His truth to the world to the end of time. It is Mary who gave us the Author of supernatural truth, and it is she who will safeguard it. That is why she is leader of the Church Militant, captain of the army of the confirmed, "terrible as an army set in battle array" (Cant. 6, 9).

The Church has no more striking way of insisting on the truth of Our Lord's presence in the Blessed Eucharist than to say that It contains the Body born of the Virgin Mary. The fact that Our Lord was born of Mary is in itself alone a reason for thinking that Our Lady operates in a particularly intimate way in the Sacrament of His Body and Blood. We may say that she gave Him to the world in Bethlehem that the world might receive Him in Holy Communion. Holy Communion makes her first gift effective. From the point of view of Our Lady, Holy Communion is the realization of what she had in mind when she accepted to be the Mother of God. Perhaps she did not know then that the sacrament would ever be instituted. But she really did wish to give her Son to men and it is Holy Communion which realizes all that is implicit in that intention.

But it is when we think of Our Lady as Mediatrix of all graces that we see that Holy Communion is her especial sacrament. Every grace that we receive comes to us through the intercession and mediation of Mary. Hence, she is Mediatrix of the graces conferred in Holy Communion. Now the graces of Holy Communion are graces of transformation into Jesus. They perfect our likeness to Him, gradually elimi-

nate all in us that does not come from Him, and subject us
entirely to Him. It is on that account that we said that Holy
Communion was the sacrament of the Kingship of Christ:
it is in It we are most completely subjected to Christ. Mary
loves Jesus and us. Both of these loves—and they are ultimately one love—make her desire ardently that we be transformed into Jesus. She wishes Him to be effectively King of
all hearts. She wishes us to grow in spiritual strength so as to
be filled with the measure of the fulness of Christ that is possible for us. She knows that neither wish can be fully realized
outside of Holy Communion and so she draws souls to It.
She prepares them to receive It worthily—she herself received Holy Communion and knows how one should prepare.
She gives them a thirst for It. They are never so closely
united to her as then. She wills all her children to be like
her First-born. He was the child after her heart. The purpose
of Holy Communion is to build us into a family where all
will be like their elder Brother: It is therefore a sacrament
particularly dear to the heart of His Mother and ours.

It is hard to miss the intensely human note struck by the
words "Mary" and "Penance." There is no need to prove
that a mother cannot be indifferent to the fate of an erring
child. His return to the family will more often than not be
the work of his mother: it will hardly ever happen that he
will return without having taken her into his confidence
beforehand.

Mary loves God and Jesus and the sinner. She reminds the
sinner, while he is yet in sin, of his Father's love for him,
encouraging him to repent, to confess his fault, promising him
certain forgiveness. She thinks too of Jesus's death for the
sinner. That death will have been in vain for the sinner if
he is not won back to repentance. Mary cannot bear to think

of as much as one drop of the Precious Blood being wasted. She loves her First-born too dearly to leave any avenue of approach to the sinner's heart untried. She prompts him with her inspirations, she tries to inflame his heart. She has the whole treasury of divine grace to draw upon in her struggle to save the sinful soul. She will not grow weary while there remains any hope—and there is hope while the sinner still lives. And if he repents, how she will receive him in the sacrament of forgiveness. The grace that cleanses his soul is her grace; it is her way of receiving him back into the bosom of the family of regenerated mankind. And will there not be many a sinner who will find a more burning joy in the thought that he is now reconciled with his mother than in any other? Such sinners need have no fear: the mother will in her good time lead them to their Father.

Spiritual writers have often shown the parallelism between the feasts of Our Lord celebrated by the Church and those of Our Lady. Since our Holy Mother the Church is the author of this parallelism we must believe that there is a real quasi-identity of life in Our Lord and Our Lady. Feasts always point to something real: they are not just occasions of subjective emotion. Our Lady's feasts can be like those of her Son only if she is really like Him. He is holy in His conception and we celebrate the feast of the Annunciation: she also is holy in her conception, for we have the feast of the Immaculate Conception of Our Lady. We celebrate His birth and hers: we celebrate His Presentation in the temple and hers also. And so the list may be extended, with the feasts of Mary based on the feasts of her divine Son, until we come finally to these of His glorious Ascension and her Assumption.

The feast of the Ascension is that of the enthronement of

Our Lord at the right hand of the Father. He had suffered and died and had thereby merited for Himself a name that is over every name, and the time had now come for Him to enter into the glory of the Father, to mount the throne that was His by right of birth and conquest, and to rule from it the countless souls that would be saved in the power of His redemption. Christ ascended into Heaven as King and Ruler of mankind. He is now throned in glory, He Who reigned once from the Cross. Death has no more dominion over Him, but He rules over all things, even death. He awaits but one event to complete His triumph—that final vindication of His claims before the whole world gathered unto judgement and ranged in view of the throne that mortal men think they may brave.

Our Lord reminded His disciples that His Ascension into heaven should not be a cause of grief: He went to prepare a place for them and us. His presence in Heaven is the guarantee of our entry there; for He is in Heaven as Our Head and where the Head is, there the members have a right to enter. But if Our Lord prepared a place in Heaven for those who will be saved through Him His first thought must have been for His Blessed Mother. He would prepare a place apart for her: she would reign with Him, He as King and she as Queen. She must wait yet a little while. The Church, the spouse of Christ, had need of the Mother of Christ, and Mary would not be out of place where there were members of her Son. But she would die. Her time of reward would come. She had humbled herself in life, even to the point of sharing in the Death of the Cross. Would there not be for her also an exaltation?

Our Lady died and was assumed body and soul into Heaven and throned Queen in the sight of God and angels and Saints. This was Mary's reward. She who had shared in the shame of her Son merited to share in His Glory. And it is thus, as Queen, that we often think of Our Lady. We see her throned high in the courts of Heaven. Angels minister to her, speed on earth to do her bidding. Saints converse with her and intercede with her for those who implore their intercession. All about her is majesty and sweetness. She is Queen and Mother. Mary like Jesus is the same today as yesterday. He is ever the Lamb Who was slain and she is ever Mother of God and Mother of men. Her throne is a mother's warm embrace to all who approach it and her majesty the height of a love that can never be equaled.

Gladdening though this picture be to the hearts that love Mary it is more than a truism to state that it falls far short of the reality. Every man-made idea of the glory of heaven is inadequate, and, if that were all we implied in saying that our description of the glory of Our Lady fell short of the truth we should be guilty of a very obvious remark. But we mean something more than this. We mean that even as man-made ideas go, this one is definitely imperfect, that it misses in fact what is of the very essence of Our Lady's royal rank: her right to rule and the exercise of that right.

Our Lord's Kingship is not limited to the right to receive homage and to be throned in honour in heaven. He rules mankind; He subjects us to Himself by His grace and directs us to an end chosen and willed by Himself. His Kingship is effective, not just honorary. It is so too with Our Lady. She rules us—though being but Queen she rules through the King—she directs us, she determines human destinies, she has all men subject to her sway. She is more than Queen in title; she is Queen in fact.

Our Lady rules mankind in that no grace is ever given to man which has not been merited by her during her life on earth and which is not now dispensed through her intercession. She determines who will receive grace and the grace that he will receive. The whole machinery of the supernatural moves when and as she wills. It is not easy to find a human analogy which will make this clear. It is as if there were a king who never issued a decree, never influenced his subjects in any way otherwise than in deference to the wishes of his queen. The full kingly power would belong to the king and the queen would have no power except through him, but the effects of kingly rule would be attributable to both king and queen, to him as having the power, to her as directing its use. It is somewhat in this way that Our Lord and Our Lady rule in Heaven. All power is His. She has no power which is not hers through Him. But He wields His power in accordance with her prayers and unless she prays His power is not exercised.

It is unnecessary to insist that there is such harmony of will in Jesus and Mary—for after all Mary's will is moved by Jesus's grace—that there can never be a question of a real conflict. But it does not follow that Mary's intercession is thereby reduced to a necessary and pleasing formality. God does not trifle in that way. Grace does really pass through Mary's hands, grace does really depend on her for its distribution. It is part of God's goodness that He allows others to work under Him in the sanctification of souls and part of His truth that their work be no mere make-believe.

We can now see the sacraments in the light of Mary's Queenship. Mary rules souls through the sacraments just as Jesus does, for she too distributes the graces that flow through the channels of the sacraments. The sacraments set us in living contact with Mary Our Queen.[1] They are the ceremonial that lends splendour to her court and the instruments of her power. Every sacrament places us in the debt of Mary as well as of Jesus; every sacrament is profession of loyalty to Mary as well as to Jesus; every sacrament is, as it were, a royal decree sealed with the seals of Jesus and Mary. The grace of the sacraments flows down to us from Mary's throne. She is Queen of heaven and Mistress of its treasures. But the treasures of heaven are treasures of grace and the seven sacraments are the seven doors of the treasury. Her right it is to open and close those doors, to regulate the distribution of her riches to the poor and the needy. She gives royally to those who come to the treasure house and wait at its seven doors; and the riches she gives us are the treasures of a great King, and she who gives them is a Queen.

Jesus is the Sun That clothes the woman, Mary, and the earth is the moon that lies beneath her feet.

[1] The Blessed Eucharist, which is the peculiar sacrament of the Kingship of Christ, is also the sacrament of the Queenship of Mary. Just as it subjects us entirely to Jesus by transforming us into Him, so it subjects us to Mary by submitting us to her desire that all men be made to the likeness of her First-born.

12

THE SACRAMENT OF HOLY ORDERS

". . . ordained for men in the things that appertain to God." (HEBR. 5, 1)

THE SOUL IN QUEST of God has found Him in many ways. And each new way was not entirely new. For though the soul at each successive stage seemed to have left the path it first followed in order to tread a new one, the ways reunited, broader and more royal, growing after each confluence of way with way into a worthy approach to the dwelling place of the King of glory. Confirmation, though something other than Baptism, proved to be a stage in the growth of him whom Baptism had made a child; Holy Communion was the food and strength of child and man; Penance, the sacrament whereby child or man might be restored to health and be fitted to grow strong by sharing once more in the bread of angels. Every way had been a way to the One God, a stage in the one quest, and every way led ultimately to the one way, the way of union in the Blessed Eucharist.

Seeking God thus, and finding Him by many ways, the soul grows all athirst for God. He is sought at all times and in all places. Within the very world of smoke and noise, or corn and grazing cattle, He awaits discovery. The universe is a sacramental thing now: it is a sign of God hidden within, and God the Sanctifier: of God in the world for the sanctification of man: it is the voice of God sounding peace and eternal joy in birds and brooks and living things (cf. Ps. 28, 3 sqq.).

The world becomes the voice of God: the world has no meaning for us unless it speaks of God to us: the world is God expressed in His work. This is a philosophy of life, and a synthesis into which everything will fit. The perfection of the world is an echo of the perfection of God. Created worth has no reason for being, except it has a voice which is not just its own. It has no glory of its very own to hymn and no right to invite us to repose at the evening of life in the calm of its made beauty. It can be, only because it can point beyond itself to Him Who is. Had it no power of pointing to God it could never be allowed the deceit of beckoning to itself. And so all things speak of God. We see His beauty in the setting sun, His majesty in the snow-capped peaks, His tenderness in mothers' caresses. He is in all things, as the lover is in his letter, as the friend on the lips of the messenger. Every day we turn the page of life to see what it will say of God, and no day do we fail to find His Name.

God is seen in the world as Cause. This too we must never forget. We grant readily that what are termed His static Perfections are mirrored in things—His Beauty, His Majesty, His Mercy, and other perfections of that kind. But above all these there is the Divine Fecundity. God is pure Being, pure Reality; God is, we may say, brim-full of being. And there is no way this perfection can be brought home to human minds so well as by depicting the Divine Essence, as it were, overflowing into the realms of the created. God need never have created; that we know. But we cannot imagine the All-perfect, the All-containing otherwise than as pouring out its riches in a plenteous stream. Hence it is that God mirrored in His works must be more than Static. In His works we need to see Him at work, that we may have some idea of what He is. And so He has made things that are causes.

Trees bring forth branch and leaf, the earth yields its fruit, the birds have their little ones—all these are so many voices of the Most-High, of Him Who is *The* Maker, *The* Creator, *The* Fount of Life. These are visions of an active God, of a God so full of being that being goes out from Him and peoples a universe with angels, men, and stars. The slightest act of causation should be to us a stunning reminder of God. God is seen most of all—because at His highest—in the activity of the causes He has made. And who can miss the note of pathos in the thought that it is most of all when they are causes that men think little of Him?

It was fitting then that the Church, which is the expression on earth of the intimate nature of God, should be a herald not only of His Holiness by the life of grace that is in it, but also of His Fecundity by the causation of grace. That is the truth proclaimed by the fact of the priesthood. Supernatural Holiness is the voice of the Holiness of God ringing in the ears of the world: the priesthood is the voice of the Fecundity of that Holiness ringing in the ears of the faithful—for the world cannot hear it or understand it. The whole Church, faithful or priests, is in some way an adequate reflection of the Lord. We see in it the riches of His Wisdom; for the Church is wise, wise as the serpent though simple as the dove. We see in it too His Mercy; for the Church has her Sacrament of Penance and her tradition of patient suffering of wrongs. We see His Purity in her spotless virgins, souls that hardly know what earth is, but which earth has hated and ever will hate. We see His Eternity in her unbroken adherence to the same truth and to the same way of life: the Church has never changed and cannot change because she is the Voice of the Unchanging. And we see in it His Riches, His overflowing Goodness, His power of

Supernatural Causation; for the Church has her priests, and they have been commissioned to give as freely of their Master's grace as has been given unto them.

It is possible to glimpse the inner meaning of the priesthood from another vantage point if we place ourselves at the centre of all Christianity, Christ. The Church is the Mystical Body of Christ. Christ lives again in His Body. The perfection of that Body is the perfection of Christ's life in it. Hence, the perfection of the Church demands that He live in His Body not only in so far as He is full of grace and truth, but in so far also as He is Priest. The Church is therefore most fittingly composed of priests as well as faithful.

Let us examine this statement a little more closely.

One of the great questions of Dogmatic Theology is that of the motive of the Incarnation. Would Our Lord have become Man in fulfillment of the present Divine Decree even if man had never sinned, or did He become Man precisely because man had sinned? There are theologians who hold that the Incarnation would have taken place had man never fallen: The Word would have taken flesh not to save man but to offer to God that most perfect tribute of praise on human lips which could come from no one less in dignity than God made Man. There are other theologians who hold that revelation, as it has been communicated to the Church by God, links the Incarnation insistently with the idea of our sin, in such wise that we have not God's authority for any other motive. Whatever be the truth of the matter—and the weight of theological thought inclines to the second view—it must never be forgotten that there is no reason for rejecting a synthesis of the two aspects of the Incarnate Word in the Person of Him Who came to save us from our sins. Even if Our Lord came on earth only because of the sin of man, it is a fact that in saving man He offered to the Father that sublime tribute of praise so desired by the theologians of the first school. Hence He is full of grace and truth as well as being Priest. He came on earth to save men; but being the Son of God He could not save men otherwise than by submitting them to Himself, by being their King, their Head, and by blending the voice of their lives into a harmony that welled ultimately from His Human-divine Heart. The two perfections were necessarily His—fulness of grace, making Him firstborn of every creature, and priestly power, by which He might offer sacrifice for them who stood in darkness and in the shadow of death. And when He won for Himself a second Body—a mystical one—He willed that His whole soul should in some way shine through the flesh of that new body, and that His Church should be His no less in her continuation of His Priesthood than in her life of God-given sanctity. There was need therefore of priests since the Mystical Christ was the whole Christ living again. In each priest is renewed the Priesthood of Christ just as in each saint is renewed His Holiness. Through saint and priest the Mystical Christ reproduces the features of the true Christ. Both must be that He may live wholly, in His dual rôle of Priest and Firstborn, once more in His Church. The visible priest is, ultimately, a tribute to the eternal, invisible, Priesthood of the one High-Priest.

In the same way then as the whole universe is a hymn to the praise of the Father, the world of the redeemed is a hymn of praise to the Redeemer. He can be seen again in His faithful. They would have no reason for their existence did they not point beyond themselves to Him. For they are not what they are in the order of grace because of themselves. They are only what He has made them to be. It would be deceit on their part were they to be and not to speak of Him: what is more still, they simply cannot be in the order of grace and fail to point more insistently to its Author than to themselves.

The priest is the visible expression of Christ the Priest. And yet, he is more still. He is the instrument of the eternal Priesthood of Jesus; for the Sacraments are causes as well as signs. So far we have considered the Priesthood only as a sign of the Divine Fecundity and the Priesthood of the Redeemer. This idea is a beautiful one which is too often neglected: but there is no reason so to insist on it as to make it appear that it is the whole truth. The priest is the instrument of the power of Christ as well as its sign. Christ works in and through His priests. His great sacrificial offering is perpetuated through the hands of His priests. His grace is poured into souls by the ministration of priests. Not only does Christ come to our minds when we see the priest with the eye of faith, but His life comes to us physically when we submit to the power He has conferred upon them. This is a terrifying reality for those called to the priesthood.

We have spoken of Christ the King throned in glory to Whom men come for life and godliness. His mighty sweep of love and reverence for the Father catches them up and offers them, and all that they are, in union with Himself in the perpetuation of the great act of Calvary. And then bending low and tenderly over man, rich with the treasures of the inner sanctuary of the Godhead, He fills souls with grace, with the grace of childhood, the grace of manhood, the grace of union. But nothing of all this is done without the priest. It is Christ in the priest who draws us into Calvary at Holy Mass. It is Christ in the priest who fills us with every grace in the Sacraments. Christ does not cease to be there because He works through a priest; but without the priest He does nothing of all this. It is true that He moves us to acts of the life He has given us without the intervention of priest or angel, for actual grace comes to us without any intermediary. But sanctifying grace and sacrifice demand as their normal condition that the human priest mediate. The priest is necessary in the present dispensation. To wish to be holy without the priest is, for a Christian, to renounce all holiness.

The priesthood is a sacrament which imprints a character in addition to conferring grace. The nature of this character can be understood from what we have just said, understood in the light of earlier chapters. Like every character, it is a power, and a consecration, and a participation in the priesthood of Christ. This last point is so clear as to need no further comment. That it is a power is also clear, for it gives the power of offering sacrifice and administering sacraments, all in subordination to the action of the great High Priest. We may pass over briefly the fact that it is a consecration, setting the ordained one apart for the exclusive life of the priestly ministry. Though this last is a point of great importance it will emerge sufficiently in its main outline from the rest of the chapter.

But there is one point that may not be glossed over. It is that of the grace of the priestly state, and the need of growth in that state. The character is of itself the power to perform priestly acts. Whether the priest be in the state of grace or not these acts will be valid for the people. If a layman assists at the Mass of a priest who has the utter wretchedness to be at the moment of celebration in the state of mortal sin, the layman offers a pleasing sacrifice to God. If further he receives a Host consecrated at that sacrilegious Mass he receives Our Lord really present within It as truly as if It had been consecrated by a saint. If all this be so, would it not appear that there is no essential connection between the priesthood of the priest and the sanctity of the priest? While admitting that he has a soul to save and should therefore endeavour to grow in grace, is it not true that considered precisely as priest he is not a better priest by being in the state of grace, nor a worse one by being in the state of mortal sin?

That this cannot be so is clear from the fact that the character of the priesthood is never conferred on a worthy candidate without being accompanied by grace. Nor is the reason far to seek. The priesthood is a sharing in the priesthood of Jesus, and He Who was our High Priest is the Same Who was full of grace and truth. No priesthood has any raison d'être on earth which is not at once a sign of and a sharing in the priesthood of Jesus. Now Jesus was not just an official, One Who had certain duties to perform for God and man, and Whose private life was lived in disregard of public duty. He was all of one piece. He not only linked God and man but was Himself linked with God and man. Linked with God by His Divinity and His created grace, linked with man by His very real Humanity, He was perfectly fitted to be the official bridge between the sinner and the Lord. And He willed—and it is His glory that that will be effective— that all who would share in His official act of linking God with man would share also His intimate character of living link. How could He will otherwise and will—as will He must—that every priest be a hymn of praise to His great glory? For if there be in the priest anything that is not Christ, that priest is a living tribute to the worth of a false God.

If we consider the priesthood in this way, not just in function of the character and mere power of valid perform-ance of certain offices, but in function of complete subjection to the living holiness of Christ the Priest, we see an amazing suggestiveness in the fact that so many of the sacramental formulae are expressed in the first person singular. The priest says "This is *my* Body," and also "I absolve thee." We know that he speaks so because he speaks in the Name of Christ and in the Person of Christ. But is it not now evi-dent that he speaks so since he speaks in the Name of the *whole* Christ? He does not speak as the instrument of a Saviour Who is Priest but not Holy, but as the instrument of the Saviour as He really is; that is to say, as the instru-ment of One Who is full of grace and truth as well as Priest; and he himself can say worthily "This is my Body" only if he is himself an embodiment of the whole Christ. "I absolve thee" falls with no strain from his lips when he who speaks is a true, though faint, reproduction of Him Who forgives. Let me say once more, that such expressions have their sacramental force even when uttered by the un-worthy. But how they are strained, how they falter, as it were, on the lips of the tepid and the sinful; "I absolve thee, but the true 'I' loves its sin. This is my Body; but my own reality is other—from Christ's Body far removed."

We find in this a suggestion which leads to a synthesis of that duality, grace and character, which in some measure proved a stumbling block in an earlier chapter. For it is at once apparent in the sacrament of Holy Orders that the grace of the sacrament is given that the life of the character be led worthily. And extending our gaze to the other sacraments we see that the same thing must hold for them also. If the character of Baptism consecrates us to the service and cult of

God our Father, it is the grace of the sacrament which enables us to do so in a way pleasing to Him. The character of Confirmation binds us to profess our faith openly; the grace of the sacrament makes our profession the tribute of a loyal heart. In the same way, it is possible for the priest to exercise priestly functions validly without being in the state of grace. But grace is necessary to perform them becomingly; and not just common grace, not the grace of a child, not even the grace of the grown man, but the special sacramental grace of the priest, a grace, which like all sacramental graces, is a principle of life and invades and transforms life in all its phases and all its resources.

We are here in face of a problem akin to that of the Gifts of the Holy Ghost. The theological and infused virtues give us the power of performing supernatural acts. But unregenerated human nature is not a congenial ground for the growth and flowering of the Divine. Hence we need gifts by which is effected a certain harmonization of the divine and the human in us—obviously by the elevation of the human—in such wise that we act quasi-divinely with ease and connaturalness. These gifts are the gifts of the Holy Ghost. In very much the same way, we may say that the priestly functions are far removed from the natural powers of man. Hence, even though the power of performing them may be conferred by the character alone—just as the mere possibility of eliciting an act of faith is given by the virtue of faith—the power of performing them with connaturalness and dignity comes from something else, from the sacramental grace. Grace adapts the man to the character. Grace enables the character to function with ease and becomingness. The character without grace is the Divine grafted on to the sinful: the character with grace is the Divine grafted on to the divinized.

We may express the same idea by saying that the grace of Orders gives the priestly mind of Christ, while the character of Orders gives us the priestly power of Christ. The power without the mind is a monster. The power with the mind is the priesthood as it was in the Saviour. We read in the Nicene Creed that Jesus came on earth "For us men and for our salvation." This is the priestly mind of Christ, expressed elsewhere so limpidly by St. Paul in the words which introduce this chapter ". . . every high priest taken from among men, is ordained for men in the things that appertain to God." The priest is mediator, and the perfect priest is he who has no aim but to mediate between God and man, who sees that any moment of his life which is not devoted to the reuniting of the sinner and his God is utter waste, shameful waste. Is not this the meaning of the statement that Christ came on earth "for us men"? The Son of God had the power of determining from all eternity what would be the motive force of His Incarnate existence. He had, we may say, the leisure of the eternal years to draw up the plan of the brief space of time He would spend on earth. And drawing up the plan He did so with infinite wisdom, made it an all-embracing plan, one which would include everything it would be worth while to do on earth. He has told us what it was, though under terms that differed from time to time; to save what was lost, to do the will of Him that sent Him, to gather men as the hen doth gather her chickens under her wing, to give life that men may have it and that abundantly—but all these are but ways of saying the same thing, namely, that His whole essence was to be a mediator, that He was entirely for the sake of men and for the sake of God. This was the mind of Christ; and with this mind and in the power of the spirit, He taught, and offered sacrifice, and instituted sacraments. But what fervour, what devotion, went into the performance of these, His official priestly acts. They were the moments when the gates were opened and the pent-up priestly mind of Christ swept triumphantly forth. The acts were passing, but the mind was ever within, ever straitening Him. That is the meaning of the grace of Orders.

From this it follows that the ordained priest should perform his priestly functions, not only validly, but under the positive direction of the grace of Orders, that is to say, under the positive direction of the mind of Christ. When He preaches he should endeavour to convince himself that he is really announcing the tidings of salvation to souls lying like sheep that have no shepherd. When he offers Holy Mass he should endeavour to put into his offering something of the intensity of the offering of Calvary: let him think of the rushing enthusiasm of the Crucified for God and souls: and let him think that he too is offering to the same God and for souls in the same need. When he administers the sacraments he should recall that he is at the moment of administration the channel of the life of Christ to souls. Christ, through him, is aflame to give Himself to souls—how He is aflame to take complete possession of them in Holy Communion!—and is he on his side aflame to give them Christ? Is the conferring of the sacrament a matter of course? Would he be as cheerful as ever if he were the cause of an avoidable delay in giving the King to His subjects?

I am not speaking just now of the theological question of the attention and intention requisite for the valid administration of sacraments. That question is one which concerns primarily the sacramental sanctification of the faithful: for if the intention be absent the sacrament simply is not conferred on them. What is under discussion now is the sanctification of the priest who confers the sacrament, and the point made is, that unless he has the mind of Christ, the administration of a sacrament will not sanctify him. It is evident that I do not mean to say that he must have an actual, explicit, consciousness of the mind of Christ within Him at every instant of His priestly ministry. But I do say that that is what he should aim at through his whole life, and that it is only by aiming at that that he will succeed in being subject in any real way to a virtual influence of the mind of Christ, or the sacramental grace of Orders, throughout the whole length of time he is engaged actively in his specifically priestly duties. It is true that it is a mistake to think that an uninterrupted actual intention is necessary for a meritorious work. But it is no less a mistake to think that therefore it has nothing to do with holiness. It is in fact, what might be termed, the Platonic idea of holiness; that is to say, it is a perfection unrealizable in normal human conditions; but it is a perfection we should ever aim to approach, because it was the perfection of Christ. He was always fully conscious of the spiritual significance of His every act, and gave to every act the full measure of His energy. We must needs be content with less, with a general direction of our lives. But this general direction can be intensified so as to approximate ever more closely to His completely particularized direction. We do not arrive at this high degree of imitation of Him by taking our acts one by one and endeavouring to make them explicitly His: this would lead the average man to lunacy. What we must do is to intensify our subjection to the wellsprings of His action in us. As priests we should endeavour to make our whole lives full of love of God and souls. If this really be effected, then every priestly act will flow in a *positive* way from those two loves, and the influence of the two loves upon activity will grow in intensity according as they are more deeply rooted in our souls. But how can they become more deeply rooted unless we give them intense and conscious care? It is therefore no exaggeration to say that the price of the virtual influence of the mind of Christ in our performance of priestly acts is actual attention to the development of that mind during our whole day. That is what is meant by saying that an actual attention is the ideal and that without it a full virtual intention cannot be realized. And we begin to see at the same time that the worthy performance of the ministry demands that the whole day, in its every detail, be passed as an expression of the grace of Orders.

What we are beginning to see is of itself not strange. If the grace of Baptism and the grace of Confirmation extend to every detail of daily life, it is small wonder that the grace of Orders should do no less. Besides, is it not the very nature of sacramental grace, that it should modify profoundly every single phase of the being and activity of the soul into which it has been poured? Was not this one of the most striking aspects of the grace of Penance, that every subsequent action of the repentant and forgiven sinner should bear the stamp of forgiven love and gratitude? Sacramental grace is not a departmental thing in the commonly accepted sense of the term, for the simple reason that the soul in its essence has no departments. Each sacramental grace is an elevation of the whole soul. There is no bit of soul left untouched to be the principle of an activity to which sacramental grace would be extrinsic. Sacramental grace is added to sacramental grace; the grace of one sacrament completes and perfects the grace of another. But there is no question of each grace having exclusive rights over some isolated part of man. Each grace is the grace of the whole man, and every act of man should bear the stamp of each sacramental grace that inheres in his soul.

We have now arrived at the point at which we can say that there is such a thing as a specifically priestly life even in those matters which are common to priests and lay-folk. This is an immediate consequence from the fact that there is such a thing as a sacramental grace of Orders; for if there be such a grace there can be no activity of the soul from which it will be absent. There is a priestly way of doing all things, no matter what they may be. Our Lord in His Life on earth performed most, if not all, of the actions that go to make up the life of a day. Yet there can have been nothing in what He did unrelated to the purpose of His coming. His carpentry in Nazareth was performed in a priestly spirit. So also His presence at the wedding feast. No matter what He did, He did it as a priest should. We may wonder how this can be, even while we admit that it must be. But there is really so little room for wonder. He simply did all that He did for the glory of His Father and the salvation of souls. The work He was engaged on did not simply matter: whatever it might be, He did it in that spirit and so did it and all things well.

It is interesting to note that we are here in presence of a problem which resolves itself in the opposite direction to a similar one met with in dealing with the sacrament of Penance. We had some little difficulty then in determining what the grace of that sacrament was, and our final solution was that it was the ontological expression of the psychological state of the repentant sinner. When it is a question of the sacrament of Orders we seem, in some extraordinarily vague way, to have no doubts about the nature of the grace. Our real problem is the nature of the psychological state which should spring from it. That is the problem which we are answering just now. The psychological state of the priest should be one of zeal for the glory of the Father and the salvation of souls. This should be his state at all times. If his mind is so, he is Christlike. He will have proved the truth of the words of St. Thomas, insisting that the priest is in virtue of his calling invited to a higher sanctity than is the layman. It is no exaggeration to say that he is invited to be a living holocaust. He can have nothing of his powers, nothing of his time, nothing of himself, for himself alone. He belongs entirely to God and to souls. Having been ordained for men in the things that appertain to God, he has had limits fixed to himself outside which he may not wander. God and souls—these must be his great passions, his only passions.

We have seen in our chapter on the Mystical Body how any soul at all may lead others to God by meriting for them through its own good works and sufferings. This is the way in which the priest too must devote himself to souls at those moments when he is not engaged in the ministry. He must do whatever he does as well as he can, that souls may draw near to God. But in his case there will be something more than is found in the lay apostle. He can hope that the grace he merits will be communicated by himself in the sacraments. He can hope to merit for others the dispositions with which they will approach himself. In this way he will really be giving of his own when he confers a sacrament. The grace of Christ will not merely pass through him as water through a channel. It will flow as it were from him, coming to him from Christ and then welling up once more in his soul too, and gushing forth into the soul before him. Such a priest was the Curé of Ars, who converted his flock as much by his mortifications as by his ministry. In him there was a perfect equilibrium between grace merited and grace communicated. In us there is such a disproportion! Grace passes through our hands, but whose are the merits? It is not our grace; we are but its ministers. We have the character of Orders; but how little the grace of Orders has wrought in us. "Neglect not the grace that is in thee . . ." (I Tim. 4, 14).

It is not possible to speak in detail of the various aspects of priestly life while still remaining within the scope of the present book. The most we can hope to do is to draw attention to certain essential or neglected points. It will therefore be understood that the following few remarks are not intended to be taken as exhaustive of the sum of priestly duties.

One specifically priestly duty is that of prayer. It is performed by the daily recitation of the Office. What should be the mind of the priest who recites his Office? He should pray as "ordained for men in the things that appertain to God." When saying the Office he prays for his fellow men. They have a right to expect that he will do it well. That is his function: it is for that he was ordained: he was ordained for men, to do all that is needful to establish them in peace and harmony with God. It does not matter whether or not he himself feels the need for prayer. The whole Church needs prayer, needs to adore, and he is the man who has freely come forward to supply the Church's need. Were the priest to go still further and think that when he prays the prayer of the Church, it is Christ Who prays in him, how could his prayer remain cold? Christ living in the Church, loving and praising the Father in the Church, breaks out into vocal prayer in the priest. When the priest prays, it is Christ and the Church, Christ in the Church, Who prays. Aperi Domine os meum—Open Thou, Lord, my lips, for my soul faints beneath the burden of prayer You have laid upon me.

There is as well the duty of preaching. Preaching is an essentially priestly work since it is a work of mediation. He who preaches mediates between man and the God of truth. Preaching tends of itself to prepare the way for the first gift of God, that of faith; and when once the faith has been implanted it tends to increase and intensify it. The priest who wishes to allow his priestly grace to influence his preaching will recall that when he preaches the word of God he is offering the gift of salvation in God's name to souls. We often read of Our Lord that He was moved with compassion for the multitude and that His compassion found expression in His teaching them. He loved the Father and loved mankind and so He gave men the knowledge of their Father. This is what the priest does. His sermon is an official offer of salvation to mankind made in the Name of the Father and in the power of Christ. It is hardly necessary to add after saying this, that the sermon should be well prepared! Nor is it necessary to mention that it should be sincere. It is an offer; Christ's offer, it is true, but the priest's as well. The priest is offering something he himself values, something which he offers because he feels the misery of mankind and desires the glory of God. This sincerity will become perceptible in his words. His hearers will feel that he has lived what he preaches. They will feel something too of strength going out from him and making them brave to give themselves entirely to God. The preacher is a pontiff, a bridgemaker, who builds a bridge of words to God and lights his bridge with faith and love.

Something has been said already in a passing way about

the manner in which the sacraments should be conferred. Though incomplete it will be sufficient for our present purpose. It were better however not to speak at all of how to offer Holy Mass than to speak of it in disjointed snatches. The priest who has learned the mind of Christ will say his Holy Mass well. That is enough for us to know. There are besides so many excellent works in which the meaning of the Mass is exposed with unction that it is superfluous to add to their number while not believing oneself capable of something new, or saying some old thing well. Let us go on then to a more neglected point, and one, besides, which is not so frequently studied, that of the workings of the grace of Orders in matters which at first sight do not seem to be immediately priestly.

It is idle to stress the fact that we are living in a time of social disequilibrium. There is no need either to point out that, as a direct consequence of social evil, it has become increasingly difficult for the layman to live a good Christian life. It is hard for the poor to be faithful to their religious duties when in spite of their prayers they must face daily the sight of starving ill-nourished children, of wives bringing forth infants in fireless and unfurnished rooms, of moody and disconsolate husbands half-crazed with hunger and frozen with despair. The question at once suggests itself: is the priest in virtue of his Orders expected to do more than other men to remedy these evils? It is not our intention to imply that priests are not doing their share and doing it nobly. But it would be well to find out if in doing it they are adding in pure generosity to the duties of a priest, or are simply giving the rein to the urge of the priestly grace within them.

Let me hint at the very outset that it is no exalted view of the all-embracing nature of the grace of Holy Orders which holds that there are certain good works to which it is indifferent. St. Paul became all things to all men that he might gain all. Was this a contribution made by Paul to the efficacy of the grace of ordination, or was it not rather his generous yielding to what that grace dictated? The priest who can bring his fellow men nearer to God by no matter what the means—provided they be good, and the price of their employment be not prohibitive—and neglects to do so, is not merely not a good Christian, he is a bad priest. The priest is made a priest that he may lead men to God. He does so immediately by prayer, preaching, Holy Mass, and the sacraments, but he is bound to use every other means as well within the limits of what is possible to him, and in using such means he acts not just as baptized, or confirmed, but as ordained.

In proof of this we can turn to a universally accepted distinction; that of the actus elicitus and the actus imperatus. An act of any virtue is said to be an elicited act of that virtue when it is specific to it, being produced by and remaining in the virtue in question and the faculty it perfects. An act is said to be an ordered act of a virtue if it be produced by and reside in a faculty other than that in which the virtue itself is, but nevertheless came into being at its command. Acts of love are elicited acts of the virtue of friendship. They are the peculiar acts in which friendship manifests itself most fully, and they are produced by and reside in the will. Good advice may be an ordered act of friendship. Friendship may prompt one to give good advice, but the advice comes from the intellect rather than the will. It is an act of the intellect produced at the behest of friendship.

We see then that it is the peculiarity of the higher virtues that they not only have acts which are exclusively their own, but they have as well the right to dictate to other virtues in the production of these latters' acts. They can draw on the resources of the whole man in the attainment of their ends. And no matter what it be that the man do, it is attributed to the higher virtue. Whether one love, or advise, or give alms, in each case the act is said to be one of friendship— elicitus or imperatus as the case may be, it is true, but still an act of friendship. When you advise a friend for his good you do not cease for the moment to act as a friend. In other words, the higher virtues have a certain amplitude of scope, such that things fall under their control which at first sight might seem to be altogether outside them. There is practically no form of virtuous action that cannot be made an act of friendship: with the corollary, that there is practically no form of virtuous action which if neglected in certain conditions will not constitute a breach of friendship.

Now the priesthood has this amplitude of scope. The essence of the priesthood is mediation, union of God and man. The actus elicitus of the priesthood would deal primarily with sacrifice and sacraments, and secondarily with prayer and preaching. This much being allowed, it has in no wise been granted that the gamut of priestly activity is thereby complete. There remains the actus imperatus of the priesthood (the term is new but the idea is old). In other words every single act whatever that can be a means to the union of God and man is capable of being used to serve the primary ends of the priestly office, and when so used becomes a truly priestly act. When St. Paul became all things to all men he acted as a priest. If he had failed to be all things to all men he would have failed in the perfection of his duty as a priest. If St. Paul were alive today he would be a social worker within the limits of obedience and possibility. Were he to refuse he would cease to be St. Paul, and model of priesthood.

Bearing this in mind, it is interesting to note that this amplitude of the grace of Orders is hinted at unmistakably in the fact that there are a number of Orders, higher and lower. There is no reason just now to discuss whether or not they are all sacraments. This would be irrelevant. What is of value is to note that the idea of the priesthood and the approach to the altar, which at first had manifested itself only in the priesthood and the diaconate, gradually extended and differentiated itself through the various interior orders, so that ultimately opening doors and ringing bells stand forth clearly as having their place in the approach of man to God and to His altar. The whole essence of our approach to God is concentrated in the priest. But the concrete integrity of our approach involves something more than an essence. In the concrete the essence must be built up into an individualized body of approach; and it is not impossible that this body will include such earthly things as bread, butter, and warm clothing.

The priest, then, as priest should interest himself in the human welfare of his flock in so far as this is a necessary condition for their spiritual well-being. There will be cases where no one will be able to do as much as he. In rural districts, where the average standard of education is necessarily low, it will be usually impossible to find a layman possessing that high degree of intelligence and initiative sufficient to suggest and carry through necessary and daring improvements, to suggest and supervise better methods of work. Even if there be such a man he will gain in confidence in himself, and will get increased support from others, if it be known that the priest is actively at his side. Bishops have the right to direct and control their priests in work of this and of every kind. But they have shown sufficiently their interest in social matters to make it clear that they wish this work to be done. Besides, is it not true that their right to direct is also an obligation to direct actively, and that any bishop would fail in his duty to God and his people who would make the whole administration of his diocese consist in a conservative clinging to institutions that served needs long defunct? A Bishop is a leader. He is bound to accept and welcome new methods of meeting new evils.

It should be no small consolation to the priest absorbed in social work to know that not only is such work priestly in that it is commanded by his priesthood, but that it is priestly also in that it opens the way to Holy Mass and the Sacraments. An actus imperatus has as end the virtue which commands it. Advice is given by friendship for the sake of friendship. The priest works for the social needs of his flock that they may be enabled to come freely and with profit to the priest; for all our sanctification is enshrined in sacrifice and sacraments. But even were this not so, it is hard to see how a priest having the mind of Christ through the grace of his ordination, and filled with zeal for the salvation of souls and the glory of God, could think that any work which helped souls and served God was not his business. St. Paul made tents. St. Paul was a priest. If it is true that there was a time when it was part of a priest's duty to make tents, does it seem exaggerated to say that there can also be a time when it will be his duty to make a new social order?

13

THE SACRAMENT OF MATRIMONY

"It is not well for man to be alone."
(GEN. 2, 18)

THERE IS A STRIKING STORY in the synoptic Gospels of a rich young man who came to Our Lord. His purpose was to ask a question which must ultimately be the one that every man asks: "What shall I do that I may have life everlasting?" He was a rich man and the answer given him was coloured by this fact, for it was expressed in terms of an attitude towards riches: "Go, sell whatsoever thou hast, and give to the poor . . . . and come follow Me" (cf. Mk. 10, 17 sqq.). To attain eternal life he was asked to give up what was most peculiarly his own.

The words of Our Saviour are words of infinite import. He spoke to the rich man, but thought of all men. And in telling the rich man that eternal life would cost him his riches He wished to convey to all men of all times, that eternal life is something which can be achieved only by an act of generous confidence.

It is not grasped, as it should be, that the law of human progress—even of natural progress, though it is not of it that we shall speak—is that man must give what he can if he dares hope to receive what he is capable of. That is what is implied in the fact that man is a social animal. To realize himself he needs the support of others. But society, even though it is for him, is not for him alone. He too must support and contribute. Should men, as a whole, refuse to give to their fellow men the result would be the ruin not only of those who did not receive but of those also who did not give; for these latter, hide the fact though they may from themselves, receive as much as, if not more than, they have ever contributed. No man is self-sufficient. All need to receive and all must give. The man who tries to work out his perfection as an isolated unit is a fool, and probably a conceited one.

That is why there is such a power in man as the power of disinterested loving; the power, that is to say, of friendship. Since man needs the help of others and is himself perfected with the assistance of others, God has given to man the power of wishing well to others for their own sakes. Had man been made naturally selfish he would be doomed to necessary frustration in life, the world remaining as it now is. Granting the rest of the universe to be as it is, it is necessary that man should have a spontaneous tendency to do good to others, to spend himself in the service of others, even to sacrifice his little all for the sake of someone else. It may seem hard to give of one's own to another. It may seem hard to expend those wonderful possibilities of achievement that one has, to wear oneself out, as it were, with life as yet unlived, and that in a straining which seems to make one's own life no more full. All this is hard if viewed from the angle of immediate results. But it is easy to one who loves, and to live life fully one must love.

The point of Our Saviour's answer to the rich man is, therefore, that eternal life is achieved by love; because to love is to give, and man must give to become fully man.

There is one love without which no man can reach eternal life, and that is the love of God and the love of all men in God. To love God is to give Him all we have. Let us not delay in taunting human nature with the too true truth that all we have is a poor gift to God. We feel the cost of the gift, for though all we have is God's it is really ours also; and being our all we feel that in losing it we lose that reserve of strength and resources which is the guarantee of success. To give all we have to God, seems to our eyes to be to make a holocaust of the future. We denude ourselves and force ourselves to live in hope and trust. We have nothing left of our own. Everything has been given to God, because that is what it means to love God. To love self is to give everything to self; to love God is to give Him everything. The rich young man did not really love God because he refused to give his riches to Him in His poor. Keeping for himself he withdrew from God, because love is impossible without some donation, and the highest love demands the greatest donation—that of the whole self.

If to achieve ourselves we must make an entire donation of self to God, we must no less make an entire donation of self to man in God. The Christian who shuts his heart to his fellow men is Christian only in name, and will lose his soul. There is therefore a deep significance in the doctrine of St. Thomas that the Blessed Eucharist received at least in implicit desire is necessary for salvation, if we consider that the effect of its reception is to make all Christians one in love. If without the Blessed Eucharist one cannot be saved, in the same way one cannot be saved without what follows necessarily from it, love of one's fellows. We have no guarantee that we love God if we do not love our brothers in God. Where is the possibility of union with Christ if there be a very real separation between us and those with whom Christ wills to be united? There is no point in mincing words here; so let us say quite clearly that the man who is not willing to give of himself in the service of others within the bounds of their needs and his capacity will most certainly lose his soul. He who will give nothing defies the fundamental law of human development and cannot but pay the price.

Without this donation of self to God and to our fellows in God no man can be saved. This donation alone is sufficient. If it be stabilized by religious profession it is the most perfect donation of all that man can make, and leads to the highest perfection of which man is capable. But man can achieve eternal life in other ways also, if in each of them he gives what the law of love inspires.

There is in the first place the more general donation of self to God and to man in God such as we have just outlined it, but without vows entering in to give it stability. This donation is sufficient to attain eternal life. It is the life of unmarried lay-folk.

There is secondly the life of virginity within the sacrament of matrimony. This too is a way of attaining eternal life. There is implied in it the general donation of self to God and to one's fellows, and a particular donation of self as helpmate and support to a partner.

There is finally the married life without the vow of virginity. Here too there is a donation which we shall consider later in detail. This donation, like all those of which we have spoken hitherto, is simply the price of a certain type of human perfection and is made in view of its achievement.

We may now compare these three ways of attaining to the full human stature through the gift of self to God and to one's brethren.

What is the perfection of man? If we turn to the world of living things we see that the living organism is perfect when all its capacities are realized to the full, and that this perfection, when realized, is accompanied by the phenomenon of fruitfulness. The fully developed animal is the one who has arrived at the perfection of bone, flesh, and muscle, that lies within the limits of its species. When so developed the animal is capable of the act of generation. In its young the animal will survive. Its young are the proof of its fitness to survive. Perfection of the self and fruitfulness are, thus, intimately connected in the animal order. With man the case is analogically the same. The perfect man is the fully developed man, and the sign and fruit of his perfection is his permanence in other men who in some way draw what they are from him as source.

He who gives himself to God and his fellow men in charity either by taking the three vows of religion or by adopting the unmarried state in the world will realize the idea of human perfection which we have just outlined (the precise difference made by the vows does not concern us at the present moment). Through union with God he will arrive at the full development of his own being. If he gives himself entirely to God, and devotes himself to the sacramental quest of God as we have indicated it, God will give Himself to him in return. He will be raised above himself up to the level of the Divine. Emptying himself of what is human and fallen, as far as is in his power, he becomes filled with the Divine. Life is his now as the human mind could never have conceived it. He is perfected with a perfection which not only realizes to the limit all that is good in man, but adds in the measure of the divine bounty the gift of a share in that Good which is peculiarly God's.

Now it is a fact that such a life will be necessarily fruitful, in the strict sense of bearing fruits distinct from the bearer. God did not intend the spiritual alone to be sterile. To turn to the great contemplatives is a proof of this. How many souls did not the great St. Theresa convert by the power of her all-pervading merits? Did not the little St. Theresa deserve to be named patroness of the missions? The souls they converted are their children. They are the fruit of their spiritual womb. The living being, when it has reached the peak-point of its development, flowers and bears fruit in testimony to what it has become. It is the same in the spiritual order. The truly great soul will bear souls, and will acquire a double permanence in them. A double permanence, I say, for such a soul will be eternal both in itself and in its work. There can be nothing more fruitful than genuine sanctity. To look on sanctity as sterile and socially worthless, is to rank it lower than the life of the plant. Fruitfulness, though not the essence of greatness, is its hall-mark. The useless contemplative is the creation of ignorance. The great contemplative is the great shaper of history.

The life of vowed virginity in the married state is fruitful in this same way. Of itself it is higher than the more usual married life. But though it be the higher we shall not speak of it in detail, seeing that it is not of really common occurrence in the Church. Our main concern will then be Matrimony in the more usual sense of not implying a vow of virginity.

Were we now asked to define Matrimony in the light of our preceding remarks the definition given would take some form such as the following: a certain mutual donation between man and woman which establishes permanent community of life and interchange of the resources of life, in view of the perfect spiritual development of each, and the generation and education of children as fruit and symbol of that perfect development (cf. III ap. Q29 a2 corp.). The rest of this chapter will consist of an explanation of this definition.

When God made Eve He explained His action: "It is not good for man to be alone." One man, left to himself, can do but little, whether we consider him in the material or in the spiritual order. Progress in the useful arts is due to the combined and successive action of many men. No one man has that grasp of the inner core of material reality which is required to wring all its secrets from it in the course of a single lifetime. So far is it from being possible to do so, that generation after generation has wrestled with the problems of sea and air and ore, and every generation triumphs over difficulties new to its fathers only to be faced by others which they will in their turn pass on for solution to generations yet to be born. And true though this may be for the natural order, is it not still more strikingly true in the order of intellect? The greatest genius of any age is the man who has best developed what his fathers before him left him as legacy. Our most brilliant flashes of thought are disguised memories. Were any man to start with the unaided resources of his intellect and, left entirely alone, endeavour to elaborate a philosophy of life or a system of morality, the result would be humiliating not for himself only, but for all who glory in the name of man. He would find perhaps a few of the more obvious principles, recognize perhaps a few of the more essential laws of morality, but there would be no synthesis, no elaboration, no harmonious structure of thought and judgement. If man has ever risen to this, it is because he has not been too proud to borrow, even when he was too proud to admit that he had done so.

Man being in need of support and help, God gave him a helpmate. The sexes complement one another. This does not mean that man cannot develop himself fully without that special partnership with woman which is known as Matrimony. Man can find in God all that he will find in woman, and far more besides. God alone can be the complement of man. The friendship of Christ is genuine and satisfying; it is not the result of self-delusion. But there is, as well as the way of perfection by union in love with God alone, a way of perfection which consists in the union with God of a man and woman united in love among themselves. This was what God had in view when He created the sexes. Isolated man, necessarily incomplete, could find his completion in a union of love with woman subordinated to union with the Almighty. And Our Saviour gave this union of man and woman its full meaning when He made of it a sacrament. For since the purpose of the union was the perfection of the united, and the perfection of man and woman, in the present order, is something supernatural (we are perfected by grace), the union which would be a condition of perfection must also be something holy, leading as it would to holiness. In other words, it must be a sacrament, sign of a holy state, and cause of the holiness of that state.

Since Matrimony is, therefore, a union in love of man with woman, and since love is essentially a kind of donation, it is important that we have a clear idea of what the donation includes. There is no difficulty about the fact that it includes a transference of rights over the bodies of the married couple. But the sacrament, being an instrument of the spiritual perfection of the man and the woman, includes as well a community of spiritual treasure. There must be a donation of souls as well as of bodies. The husband has first right to a share in the prayers and merits of the wife, just as she has first right to a share in her husband's prayers and merits. They have a right to the pooling of their spiritual outlook, to a communication of ideas, especially of spiritual ideas. That is but one of the ways in which one is the complement of the other. One should be interested in the other's salvation, should be ready with advice, with good example, with patient resignation when nothing else is of avail. It is fundamentally absurd to think that the possibilities of union between man and woman are purely in the order of the flesh. The greatest of all unions is that union of souls of which I am now speaking. Husband and wife are truly one in the highest sense only when their souls are united. The soul of each should be an open book in which the other may learn what is yet hidden of the way of spiritual progress. One has what the other has not. Both stand to gain by mutual trust and generous devotion. They should love one another in truth—love, that is to say, by giving what is worth giving, the goods of the soul.

Since this union between man and woman is a holy, sacramental one, it must needs be permanent. When God joins man and woman together that they may work out their salvation together, it is certainly His intention that their union endure as long as their salvation be still to be accomplished. Nor is permanence anything less a consequence from the fact that the marriage union is destined to complete the insufficiency of the isolated individual. For permanent support is precisely one of man's greatest needs. A man will face almost untold difficulties if he feels that there will be always someone who will understand him and be grateful for what he has done. This holds for spiritual as well as for material difficulties. Spiritual progress costs many a struggle, and it is good to relax from time to time in the company of one who understands. But this need for understanding and support is certainly not met if marriage be something that man can undo. What man needs is a support to which he has a right no matter what be the attitude of purely human powers and forces. In other words he needs indissoluble union of husband and wife, guaranteeing to each help and understanding while life is still to be lived. The very indissolubility of marriage is, therefore, holy, for it is a cause and condition of holiness.

It is common to point to the many failures in marriage as a proof that indissoluble union between man and woman is good for neither. Unfortunately it is only too true that many marriages do seem to fail in their purpose. But the reason for the failure—or at any rate for many of the failures—may be nothing more than a lack of understanding of the great law of human happiness which we enunciated at the beginning of this chapter—that the price of real growth and happiness for man is that he give. Man must give to God in order to save his soul. Husband and wife must be ready to give the one to the other if their married life is to be—as it should be—a condition of life in which salvation will be easier for both than it would have been had they never married. To get out of Matrimony all that is in it, husband and wife must be willing to give to one another all that they have to give. They must give patience, understanding, love; they must be willing to waive their private rights and fads. If both do this then both will gain, because if both give to the limit of their capacities then both will receive to the limit of what is possible. But if, as happens so frequently today, both enter matrimony to receive, then both will give but grudgingly and receive but rarely. When I say that this idea of giving tends to become obscured today, I am saying, too, that the idea of genuine love has been lost as well. Love is disinterested; he who marries for love marries that he may give. If one marries to receive, that is because one loves oneself only. True love is a discipline, something that purifies, that empties one of self. And it is only when one is empty of self that one can be full of God.

There is another reason, too, why so many marriages fail—though it would not be correct to look on this as a reason quite different from the one just given—and it is that so many people today have false ideas regarding the things that are worth having. Married folk, especially when they have a family, find that much of the pleasant things of life are no longer for them. They have no time for cruises, for frequent visits to the cinema and the theatre; they must be home early if they go out for tea; they are expected to be rather reserved in bearing, to refrain from the sports of youth—the list might be continued indefinitely. Marriage becomes a round of "don'ts" and "can'ts." Why not dissolve it and experience life?

It is clear that the modern misunderstanding of the elementary principle that one must give if one will live is at the root of this difficulty also. But there is something more in it as well—ignorance of the things that are worth while. Those who wish to experience life to the full should try to learn that married life is a very full and intense form of life. There is more in the life led fully under the guidance of the grace of the sacrament of Matrimony than there ever will be in tours and cruises and social flutterings. Modern amusements are really an escape from life. By yielding to superficial and fevered impressions and emotions they blind the mind to the fact that genuine experience and intense life is something that must be wrung from one's surroundings. The best things

—the things of the Spirit, which are really the things that are worth while—are hidden deep down beneath the surface of married or single life. They are found by digging beneath life, not by dancing on its surface. The truth of the matter is this, that the most thrilling experience in this world is the friendship of God in Christ, that there is depth of life and genuine satisfaction in full acceptance and understanding of the duty of disinterested love of wife and children. But it is no less true that nothing of all this can be felt except by one who lives it. To those therefore who speak of the boredom of respectability there can be only one answer. Have you ever tried with all the fervour of heart and soul to be respectable? If not, what do you know of what respectability can yield?

In all the works of God there is order, and He has established a certain order of dignity within the matrimonial union no less than in all else He has made: "Let women be subject to their husbands, as to the Lord: Because the husband is the head of the wife, as Christ is the Head of the Church . . ." (Eph. 22–23). Under this respect the grace of the sacrament of matrimony is one which enables the husband to be a worthy head of the family, and the wife to help in loving subjection. But every word of all this is an insult in the ears of emancipated woman. Woman is equal to man, better than man when she gets the chance! Think of the intelligent, highly strung woman subject to the slow unimaginative dealer in soap! . . . Let us take for granted all that may be said on the advisability of finding a partner in life with whom you will live in harmony; but there remains a still more fundamental point—whether or not subjection is shame.

God has made His universe in tiers that the higher may communicate of their being and strength to the lower. There is no shame in accepting from a higher what you need and have not got of yourself. Now there is something that woman needs which she can get from union with man, and the condition of getting it is that she bend down to accept it. A married woman has a sense of security that her unmarried sister cannot have, and her security comes from her being in the care of a husband. Here, once more, we are stating a fact. It is useless to prove it, because it is denied only by those who deny every premiss by which it might be established. The most practical thing to do is to indicate how the opposite belief arises and to show the fundamental error on which it rests.

The belief that woman is equal to man and gets on quite well without him arises automatically where young boys and girls are educated together and mix freely on terms of absolute equality. There is no reason why it should not happen fairly frequently, that in a school where boys and girls are in the same class—and this holds with even more force for universities—there should not be a fair number of girls very nearly as intelligent as the best of the boys and certainly more intelligent than the worst. The same thing will happen in sports, plays, musical societies. At once the sceptical attitude emerges; where is the vaunted superiority of the male? What has not been seen is that under such a system of education male and female never meet as such—except perhaps illicitly. The woman who knows nothing of man except how intelligent he is, or how well he plays tennis, has never met a man at all. Sex is something deeper than diversity in intellectual and physical power, even though it normally manifests itself in such diversity. What is it then? Were we to say that it is just sex and nothing more we should have given the best possible answer, for like every ultimate, sex cannot be defined in terms of anything else. But for the sake of satisfying those who have followed thus far, it may be said to be that in male and female which makes them complementary in the matter of life and experience of life, and which, in consequence, is quite compatible with an inverse order in goods of soul or body. Can there be such a thing? Once more you must turn to him or her who has the genuine experience lived sincerely. Ask the gifted lady graduate how she can be happy with her prosaic husband. The answer can only be that she and he came to the sacrament as woman and man, not as bridge partners, nor a debating team, and that, consequently, both she and he now know life as never before.

The fundamental error on which rests the belief that submission to man is degrading for woman is that rights can be guaranteed only by mistrust and force. In other words, it is based on an extension of the idea of class warfare. Class warfare is the theory that the good of the lower can be attained only by the overthrow of the higher. The only guarantee of rights is a rigid levelling which will destroy radically the power of one to rule over another. Now, it is certainly part of the Christian scheme of things that rights should be guaranteed. The value of the welfare of the classes termed lower is something absolute in the Church's eyes. It is an issue on which the Church may not yield an inch of essential terrain. But the Church, and God in His Church, envisages the welfare of the poor as achieved without strife. The right of the poor to a becoming livelihood should be guaranteed in the first place by the law of Justice and Charity at work in the rich. The Church sees the first guarantee of the rights of the poor in the obligations of the rich. We may go so far as to say that the whole point in being rich is to be able to help the poor; "Make unto you friends of the mammon of iniquity" (Lk. 16, 9). It is God's plan that the poor be cared for by imposing the obligation to provide for them on those who

have money. The attitude of the poor should then be one of
faith in the rich as such, not hatred and mistrust. To teach
them to hate the rich as such is to replace the law of love by
that of the jungle. Now something of the same kind happens
in Matrimony. The wife is bound to be subject; but the husband is bound to care for his wife in love; "Husbands, love
your wives, as Christ also loved the Church, and delivered
Himself up for it; . . ." (Eph. 5, 25). To put the thing in
the most selfish way possible: it is in the interest of the wife
to be subject, because it is only by the channel of subjection to
her husband that she will get the peculiar worth of the sacrament; for the husband is on his side bound to rule the family
for her good, and cannot rule it so if she refuses to have him
at the helm. It is evident of course that she is not asked to be
the slave of man: she is his partner. But where the goods of
Matrimony are concerned she is the junior partner of the
firm, and should accept her condition in love and trust. Her
reward on earth is very great.

The union of man and woman is the sacrament of Matrimony; being a union which leads to the perfection of both it is
necessarily fruitful. Fruitfulness, as we have said, is the sign
and crowning of what is perfect. It is no accident that the
physical act which is most expressive of the oneness of man
and wife should also be that by which their union is normally
blessed with children. This indeed is no accident but a visibly
coherent element in a splendid whole. The marriage act is
something unutterably sacred. It is the expression of the stage
of spiritual growth of the married pair. It is not something
which is allowed them by way of license, but something in
which their spiritual life finds its completion, something
elevated by the sacrament up to the level of sacred mystery,
bond of common holiness, hope of common spiritual fruitful-

ness. The impulse to the marriage act should be the fervent desire to perpetuate the life of grace on earth as it has been lived and relished by husband and wife.

Hence it is that a recent author[1] could state that the noblest element in the virtue of modesty is not the instinct to hide what one is ashamed of, but the quasi-religious instinct to keep a veil over what is sacred. Everything that has to do with the marriage act is made sacred by the grace of Matrimony. The fruit of the act is an immortal soul: the principle of the act is two immortal souls made as it were one. God has thought it all out as a wonderful example of His confidence in man, committing to man the duty of peopling the earth with souls fit for heaven. The success of heaven, we may say, depends on the success of Matrimony. God must have given and all-conquering power to our humano-divine love, seeing that He confided to it so formidable a task!

There is always a lurking suspicion that the person who speaks of children as being the fruit and sign of the perfection of their parents is indulging in fanciful metaphor as long as nothing more than the mere generation of the child is considered (though the suspicion is unfounded even then, as a little reflection will show). But the moment we observe that the child is the fruit of its parents more by education than by generation we see that what appeared to be metaphor is simple fact. The child is the fruit of the souls of its parents more even than of their bodies: the whole reason of its being the fruit of their bodies is that there may be no doubt as to the souls whose privilege it will be to mould and form it. And it is most of all in the moulding and formation of their children that parents give evidence of their own spiritual matu-

[1] cf. *Love, Marriage, and Chastity*, by Fr. Mersch S. J., Sheed & Ward, p. 53.

rity, and ensure for themselves and all that they stand for that permanence which we said was one of the ends of generation.

St. Thomas explains this when he tells us quite simply; "Education is the end of procreation" (Suppl. Q49 a2 adI). The husband and wife who have come together in the union of Holy Matrimony have learned the meaning of God and life, the one from the other, and the one with the other. They have now reached spiritual maturity—not that there is nothing more to learn, nothing more to experience, but that they have pulsed together with the thrill of a life that was real though they had not known and could not know the thrill of all real life. They have now a treasure which by a natural impulse they tend to communicate. They tend to radiate life: life of the body, for they are man and woman, life of the soul, for they are husband and wife. Their urge to communicate is then far from exhausted by the generation of children. They have more to communicate than life of the body, for they are rich in life of the soul as well. The personal education of their children is consequently their right. They will live in their children. Their children will learn of them what life is. Their children, growing within the framework of the parents' synthesis, will be the parents' guarantee of the validity of all they hold worth while. The parents will feel that they are makers of destinies, shapers of the world, co-workers with the Almighty. They will have achieved souls—what greater proof of their own right to endure and of their title to immortality? And the father will live in his son and the mother in her daughter when son and daughter will one day in their turn announce the worth of the truth and beauty that their parents had claimed undying.

Unfortunately there are parents whose aim appears to be to confide their children as soon as possible to nurses and after that to pack them off at the earliest opportunity to a boarding school. It is usual to tax such parents with laziness and neglect, and this is right. But it is far more to the point to tax them with sheer ignorance, because the parent who neglects to train his or her child simply flings away the greatest opportunity that will ever be offered of doing something really worth while. If parents have convictions, even if they be but purely natural ones, they need to be particularly blind and insensible not to see the appropriateness, and feel the urge, of making them the convictions of their children also. To have a child is to have the most tangible of all opportunities of perpetuating one's own personality. Parents are supposed to be mature enough to know what life really is. They should feel the urge to bear the fruit of this maturity. They will bear it by educating their children, by being solicitous with regard to their outlook, by encouraging their virtues by rooting out their vices. All this is the work of a grown person and the most evident proof of the "grown-ness" of the person who performs it. There is one experience which is altogether unique in this world, and that is the experience of the parent who sees a child stand up, as it were spontaneously, for what a parent values, and knows beyond all shadow of doubt that the child does so because of the manner of the education for which the parent was, under God, responsible. Is it a trifling thing to hear a child say its prayers as prayers should be said, and to know that that is your doing; to see it receive its King and know that you brought it to the altar? Are such things as these but trifling recompense for missed parties and impossible cruises? Once more must it be said that only the true parent is qualified to reply, and such a parent can give but one answer.

It was necessary to uphold unswervingly the father's right

to first place in the family even while showing that the mother suffered no injustice thereby. But over and above the fact that she suffers no injustice, it is to be noted that precisely in this matter of the education of children mothers have one of the greatest compensations for whatever may be hard in their lot. It is normally the mother rather than the father who can relive best in the children. The reason for this is that the actual education of the children falls usually more upon the mother than the father, and, if we speak of early education, is almost exclusively a matter for the mother. Ultimately the responsibility for the education of the children is the father's. But it is usually impossible for him to take charge of it himself. He is forced, as it were, to leave it in the mother's hands. It is usually the mother who teaches the children how to say their prayers, who notices their failings, who prompts them to do good. It follows necessarily, therefore, that it is most of all the mother who will relive in them. Of course mother and father are supposed to be one in souls as well as in body, so that the life of the mother in the child is the life of the father as well. But there is clearly something more intimate in the relationship which education sets up between child and mother than between child and father, while the child is young at any rate, with the result that the mother's reward on earth is proportionately greater, in the measure in which her position is less exalted.

Matrimony is therefore a sacrament not of a moment but of a lifetime. Its reception is something that passes; its grace, and obligations, and rewards, remain. The grace of the sacrament has as precise end that there may be a life of union of soul and body between husband and wife, that they may be the one united with the other in view of their union with

God by grace, and they may bear the fruit of their union in God in children who will be worthy of their Father in Heaven. It was pointed out in the opening chapter that life is a quest of God. We saw subsequently that God is found by grace and that grace is given by the sacraments. Matrimony is, therefore, a way of finding God. Marriage will be all it can be only if those who enter upon it do so in order that they may be more closely united to God than would be possible for them were they to remain in the world. People do not marry and then try to save their souls in the married life. They marry that they may save their souls. Salvation is not an accessory to Matrimony; it is its whole point. A newly married couple should find that Matrimony should make them more appreciative of the sacraments than ever before, for it should lead, by the fact that there are now two interested in the salvation of each, to a deeper appreciation of the mystery of grace and a more burning thirst to drink of the founts of grace. A husband or a wife who does not consider it the first duty to excite the other partner to love of God has no idea of what Matrimony means. Yet, how common it is to find wives who give their husbands no rest from their importunate suggestions of how to get promotion or how to cut a successful social figure, and never think it their place to hint that the last Mass on Sunday and reception of the sacraments at very wide intervals is less than they could both do if they really tried. Are there not parents, too, who feel the bitterest shame if their children do poorly in a school examination, but look on their ignorance of the truths of their faith as something which is not so much the fault of the family as of teachers and priests? Shame and confusion should fill the soul of a parent who finds that his child knows more about film-stars than about God. What is the family for, if not that the parents may have an opportunity of doing something worth while by sanctifying themselves and their children? [1]

It would be inexcusable to close even so brief a treatment as this of the sacrament of Matrimony without mention of the Holy Family. In the Holy Family the Catholic husband and wife will find the model of what they should be and do: the model of union between spouses, and of fruit in children.

Mary and Joseph lived together only that each might live the more intimately with God. They were two souls, searching hand in hand for God, who might have been two souls searching for Him unaided, but selected rather to find Him together. Mary must have been an ineffable lesson to Joseph, and I think that Joseph cannot but have been the occasion, at least, of progress to Mary. They must have prayed together when the day's work was over, the one suggesting to the other what should be the object of their prayer and what its form. When Joseph was tired, and sheer fatigue and disappointment, perhaps, cast some slight shadow on the brightness of his vision of God within him, Mary would have noticed that for the moment God was not all to him that He had been, and her gentle comfort would draw Joseph out of himself to her in love of her, and out of her and himself to God in love of God. Two seers they were that spoke to each other of the vision of the Eternal Beauty; two runners they were, that ran to God with words of strength and encouragement on the lips of each; two lovers they were, that loved one another only because each was a temple where they could love God too; two human beings, they, that did what man and wife will do while grace is strong.

[1] The family Rosary is a most efficacious means of making the family a principle of spiritual growth for its members.

Mary and Joseph are models to parents also in their Child. Joseph was not father of Jesus according to the flesh. But it were foolishness to think that on that account something was lacking to the perfection of the bond between Joseph and Mary. Their marriage was a true and complete one, and it was fruitful, too, to both, not by the generation of the Son of God but by His education. A staggering truth, that! Mary and Joseph educated Jesus, and in that they are models to all parents. Parents are to educate their children as Mary and Joseph educated Jesus! Jesus was truly educated by His parents, for they assumed during His early years the direction of His acquisition of experimental knowledge. Though He knew all things, He willed, too, to learn all things, and it was the duty of Mary and Joseph to take charge of Him in the fulfillment of this Will. They must have undertaken it with extraordinary reverence—to educate the Incarnate Word! Reverence should mark the attitude of every Christian parent in regard to a child, for the child is called to be a second Christ. To educate a child is to endeavour to mould the mind of the Son of God. He is within the child, seeking expression in him. The parent has as much power to determine the extent to which Jesus will live in his child as Joseph and Mary had to determine the purely human mind of Jesus. The vital importance of the place of the education of the child in the plan of Matrimony can hardly be more strikingly manifested than in this union of Mary and Joseph, which was a genuine matrimonial bond, but in which the Child appears as to be educated, not as to be generated. Generation without education is a small thing: education without generation is of itself complete.

"This is a great sacrament; but I speak in Christ and in the Church" (Eph. 5, 32). The great St. Paul, inspired by the

Holy Ghost, spoke of Matrimony. And since it was God Who spoke through him, he spoke of Matrimony as it is in its highest essence—as a descent of God and the life of God on earth, rather than as a toilsome ascent of man and the life of man to God. Our treatment has been more humble. We have begun with the lowest in Matrimony, its natural basis, and worked slowly up to what was higher, its spiritual significance. St. Paul's words come then as crown to all that has been said so far. They are the full glory of marriage seen in the mystery of its Author.

The words we have just quoted from the Epistle to the Ephesians are preceded immediately by the verse: "For this cause shall a man leave his father and mother and shall cleave to his wife, and they shall be two in one flesh." Then come the striking words: "This is a great sacrament [that is to say, a great mystery]; but I speak in Christ and in the Church." What exactly is the mystery? The answer is evident from the close sequence of the two verses. The great mystery is that a man should leave father and mother and cleave to a wife, but its greatness consists precisely in its being a figure of what Our Saviour did. For Our Saviour left, we may say, Father and Mother, and took to Himself a spouse to whom He is indissolubly united. He left His Father, when taking flesh He came on earth. He left His Father, while still, it is true, remaining one with Him. But one may speak of His really leaving Him; for in the eyes of the world the invisible unity of Father and Son was overshadowed by the visible distinction of Incarnate Word and Eternal Father. He left Mother also. He was born of the Jews and therefore born into the synagogue. But He left this Mother to win for Himself a glorious spouse, the Church, who, unlike the synagogue, He could present to Himself, unwrinkled and unspotted. On the Cross He left His own Mother Mary for a time, as well. "Mother," He said, indicating St. John, "Behold thy son," for the Son born of her womb was about to die. And His death was the price of His spouse, the Church. So, leaving Father and Mother, He took to Himself the Church as spouse. And He and the Church became two in one flesh; for the Church is His Mystical Body. That is the ideal of marriage; Christ cleaving to His Church, Christ in union of life with His Church, Christ fruitful in His Church.

It is usual to point to certain details in which the parallel between the union of Christ with His Church and the union of husband with wife can be clearly seen. The union of Christ with the Church results in the sanctification of the Church; in the same way the union of husband and wife is in view of the sanctification of both. The union of Christ with the Church is fruitful in bringing souls to eternal life; the married state is one which issues normally in children rich in the life of grace. The union of Christ with His Church will never be broken as was the union of the synagogue with the God of Israel; husband and wife are indissolubly united. Finally, it is noted that Christ has but one spouse, the one true Church; in the same way the love of the husband is to be consecrated entirely to one wife.

These points embrace the main individual manifestations of the mystery of Christ and His Church in the sacrament of Matrimony. But one cannot conclude better than by insisting that what is still more fundamental than any individual point is the great central reality that the union of husband and wife is the Mystery of the union of Christ and the Church working itself out in two human lives. Matrimony is not just something that resembles the union of Christ and His Church in certain respects; it is the union of Christ and His Church in one of its most sublime realizations. Husband and wife united in Matrimony mean nothing more than Christ united to His Church in a certain way. Their marriage had no meaning therefore except that it was a new capture of their souls in the bonds of the love of their King and Spouse. Two souls enter the married state not so much that they may be the spouses the one of the other as that both may be spouses of Christ. And so, the point of Matrimony for them in their individual lives is that it enables them to learn in their love for one another what should be their love for Him Who is the true Spouse of souls. The mystery of the Mystical Body shades over for them into the mystery of the Bride and the Bridegroom: one mystery, it is true, but with a nuance of tenderness and self-oblation. And they and God are caught up into a new oneness. And they know themselves in the words of St. John: "And I . . . saw the holy city, the new Jerusalem, coming down out of heaven from God, prepared as a bride adorned for her husband. And I heard a great voice from the throne, saying: Behold the tabernacle of God with men, and He will dwell with them. And they shall be His people; and God Himself with them shall be their God." (Apoc. 21, 2-3).

14

THE SACRAMENT OF EXTREME UNCTION

". . . bound up his wounds, pouring in oil and wine."
(LK. 10, 34)

WE HAD OCCASION to refer in an earlier chapter to the idea of integral Christianity, which was described there as being the subjection of the whole man to the whole truth, or, better still, as the subjection of the whole man to the Whole Truth, Jesus Christ, Incarnate Truth. Something remained implicit in this description which must now be exposed. It is that there is such a thing as the whole man, and that sanctification is a matter for the whole man. The present moment is very opportune for doing this, since the sacrament of Extreme Unction is nothing more than the last attempt of God in His Church to effect the sanctification of the whole man through the harmony of the parts of man. And being the last, it is in some way the most striking. We see in it as nowhere else— except perhaps in the ritual which precedes the administration of Baptism—the embodied truth of the possibility of soul made holy by flesh, and of flesh made immortal by soul.

There is no more appropriate note than this upon which to close a treatment of the sacraments. Its appropriateness explains why, even at the risk of becoming tedious, we return once more to an idea elaborated in the second chapter, and touched upon once more at the beginning of the chapter on the priesthood. But its appropriateness is something more than a matter of intellectual harmony and fitness. It is appropriate for the soul, too, that it become the captive of the idea of the whole universe as a possibility of its sanctification. This idea is nothing more than the bare truth. It is a fact that nothing ever enters into contact with a soul—and more especially with a soul in the state of grace—which has not within it a God-given power of sanctifying. God does not make as man does. There is no material over which man has such control that he can make out of it something in which the perfection of the whole will be compatible with the perfection of each of the parts. Man can work passably for one end, less passably for two or three. But no man can work in such a way that not only will the end be end, but the means will be ends too in their own right; work that is to say with materials of which each component part will have its own inviolability, rendering it a crime and a moral impossibility to sacrifice in the slightest way the most insignificant of details even in view of a greater harmony in the whole. That is the way in which God works in the world of souls. There is an end in that world—the glory of God in His Christ—and to that end each soul is but a means. But each soul is an end as well. For to each soul is subjected all that is below it, whether animal or bird or plant. And each soul is equated to every other soul, in such wise that none may be sacrificed for another, and the full and perfect development of any one and of all is not only compatible with, but is conducive to, the full and perfect development of any other and of all others. To think that God made all things for me alone is not to bid my soul batten on pastures of common right. God has made the world for me alone, and for each and every other individual alone as well. He has made a world in which essential interests cannot clash. We cannot make such a world—I wonder do we ever try, even?—nor can we easily conceive of it. But to be God, to be Harmony and Omniscience, is to have this power. And to be a soul with a capacity for the divine is to have need of a Maker Who can fashion a world of the kind.

The institution of sacraments in which things and words of earth become official channels of grace is a mental preparation for the acceptance by faith of the wider truth that the whole world is in a manner sacramental—that is to say, that the whole world is a sign of the sanctifying will of God in our regard, and that it is as well the channel of this will. But not least among the things of this world which impact upon the soul is the body of man. The body therefore must have, no less than things farther removed from the soul, an altogether essential role to fill in the drama of human holiness. Holiness cannot be a thing of soul alone, as clearly it cannot be a matter of body alone. It must be a matter of soul and body, of soul through body—terminating wonderfully, in the life of glory, in superabounding holiness of body coming to it from soul.

This is the point of those ceremonies anterior to the Baptism proper in which the organs of the various senses and the members are signed with the sign of the Cross. The Christian about to enter upon the way of Christianity needs a special holiness of body because his body is about to be called to the function of instrument and partner of a divinized soul. The very administration of the sacrament is an example of soul sanctified through body. It is through the washing of the body that the soul is made clean. Similarly it is through the anointing of the body that the soul is strengthened in Confirmation, through the nourishing of the body that the soul is nourished in Holy Communion, and so on through all the sacraments. The body becomes in very truth a temple of the

Holy Ghost. He resides somehow in the body; not just in the soul, but in the body as well. Every bodily action is capable of an eternal signification, every bodily contact can be the channel of an infusion of the divine. This is life, sacramental to the utmost, and life as God has made it and means it to be lived. In the quest for God the body is the hands of the soul. And this cannot be otherwise since God became Incarnate and the Will of God first appeared in forms of earth.

But though the union of soul with body be a means to the spiritual perfection of the whole man, this union will cease to be. Man is not made for death, but man will certainly die. His body is such that of its whole being it tends to dissolution. His soul is such that with its native powers it cannot retain beyond a certain space of time its slender hold on flesh and blood. The soul is of itself eternal. But it cannot communicate its eternity to a body. It can shape a body out of the formless mass of primal matter for a while and then, as it were exhausted, its power declines, and the body it formed, and loved, and even needed, is torn from it. The soul emerges from this ordeal incomplete. It is the lowest of spirits, not so far above matter as to be altogether independent of it; and even when quickened by grace, even when enraptured by the vision of the Three in One, it retains its capacity for union with the material, and demands that union as the final complement of its bliss. It is only when we find ourselves in danger of death that we see how the soul cries out with its whole being for the body. What dread and anguish when one seems to be caught inescapably in the whirlpool of some accident. There is no sigh of relief that at last there will be an end to the period of the soul's imprisonment in flesh, no wild leap of joy such as would be did the soul bound, even before it is forced to do so, into the clear air of incorporeal felicity. There is but pain, but shrinking and dread. And could it be otherwise when even the soul caught up in glory retains that love for the body which is the meaning and cause of the final resurrection?

The soul is made for the body and yet must lose it. The soul is sanctified through the body. There can be no doubt therefore that that final moment when the soul will be separated from the body, the instrument of its sanctification, will be of supreme moment for spiritual growth or ruin. The moment of death strikes at the very principle of our holiness —soul made holy by body. After death there can be no more growth in holiness. Death itself is the last instant of growth; and because it is one which strikes at the foundation of human spirituality it called for a special sacrament to make it fruitful. The sacraments stand at all the cross-roads of life. Where can they be more necessary than there where life, as we know it, melts into death, and death, as we can see it, is the prelude to a life beyond our imagining or a death beyond our wildest fear? There needed to be a sacrament to mark the end of the whole sacramental system. Death removes the soul beyond the power of this world—except in so far as prayer can reach it. It has no longer a hand to catch God in the things that pass, for now no things will pass. Its last outstretched pleading will be answered by the anointing of Extreme Unction— and then it goes to face God in immutable fixity of look, or to turn for ever from the Face it refused to recognize when It walked the streets and lanes of earth. At such a moment there must be a new sacrament—one that will be at once our last sanctification and our strength to face the great parting. Or let us be still more precise and say that there must be a sacrament which will be our last sanctification precisely in being the strength to face the great parting. For if our union of soul and body is a fount of grace, our separation of soul and body is the last draught we shall drink thereat, and we have need of vigilance and calm that this final opportunity be not squandered.

There is therefore an immense power of sanctification in death. Death is the moment when the alternative, Will the body debase the soul or will the soul elevate the body? is faced for the last time. This is the great alternative of life too. The body is the instrument of the soul; it was made for the use of the soul. But its demands are more insistent than those of the soul, and the human person is dragged, sometimes even half unwillingly, but never wholly unwillingly, to side with the body against the soul, and to thrust what is god-like in him down to the level of what is clay. The alternative comes with biting clearness at the moment of death. Will the body drag the soul to hell, or will the soul lift the body up to a share in glory? And the answer each man will make depends on how he will use his God-given body at the moment of death. Should he regard it and all it stands for as of ultimate worth, he will lose everything; should he throw it away gladly, rejoicing that even at that supreme moment there is some gift he can make to God in expression of his love, he will save all—even the body, which will be his again when the angel sounds the great trumpet. And even while this choice is as yet to be made, the soul is united to the body and to little else—in fact to nothing else, for what remains the object of vision of the glazed eye, what is felt by the blue cold fingers? The soul must make a choice such as it never made before, and there will be but one place where it will find God and light—in the body which it is called to renounce.

That is why Extreme Unction is an anointing of the body and its senses. At the moment of death the body is called to be the channel of the divinity as on no previous occasion. The body needs to be purified that it may be worthy. It does not need to be purified precisely in so far as it is a body, a three dimensional thing. It needs to be purified in that part of it which can bring us near to, or withdraw us from, God—that is to say in the senses and the principal members. For the senses are called on to see and hear and taste and feel God as never before: to see Him in a sightless eye, to hear Him in a muffled throb, to taste Him with parched lips, to feel Him with nerveless hands. They need a special purification that they may rise to the level of their last great task. They have become the only channel by which God may come to the soul through a thing of this world; and that is the only way by which He has determined to come, right up to the moment when the world will be no more for the soul. There is an amazing oneness and consequence, a startling though tender logic in the approach of God to the soul. There are alternatives in His way of coming, but they are nothing more than forms of one invariable method. And here at the last most solemn moment, when the soul is about to be shorn of the body, God approaches by what may be termed method without form: approach in what appeals to the body is replaced in the final test by approach through the body itself.

From this it follows that the sacrament of Extreme Unction is not a sacrament of the dead in the sense in which this may be said of Baptism and Penance. Its primary object is not the remission of sin at all. It forgives sin only when it finds unforgiven sin of which the now repentant sinner is unaware, or known sin for which he has at least general attrition. What Extreme Unction does primarily is to cleanse the soul from the remains of sin, that is to say, from that spiritual weakness or debility which remains over in our souls as the result of actual sins, even after these sins have been forgiven. Actual sin is forgiven regularly as to its guilt and eternal punishment by the sacrament of Penance. But Penance does not wipe out that physical contamination of the body, by which having once been the servant of free and deliberate sin, it becomes less fit to be the channel of God's coming to the soul. If the senses sin they become fit to see or feel or hear sin. A man who has frequently sinned with his eyes will find enticement to sin in objects that are at the worst indifferent for other men. Even when the guilt of his sins of sight will have been washed away, this corporeal, or physical, tendency to sin will remain. It will no be easy for him to see God in His creation. And how will he see God with the glazed eye of the dying? Every vague form, every shapeless mass, will be an invitation to sin or a thrust towards despair. That is what is meant by the remains of sin that must be wiped out by Extreme Unction. Its grace gives a special power to overcome the earth-bearing tendency of a body that has consorted freely with earth. Its grace is a purifying grace, making the body more fit to serve the soul and now most of all, when the soul stands in greatest need of a God-like and disciplined body.

Every spiritual purgation at the same time unites the soul with God and illumines it with His brightness. The distinction between purgative, illuminative, and unitive is more a distinction of aspects of a single process, than of stages in a triple process. And the fact that at one time one aspect, at another time another aspect, will be more in evidence is no reason for understanding the distinction otherwise than as we have done. The sanctification of the soul by the grace of Extreme Unction is a single spiritual process. We have noted its purgative aspect. But there are two other aspects as well. It is illuminative and unitive also. These two aspects are fundamental to any correct understanding of the sacrament.

With regard to the illuminative aspect, it is easy to conclude from what has so far been said, that the whole reason
of the purgation of the senses in this sacrament is that they
may be fitted to see God in the greatest of all physical purga-
tions, that namely in which the body is torn from the soul's
grasp. This is equivalent to stating that the vision of God
achieved during life in mortification is intended to reach its
climax in death, the exemplar of all mortification. It is a fact
that God is to be found in the cross as nowhere else. What
the reason may be is no concern of the present moment; it is
enough for us that the fact be indisputable. From the moment
when God Incarnate mounted the Throne of the Cross to
draw therefrom all men to Himself, it is on the cross that all
men must find Him. He is most present to us in a world of
pain, a world of disappointment: a world of pleasure, a world
of realized ambitions is a world that feigns to explain itself,
and to have no need of the explanation of a suffering Saviour
Who wills to mould us to His Own Image and likeness. And
this being a fact, is it strange that the greatest revelation of
God must necessarily be that unveiling of His face when the
fabric of the body is rent in twain and He is first half-
glimpsed behind it, giving meaning to our anguish? Does
not this explain why it is that the grace of final perseverance,
that is to say the grace of dying in the state of grace, is
something that cannot be merited? To die in the state of grace
is to accept the vision of God in the pain of the greatest of all
crosses—greatest, that is to say, not just that it is greater than
any other, but that it is the type and exemplar of all others, in
that it is *the* supreme human cross and no other cross is hard
except in that it is a foretaste of death. To have accepted the
vision of God in trials no matter how severe is no adequate
preparation for His vision at our last dread hour. Trials of
life are but shadows: death is their great reality. Crosses of

life are not foretastes of death: they are but faint copies. Death is unique, inimitable. We come to death as to the unknown; to seek to know death in the experience of any other pain, no matter how great, is to ask the secret of the thunder of the raging sea from the fretful wisp of spray that falls lifeless at one's feet far inland. The sorrows of life are but the spray tossed from the ocean of the grief of death; and one's first view of that mighty ocean, bursting on eyes that have rested a lifetime on meadows and flowing streams, cannot but be terrifying, cannot but wring a gasp even from the soul supported by grace.

To see God in death is unique among the phenomena of spiritual illumination. To be united to Him in death by grace is also unique. The grace of union with God at the moment of death is entirely gratuitous. We have seen why this must be so, if we understand death as it normally is, a gradual passing, by way of sickness from this world to the next. (It is clear that what we have just said does not claim to explain why every grace of a happy death, even if death be painless and unexpected, must be something gratuitous; that is but an aspect of the mystery of gratuitous predestination.) If then the grace of a happy death be something *sui generis*, the union produced by that grace must be similar in character. It is a union with God which is immediately preparatory for union with Him in the face to face vision of glory. It is a union which is a preparation for the greatest of all unions. And now we see once more why the primary reason of the sacrament must be not the forgiveness of sin, but something higher, something more subtle and refined. The preparation for the greatest of unions must be the removal of the last and most subtle of obstacles. Sin is not an obstacle of this kind. Sin is crudest ungodliness. What is subtle is the trace of forgiven sin, the earthiness that remains as sin's legacy, creaturehood that tends to contentment with the creature. This is the last obstacle to union with God, and must therefore be the object of the last sacraments.

There is another reason too why Extreme Unction considered under its unitive aspect should involve a purification of the bodily. It is that its purpose is not merely union of the soul with God in the moment of death, but union of the soul with God in Glory, and union of the body with Him too through the body's sharing in the soul's bliss. It is a great thing that a body should be called to be the partner of a soul vivified by grace. That is why the body is anointed before Baptism. But it is greater still that the body should be called to be the partner of a soul wrapt in the clear vision of the Divine Essence. The body will need a thorough reformation in order to be worthy of its beatified soul. It is true that this worthiness comes to it through the preternatural gifts which God will confer on it when it rises glorious from the tomb on the last day. But it is in the wise designs of God that man should progress even on earth up to the very threshold of glory. The grace of the soul in glory will be no more than was the grace of the same soul on earth. And if the body in glory will have an utter unworldiness, it is the mind of God that that unworldiness be achieved, by way of disposition, here on earth also. Extreme Unction does that. It gives to the soul the power to spiritualize the body through the supreme cross of death. The price of a glorified body is the sacrifice of the body of flesh, and this sacrifice is made as it should by that soul only that is utterly free from the clinging earthiness of past sin. There is a wonderful unity in this sacrament. Every aspect dovetails into every other. It is unitive through purgation, purgative by illumination. It purifies the body by strengthening the soul. It purifies the body that it may unite the soul to God and the body to the soul in the bliss of glory. Every aspect is but an aspect. The reality is one— the whole man finding the Lord by the way of the cross of death.

Where will the soul find the strength to bear this final cross? In Faith, and Hope, and Love. Faith shows the value and meaning of the cross. Hope, that virtue whose formal motive is the Divine Omnipotence, gives us some little of the strength of God, and of the strength of the dying God-man. Love makes the cross light to bear; to love is either not to suffer or to love one's suffering. St. Thomas single out Hope as being in a special way the fruit of the sacrament. Hope is the attitude of the soul that is faced with an evil which it can overcome. Death is an evil, the greatest of all purely human evils. It is not an easy thing to face death. And to face a death fraught with eternal possibilities is something harder still. That needs superhuman strength, divine strength. Hope in the face of this death comes from the possession of the God of all Power within one's soul. God is within the dying Christian. He has come to him by the way of the sacraments, and for the last and definitive time by the way of the last Sacrament. He is there with His Omnipotence, and with that Mercy too which makes Him lavish in the use of Omnipotence. There is no room left for dread or shrinking. Hope will arise, humble and contrite Hope, that is no less confident and exultant Hope. To die in the Lord is to die in Hope. It is to have achieved what was for man utterly impossible, and to know that the achievement was the work of One greater than man.

The oil of Extreme Unction is the oil of Hope. It is gentle and soothing; it is strengthening. It penetrates the tissues of the body to symbolize the penetrative power of its grace. Nothing that is weak and human will escape its healing touch. It will strengthen the last weakness of the spiritual athlete, the languor and sluggishness left by forgiven sin. And Hope will be perfect, and Strength will pervade weakness.

It is good to give sensible body to these thoughts by the remembrance of the ideally happy death of the great St. Joseph. His death was made light by the presence at his side of Christ the Power of God, and Mary, symbol of the Mercy of God. The Author of grace and the Mother of Compassion were near him. They were at his side, not just as thoughts are near us, but as living beings are. We die in the same conditions. We are strengthened in Hope, not merely by the thought of Jesus and Mary, but by the physical presence of Jesus and Mary. Their presence is perceptible only to the eye of Faith and Love—and Faith and Love are surely the best companions of Hope—but that does not mean to say that their presence is not real. It is real and fruitful. Our Lord is the Crucified and Mary is the Mother of Sorrows. If we miss their presence in the cross of death, death is nothing more than horror. To see God in the trial of death is to see God in Jesus and Mary. Death, as death now is, is meaningless without them. God could not allow us to die if they were not present to give death its worth.

Yet, though Jesus and Mary be at the bed-side of the dying, and though the dying man has a vision of them such as he has never had before, it is but human to think of the unshared loneliness of death. One dies alone. The eyes fail. Voices grow indistinct. It is no longer possible even to feel the hand that presses. Friends and loved ones are there— but they are cut off from the dying man and he from them.

But these are human thoughts; they are true of only half the reality. They are more true of the bystanders than of him who dies. The bystanders are cut off from the dying man, but he is close to God. They feel with the stab of clear perception, that he is going *from* them. He feels that he is going *to* God. He is alone in this world because he is now more with God than man, and God is not of this world. Yet the faithful of the world draw as near as they may, for they know that though God be at the door of the soul He may yet be refused entry. So they pray. There is no gate into the soul open to them but the gate of prayer. Exhortations remain unheard. The Church is with them at that moment. She brings her greatest treasure with her, a sacrament. And for the only time in the whole range of sacramental sanctification, does the Church too come to the soul with words of petition on her lips: "By this holy anointing and by His own most tender mercy may the Lord forgive thee whatever thou hast sinned by thy eyes . . ." The Church senses that the soul before her is about to pass from the tribunal of the Mystical Body to that of the King of Glory. And though she still has power of conferring grace and of loosing and binding, even in regard to the dying, the dread solemnity of the moment makes her plead when she could with reason command. The bystanders are lonely and the Church is lonely too. She can yet touch the soul sacramentally, but she senses the peculiar worth of the way of prayer.

The loneliness of the bystanders is the price they must pay that the dying man may have his horizon peopled with the angels and the saints. Their loneliness forces them to their knees, and it is on their knees that they can be of most help to the dying. God alone can act immediately on the dying man. The prayers of friends will move God to be merciful to him. They are as yet in the world of faith and their faith moves them to prayer. He is on the brink of vision, and his vision will be assured by the prayer of their faith. Even for those who remain there will be a kind of vision. They will have seen in the dying man the nothingness of all that is not God. His death is for himself a vision of God; for his friends it is a vision of this world, the truest they will ever have.

Sacrament differs from sacrament in dignity. It is possible to establish a certain sacramental hierarchy with the Blessed Eucharist as the crown and end of all others. Without discussing the order of all the sacraments relatively to one another, it may be noted with St. Thomas that Extreme Unction is of greater perfection, though of less necessity, than Penance. It is possible to conceive of a sinful world, such as the present one is, without a sacrament of Extreme Unction. But it is hard to conceive of it without Penance. And he develops his point by indicating an analogy between the relationship in which Extreme Unction stands to Penance and that in which Confirmation stands to Baptism. Confirmation brings to perfection the grace infused at Baptism. By Baptism we are made children of God: by Confirmation we become men in His service. Now something similar takes place when we receive Extreme Unction. Its effect is to perfect the work of the sacrament of Penance. And this it does in two ways.

Penance is the sacrament of forgiveness of actual sin. But forgiven sin remains on in the soul in the form of spiritual weakness. In removing this weakness Extreme Unction perfects what the sacrament of Penance had left unfinished.

There is as well another way in which it perfects the work of Penance. We saw that the permanent effect of the sacrament of Penance was the spirit of penance, or what spiritual writers term as well, the spirit of compunction. This spirit is the conviction of past sin. But there is something that may be added to this even though it be necessarily connected with it—and that is the conviction of present weakness. That is the peculiar fruit of Extreme Unction. In terming it the peculiar fruit of Extreme Unction, I do not mean to imply that the spirit of penance contains nothing at all of the idea of a conviction of present weakness. The contrary has been stated with sufficient clearness in the chapter on the sacrament of Penance. What is meant is that the immediate effect of Penance is a spirit of sorrow for past sin whatever else may follow, whereas the immediate effect of Extreme Unction is a conviction of present weakness. Extreme Unction is more immediately concerned with the effects of sin than Penance is. Penance is concerned first of all with sin itself.

From this there follows the fundamental conclusion: the dying man will appear before God penetrated with a conviction of his utter nothingness. He will appear before God knowing himself as he really is. He will appear before God a sinner—a forgiven sinner, it is true, but a sinner, marked with the healed scars of his sins. And this is the whole of Christianity in so far as Christianity means a state of the individual. Christianity is not just the life of grace: neither is it just forgiveness of sin. It is the life of forgiving grace, and the life of vivifying forgiveness. The true Christian is the Christian as he is when he is ready to meet God. He is prepared for this meeting by a sacrament which is a confession of weakness—but weakness strengthened by the oil of the Divine. That is the term of his quest of God.

CONCLUSION

"He sent His word, and healed them: and delivered them from their destructions."

(PS. 106, 20)

IT IS ALWAYS WELL to review a new series of ideas when one has reached their term, and endeavour to seize them all, with their varied tints and ripples of light and shade, in one comprehensive sweep of the mind's eye. Perhaps nowhere is this need felt more than in spiritual matters. For the mind has some unconscious conviction that the spiritual, like God its Author, must be simple and all of one piece, and passes with a sense of disappointment from any presentation of spirituality which ends on the note of multiplicity of parts. There has necessarily been a great deal of analysis in this brief book. To synthetize what we have so laboriously taken asunder would demand another of equal proportions. But there is a far better synthesis than any we could attempt: that namely which the Holy Ghost effects in our minds through His gifts, taking the scattered ideas that lie in cumbersome profusion in our minds, heating them in the fire of His charity, and welding them into an affective rather than a mental oneness, where they will all light up the soul with the same bright shining love. This is the synthesis which our souls do really need; and it comes not by study but by prayer.

It is, however, not impossible to give some inadequate idea of the central theme of the preceding chapters—not indeed in order to dispense with the work of the Holy Ghost, but rather to prepare the way for Him and to excite in souls the desire of His coming. And we are fortunate in that St. Thomas has already done so in his prologue to the fourth book of the Commentary on the Sentences. We can do no better than to borrow his ideas and lend them words of our own.

By the sin of Adam the human race incurred death and infirmity: spiritual death, through separation from the Fount of all life; spiritual infirmity, through the loss of grace, which was the perfection and beauty of the soul. To restore man under these two heads the Eternal Word intervened. The Word of God, being Eternal Wisdom, is the fount of all life (cf. Eccl. 7, 13) and hence can restore the life of fallen man. Being as well the Power of God—"By the *word* of God the heavens were established; and all the power of them by the spirit of His mouth" (Ps. 32, 6)—He can strengthen our infirmity and support our weakness.

"But the word of God is living and effectual, and more piercing than any two-edged sword" (Hebr. 4, 12). Hence it was fitting, in view of the weakness of human nature, that the Word should not come to our aid in the full splendour of His glory and might of His power, but that He should heal our ills by assuming to Himself a nature, weak and infirm like ours in everything but in sin. And so the Word was made flesh and dwelt amongst us, and moved among men healing them of their ills, restoring to them the life of grace, for "Virtue went out from Him and healed all" (Lk. 6, 19). God, in truth, sent His Word Incarnate and healed mankind through Him and delivered them from the destruction of their sin (cf. Ps. 106, 20).

The Incarnate Word of God is therefore the great Physician of our souls. Coming to heal us He made His Sacraments as it were "sweet confections . . . and ointments of health" (Eccl. 38, 7) by which His healing power would be communicated to mankind till the end of time: "The Most High hath created medicines out of the earth" for He used in His sacraments the things of earth as medicines of our souls—"The virtues of these things is come to the knowledge of man, and the Most High hath given knowledge to men that He may be honoured in His wonders. By these He shall cure and shall allay their pains . . . and of His works there shall be no end. For the peace of God is over the face of the earth" (Eccl. 38, 4–8). And these healing things— which are life to the dead—His sacraments, are, like the great Physician Himself, word of God and thing of earth: He, the Eternal Word living in human flesh, and they the word of His minister, able through Him to make elements of earth life-giving. He Who is Word and Flesh instituted sacraments that were form and matter.

"All flesh is grass, and all the glory thereof as the flower of the field . . . The grass is withered, and the flower is fallen: but the word of the Lord endureth for ever" (Is. 40, 6–8). We are sick; we wither; we fall and die. The Incarnate Word—Our King and Saviour—endureth for ever. "Thanks be to God for His unspeakable gift" (2 Cor. 9, 15). We hear His voice: "Say to the faint-hearted: take courage and fear not . . . God Himself will come and save you. Then shall the eyes of the blind be opened, and the ears of the deaf shall be unstopped. Then shall the lame man leap as a hart, and the tongue of the dumb shall be free: for waters are broken out in the desert, and streams in the wilderness . . . And the redeemed of the Lord shall return, and shall come into Sion with praise, and everlasting joy shall be upon their heads: they shall obtain joy and gladness, and sorrow and mourning shall flee away" (Is. 35, 4-10).